Private Wealth
IN RENAISSANCE FLORENCE
A STUDY OF FOUR FAMILIES

Private Wealth

IN RENAISSANCE FLORENCE

A STUDY OF FOUR FAMILIES

BY

RICHARD A. GOLDTHWAITE

PRINCETON, NEW JERSEY
PRINCETON UNIVERSITY PRESS
1968

To my parents

Acknowledgments

THIS project was originally a dissertation begun under the direction of the late Prof. Garrett Mattingly, who, however, died before it was completed. It was his lively and stimulating interest in the original idea which more than anything else set me on my way, although the result is hardly worthy of the great tradition he represented. To his successor at Columbia University, Prof. Eugene F. Rice, Jr., I am deeply grateful for the kind and generous attention given me in the final stage of the dissertation and for the continuing interest he has shown in my work.

For material support, my thanks go to the trustees of Oberlin College for a Haskell Traveling Fellowship, which enabled me to spend a year in Florence to work on the dissertation. Subsequently, a fellowship from the Folger Shakespeare Library and especially generous support with release-time from teaching duties as well as funds from Kent State University made it possible to do post-doctoral research and to put the material in its present form.

I owe much to the staff of the Florentine archives for the courteous patience and assistance with which they introduced a foreign novice to the wonders of their treasury; and along with many who have worked there, I am particularly indebted to Dr. Gino Corti, who selflessly put his enormous fund of information and remarkable archival skills at my disposal. I must also thank the Guicciardini family for permission to use their impressive (and comfortable!) archives.

Having worked on this project for several years, I am indebted to a host of friends and colleagues who have all along the way offered invaluable assistance of various kinds, often unbeknown to themselves. Three, however, call for special mention: Mrs. Florence Edler de Roover, for her generous

Acknowledgments

help in clarifying Florentine business practice; Professors David Hicks and Marvin B. Becker, whose friendship and conversation has been a constant stimulation from the beginning to the end.

March 1968   R. A. G.

Contents

Tables

List of Tables

List of Tables

SELECTIVE GENEALOGIES

Private Wealth

IN RENAISSANCE FLORENCE

A STUDY OF FOUR FAMILIES

ABBREVIATIONS

AC:	Archivio Capponi
AG:	Archivio Guicciardini
A Gondi:	Archivio Gondi
ASI:	*Archivio storico italiano*
ASF:	Archivio di Stato, Florence
BNF:	Biblioteca Nazionale, Florence
CS:	Carte strozziane (with Roman numeral indicating series)

Introduction

PROBABLY no history of a city has been more closely examined than the history of Florence; and there can be little doubt that, apart from the intrinsic fascination of the city's rich cultural tradition, much of the magnetic force that continues to attract historians emanates from the city's seemingly inexhaustible archival resources. Florentines were remarkable record-keepers; in documents ranging from historical chronicles to personal accounts they kept track of the events of their lives (and it is no coincidence that the history of both historical writing and accounting is based on the Florentine evidence). Their documents have survived in such quantity and variety that today the city's archives have almost no equal in the extent to which they can be made to yield up the secrets of her past. Yet despite the continuing scholarly assault, there are still vast collections of documents which, far from having been explored, need to be merely charted; and it can hardly be said that Florentine studies, as extensive as they are in range of topics and as intensive in archival research, are yet exhaustive in exploiting the remnants of the city's historical past. For this reason alone, Florence will likely remain the favorite of Renaissance historians for some time to come.

It is the public record on which historians have for the most part fixed their scrutiny, but Florentines were remarkable keepers of records in private as well as public life. In a highly individualistic and capitalistic society like theirs, considerable value was obviously put on writing and accounting as devices for maintaining records of their numerous farflung and protracted economic activities and of their complex relations with one another; and it is not surprising that in the early literary tradition of paternal advice the Florentines are quite explicit on the importance of the written record. "Always, whenever you have a document drawn up," cautions

Introduction

Paolo da Certaldo in the mid-fourteenth century, "keep your own book, and write in it the day that this is done and the notary who does it and the witnesses, and why and with whom you do it, so that if you or your sons have need of it, you can find it."[1] "Paper costs little, and often it returns a good profit," is the maxim of an anonymous contemporary.[2] And, of course, the importance of keeping the record of getting and spending is particularly emphasized. "Make sure that in your books is written what you are continually doing, and don't ever pardon the pen . . . ," insists Giovanni Morelli.[3] For an example of one who never spared his, Giannozzo degli Alberti, in the famous dialogue on the family, points proudly to one of his ancestors, Benedetto, who "always [wrote] down everything, every contract, every receipt and expenditure outside the shop, and so often [looked] over everything that he almost always had a pen in hand."[4] Benedetto used to say, according to Giannozzo, that "he did so well in business, always having his hands stained with ink";[5] and a few years later Giovanni Rucellai took the very words and set them down in his *Zibaldone* as the best advice he could give his sons for conducting their affairs.[6]

All this advice was well taken, the habit was formed, and over the centuries there was a vast accumulation of all kinds of private documents. Originally considered of interest only to the family, they today constitute a rich mine for anyone working in social history. This material includes the kind of things one would expect families to collect, such as notarial records, letters and diaries, property deeds and account books

[1] *Libro di buoni costumi*, ed. Alfredo Schiaffini (Florence, 1945), p. 144.

[2] Gino Corti, ed., "Consigli sulla mercatura di un anonimo trecentista," *ASI*, cx (1952), 118.

[3] *Ricordi*, ed. Vittore Branca (Florence, 1956), pp. 228-29.

[4] Leon Battista Alberti, *I primi tre libri della famiglia*, ed. F. C. Pellegrini (Florence, 1946), p. 322.

[5] *Ibid.*, p. 321.

[6] *Il zibaldone quaresimale*, ed. Alessandro Perosa (London, 1960), p. 6.

—but it is these latter that exist in the greatest quantity. True to that capitalistic spirit that made their fortunes—and the history of the city as well—Florentines were keen in keeping track of every *lira, soldo,* and *denaro* passing through their hands and quick to perfect techniques of accounting. If they did not actually invent double-entry bookkeeping, it is certain that by the mid-fourteenth century it was a well-known procedure, and that by the mid-fifteenth century it was a generally accepted practice even in keeping house-hold accounts. Moreover, in other respects Florentines refined the organization of accounts to a degree unknown in the rest of Italy. Bookkeeping was likely to be a part of a boy's education, and Florentines kept accounts even of household expenses as a matter of habit—even women could keep a respectable set of books.[7] Although they lost their commercial and financial ascendancy in Europe, Florentines never lost this habit of keeping accounts, and over the centuries their records kept accumulating. Today the Florentine archives abound in the account books of their personal businesses and fortunes, many of them still in the possession of the family (and a few still growing with each year's additions), but an impressive number of them are in the public domain and easily accessible to any scholar who wants to strike a rich vein of materials for social and economic history.[8]

[7] Both the mother and the widow of Filippo Strozzi *il vecchio* kept their own accounts, which survive; and in her letters to her sons, his mother occasionally refers to posting figures: Alessandra Macinghi negli Strozzi, *Lettere di una donna fiorentina del secolo XV ai figliuoli esuli,* ed. Cesare Guasti (Florence, 1877), pp. 117 ("ho posto a suo conto. . . .") and 152 ("hottene fatto creditore al Libro mio"). Francesco Guicciardini comments that his grandmother knew how to use the abacus; "Memorie di famiglia," in *Scritti autobiografici e rari,* ed. Roberto Palmarocchi (Bari, 1936), p. 30. In Boccaccio's tale of how the Genoese merchant Barnabò Lomellin was deceived about the faithfulness of his wife, he tells us that this remarkable woman knew how "leggere e scrivere e fare una ragione"; *Decameron,* II, 9.

[8] For a brief indication of the numerous family archival collections to be found in Tuscany, see "Notizie degli archivi toscani," *ASI,* CXIV (1956), 414-40; CXVIII (1960), 359-73.

Introduction

Although family documents of all kinds survive in some quantity from the fourteenth century onward, the further one goes back in the history of a family the fewer documents he is likely to find. The oldest account book dates from 1211, but it is not until the mid-fourteenth century that an appreciable number of them can be turned up. The great accumulations, however, date from the second half of the sixteenth century; and for the following two hundred years there are innumerable collections that have virtually complete sets of accounts for each generation over the entire period. The sheer bulk of some of these almost defies research into the history of even one family. Before the second half of the sixteenth century, however, most collections thin out considerably. Much of the material for the period of the Renaissance is very fragmentary, representing only a small fraction of what originally must have existed. For isolated individuals there are bits and pieces and occasionally even a fairly comprehensive series of account books; but the famous case of Francesco di Marco Datini, the merchant of Prato over five hundred of whose books survive, is most exceptional even by Florentine standards. Consequently, for the family as a whole over several generations, the record is not nearly as complete as it is for later periods. Nevertheless, the mass of materials dating from the Renaissance, from the fourteenth to the mid-sixteenth century, though more widely scattered and fragmentary, is impressive; and for some families enough fragments exist from several generations to establish something of a continuity in the documentation and to make it possible to trace the fortunes of a family over the entire period. Certainly in other Italian towns family materials have not survived in such considerable quantity for this period;[9] and

[9] Judging from published studies, one has to conclude that family materials in archives of other Italian cities are not very numerous; account books dating before 1500, for instance, are very rare. In his study of Genoa, Jacques Heers can muster only enough information to make a weak presentation of two families in the fifteenth century:

the very existence of such records in Florence, offering the historian an entry into the social world of the fourteenth and fifteenth centuries, is enough in itself to vindicate the city's preëminence in Renaissance studies.

Although these abundant materials invite the study of the economic history of many Florentine families, holding out the possibility of considerable knowledge about private wealth and general economic conditions in Renaissance Florence, this entire realm of social history has hardly been explored by Florentine historiography. Only economic historians have made studies of family account books, seeking to find in the records of family companies something about the origins and nature of early business organization. Even at that, in confining themselves to the dynamic phase of the growth of Florentine international finance and commerce, they have studied only the very few isolated account books surviving from the early fourteenth century and thus have tapped only the surface of this vast deposit of economic records. Moreover, business historians, with the notable exception of Armando Sapori, seldom regard these business documents in the context of family records.[10] Even literary records left behind

Gênes au XVe siècle: activité économique et problèmes sociaux (Paris, 1961), pp. 544-49; and Heers has published the one account book which survives: *Le livre de comptes de Giovanni Piccamiglio, homme d'affaires génois, 1456-1459* (Paris, 1959). For Venice the surviving books of one fifteenth century merchant have been examined by Frederic C. Lane, *Andrea Barbarigo, Merchant of Venice, 1418-1449* (Baltimore, 1944); but there is apparently much more material yet untouched. In Lucca family records are very sparse and there is only one book of *ricordi* for the sixteenth century: Marino Berengo, *Nobili e mercanti nella Lucca del Cinquecento* (Turin, 1965), p. 34 n. 2. In the only two intensive studies of the economic history of Italian families which I know, documentation from family records for the period through the Renaissance is very feeble indeed: Giuseppe Mira, *Vicende economiche di una famiglia italiana dal XIV al XVII secolo* (Milan, 1940), a study of a family of the Lombard nobility; and Stuart J. Woolf, *Studi sulla nobiltà piemontese nell'epoca dell'assolutismo* (Turin, 1963), a study of three families from the sixteenth to the eighteenth century.

[10] See his various studies on fourteenth century family businesses,

by families, such as diaries and *ricordanze*, which for the period around 1400 are particularly numerous—perhaps more so than for any later period—have hardly been placed in their context as family documents although like most literary sources, which yield their substance more readily and profitably than something like account books, they are well known by Florentine historians.[11] The record of the family, in short, is a reasonably full one, but it has hardly been touched; and the many questions one might ask about the family and its history in Renaissance Florence must for the moment remain unanswered.

This study has been undertaken as a first step to exploit these archival resources in Florence and to study family history as an approach to Renaissance life and civilization. The selection of these four families—the Capponi, Gondi, Guicciardini, and Strozzi—was made primarily for the single reason that their extant documents seemed to be the most suitable for getting sufficient detail over a number of generations to give their histories significance. In all four cases the records are fullest for the period of the late fifteenth and early sixteenth centuries; but, in addition, for the Strozzi there are a number of books going back a couple of generations to the beginning of the fifteenth century; and for the Guicciardini, there are two isolated but comprehensive books from the second half of the fourteenth century. Otherwise the point of

---

now collected in *Studi di storia economica, secoli XIII-XIV-XV* (2 vols.; Florence, 1955), especially "La famiglia e le compagnie degli Alberti del Giudice." Of interest also is Victor Rutenburg, "La compagnia Uzzano (su documenti dell'archivio di Leningrado)," *Studi in onore di Armando Sapori* (Milan, 1957), I, 689-706. For bibliography of family business documents and studies of them, see Sapori, *Le marchand italien au moyen âge* (Paris, 1952), pp. 5-10.

[11] There is a very useful discussion of these sources for family history by P. J. Jones, "Florentine Families and Florentine Diaries in the Fourteenth Century," *Papers of the British School at Rome*, XXIV (New Series: XI) (1956), 183-205. Cf. the bibliography of I. Del Lungo and G. Volpe, eds., *La cronica domestica di Messer Donato Velluti* (Florence, 1914), pp. XII-XXIV.

Introduction

departure for these studies has been the *catasto* of 1427, which provides the first full documentary evidence of a family's financial position. Subsequent *catasto* reports, although less reliable, have been used for lack of other documentation until the record can be filled in from private account books, which for all these families exist in impressive quantity beginning in the late fifteenth century.[12]

Although the wealth of the family is thus the central interest, there has been an attempt to relate that wealth to other aspects of the family's history, especially its political position, although this relation has not been understood as one of cause and effect. A remarkable variety and quantity of noneconomic

[12] For the period before 1427 there are records of various *prestanze* which reveal individual payments; they are useful in ranking citizens according to the size of their tax payments and presumably therefore are an index to relative status of taxpayers. The records of the famous *catasto* of 1427, on the other hand, contain complete inventories of private wealth for each householder and they are the inevitable first stepping-stone in exploring private wealth. The *catasto* continued to be levied up to 1480, but unfortunately the reports after 1427 are not reliable. The authorities found it too difficult to check reports of liquid wealth and the good citizens found it increasingly easy to falsify this part of their financial statements. Sometimes they entered the kinds of investments they had but added a variety of specious excuses for not declaring any values. Eventually some eliminated business investments altogether from their reports. As long as Florentine wealth was founded on a commercial and industrial economy, any inventory of a man's wealth which excluded his business investments has a very limited value. For this reason the reports after 1427 are at best only suggestive of the kinds of investment which a citizen might have; and the tax paid is not even indicative of his relative financial status among all taxpayers. By 1480 the *catasto* had become in effect a tax on real estate only, and this fact was acknowledged in the new tax legislation which introduced the *decima* in 1494. The *decima* was strictly a land tax and was the basic direct tax of the state throughout the ducal period.

On the operation of the *catasto*, see Giuseppe Canestrini, *La scienza e l'arte di stato* (Florence, 1862); Otto Karmin, *La legge del catasto fiorentino del 1427* (Florence, 1906); C. F. Pagnini della Ventura, *Della decima e di varie altre gravezze imposte dal comune di Firenze* (4 vols.; Lisbon and Lucca, 1765). For comparative purposes in ranking Florentines by their wealth, there are useful tables which summarize the *prestanze* of 1403 and the *catasto* of 1427 in Lauro Martines, *The Social World of the Florentine Humanists* (Princeton, 1963), App. II.

materials relevant to family history have survived in Florence, and it is possible to put a good deal of flesh on the economic skeleton of a family's history. In the Archivio di Stato abundant documentation for the construction of family trees can be found in the extensive notarial archives and in various official records kept of baptisms, marriages, deaths, and other such vital statistics. Fortunately, in the seventeenth and eighteenth centuries genealogists assembled much of this information for leading families, and their work survives in numerous manuscripts located in the Archivio di Stato and other public collections. In the nineteenth century additional genealogical research was undertaken for a few important families and made available in published form. These genealogies are more than mere family trees. In sketches of individual members of families there is much information which has been carefully and laboriously sifted out of the numerous Florentine diaries, chronicles, and histories; and also usually included are lists, extracted from archival sources, of the most important political offices held by members of these families. Consequently, the historian of Florentine society is spared the labor of much genealogical spadework necessary to the study of the history of a number of leading families, and he has at his disposal to begin with a sound genealogical tree and a wealth of biographical information on individual members.[18]

[18] The most prominent nineteenth century Florentine genealogist was Luigi Passerini, much of whose work was published in Conte Pompeo Litta, *Le famiglie celebri italiane* (15 vols.; Milan, 1819-1902). A number of his genealogies of Florentine families were published in separate volumes which contain considerably more information than is found in Litta. These include the Alberti, Altoviti, Corsini, Ginori, Guadagni, Niccolini, Panciatichi, Passerini, Ricasoli, and Rucellai; see Attilio Pagliaini, *Catalogo generale della libreria italiana* (3 vols.; Milan, 1900-1905). Passerini's manuscripts are in the Biblioteca Nazionale in Florence and they are also useful. Another useful genealogical compilation in manuscript in the Biblioteca Nazionale is the Poligrafo Gargani.

Litta is the standard genealogy for Italian families; but see also: Demostene Tiribilli-Giuliani, *Sommario storico delle famiglie celibri*

Introduction

These are the materials, then, for the study of the Florentine family; and the procedure for pursuing a family history will be partly determined by the kind of materials which are to be used. In the few valuable studies on Florentine family history which have been made recently, the approach has been what one might call deductive, the procedure having been to collect the individual names within an entire cognate group as they appear in all kinds of archival records with the hope of thereby discovering what kind of real relations might have reinforced blood relationships. Since these studies have been inspired mostly by political interests and have focused on families which have left behind very few of their own records, they have concentrated on official public sources. Consequently, in taking an approach from outside the family such studies have not been very successful in penetrating the inner vitality of the familial organism; and furthermore, their scope has been limited by a time span of usually only a couple of generations. And finally, all of these studies have been based on the unexamined assumption that an entire cognate group is indeed a family in a meaningful sense, that is to say, that it has a unity which is more than just genealogical.[14] An alternative approach to the whole problem is

---

toscane (3 vols.; Florence, 1855-63); and Vittorio Spreti, ed., *Enciclopedia storico-nobiliare italiana* (6 vols.; Milan, 1928-32). On the Acciaiuoli, Lanfredini and Niccolini, see the following popular works: Curzio Ugurgieri della Berardenga, *Gli Acciaioli di Firenze* (2 vols.; Florence, 1961); M. Mansfield, *A Family of Decent Folk: 1200-1741* (Florence, 1922); Ginevra Niccolini di Camugliano, *The Chronicles of a Florentine Family, 1200-1470* (London, 1933). The enormous bibliography on the Medici is now compiled in Sergio Camerani, *Bibliografia medicea* (Florence, 1964). On the Strozzi, Capponi, Gondi and Guicciardini, see the bibliographical notes below.

[14] G. Brucker, "The Medici in the Fourteenth Century," *Speculum*, xxxii (1957), 1-26; and the various studies of Lauro Martines: "La famiglia Martelli e un documento sulla vigilia del ritorno dall'esilio di Cosimo de' Medici (1434)," *ASI*, cxvii (1959), 29-43; "Nuovi documenti su Cino Rinuccini e una nota sulle finanze della famiglia Rinuccini," *ASI*, cxix (1961), 77-91; *The Social World . . .*, pp. 199-237 (sketches of five families into which humanists married).

taken in the following studies of four families. It arises from the almost exclusive concentration on family materials and might be called, by way of contrast, an inductive and internal approach, working with the individual family unit and its own economic records. Here, attention will be focused on the family unit, or household, as defined by the economic bonds reflected in the account books. The transformation of these units through time as a result of the genealogical process of furcation and the consequent loosening of bonds, the disintegration of older units and formation of new ones, is traced as far as is practicable through the existing records; and the ultimate objective is to uncover some patterns in this process of transformation of family groupings over a number of generations and to understand something of the dynamic of that process. Because the documentation is often exclusively economic in nature, family units are observed primarily in terms of their financial or economic ties. One cannot, of course, overrule the possibility that economic bonds may not have been coincident with other bonds arising from political interest, from social or class status, or simply from familial affection, but there can hardly be any doubt that economic relations are among the most concrete for the historian to define. The advantage of this approach, in short, is that one can establish a solid body of material from which a meaningful, if limited, definition of the Florentine family can tentatively be formulated.

It has been almost a generation since Lucien Febvre made his appeal for the study of family history as one of the surest touchstones to the life of an age,[15] but very few historians

---

In addition, see Jones' article. For studies of families in the earlier, communal era, see: Elizabeth von Roon-Bassermann, "Die Rossi von Oltarno: ein Beitrag zur mittelalterlichen Sozial- und Wirtschaftsgeschichte von Florenz," *Vierteljahrschrift für Sozial- und Wirtschaftsgeschichte*, LI (1964), 235-48; and the sketches in Berthold Stahl, *Adel und Volk im Florentiner Dugento* (Cologne, 1965).

[15] "Ce que peuvent nous apprendre les monographies familiales," *Mélange d'histoire sociale*, I (1942), 31-34.

responded with the kind of solidly based monograph he envisaged. Recently, the sociological approach of Philippe Ariès has had a greater impact,[16] and his interpretation of the family in early modern European society has generated considerable interest in the role of the family in a society and the significance of its transformations. It is, in fact, safe to say that, thanks partly to Ariès, the family has become a central theme in the speculations of the modern social historian. But for all that, there are still not very many significant case studies of specific families, and in their absence this more ambitious sociological approach will remain defective. For the period of the Renaissance there are so few studies of the family that it is difficult to make very many generalizations about it, not to mention the impossibility of even defining the term.[17] Perhaps these studies of four Florentine families will contribute some of the substance for a clearer formulation. But meanwhile, particularistic studies of families are not without their own rewards. As Febvre observed:

Les monographies de famille posent des problèmes plus rares, plus délicats, plus particuliers. Elles mettent mieux en contact avec la vie. Elles provoquent des surprises, des étonnements. Elles révèlent des accidents. Elles inquiètent. Elles font réfléchir.

[16] *Centuries of Childhood. A Social History of Family Life*, trans. Robert Baldick (New York, 1962).

[17] In his survey of the period Jacques Heers concluded, "il ne semble pas possible de répondre nettement à la question: Qu'est-ce la famille vers la fin du Moyen Age?" *L'occident aux XIVe et XVe siècles: aspects économiques et sociaux* (Paris, 1963), p. 299.

Chapter i

THE ADMINISTRATION OF

PRIVATE WEALTH

THE history of accounting has been written primarily with an eye to the keeping of business accounts. Accounting, after all, developed in response to the growing complexities of Italian business organization and most of the early evidence of Italian account books are primarily records of those businesses. Even today accounting is associated with some kind of formal economic organization and not usually, for example, to something like household management. But in Florence in the early fourteenth century business organization was not distinct from the family; and since its capital was but a part of the family patrimony, account books included all the family's financial affairs, private and domestic as well as those strictly concerned with business. In confining themselves to examining account books as business records and judging them against sound business practice as we consider it today, historians of accounting have generally overlooked the use of accounting techniques by Florentines to administer not just their businesses but their entire fortunes. Yet even after company organization became distinct from the household with its own set of books, Florentines continued to keep precise records of their total wealth, employing the methods of accounting and even improving on them. Anyone who looks over family financial records from this period cannot fail to be impressed with the persistence of Florentines in categorizing and organizing their various economic activities, from the household to an international bank, so that by merely glancing over their records they could readily assess with considerable precision and detail the state of their wealth. From the fourteenth to the early sixteenth century the refinement of their methods in this respect is remarkable; and the account books used in this study, if laid out chronologically, illustrate that course of continual refinement.[1]

The oldest books used in this study, and the only ones dating from the fourteenth century, are the books of Piero Guicciardini and his son, Messer Luigi, covering the entire second half of the century (1344-1404).[2] These books are not business records and they have nothing to do with the extensive commercial and banking interests of the family. They are, on the contrary, strictly private records of the family's capital investments mostly in land but also in business. They

---

[1] In the essential elements of accounting procedures there is nothing unusual about the books used in this study. For the most part, these ledgers are standard books of *debitori e creditori*, frequently with a brief *ricordanze* section at the end; and correct double entry accounting is employed in virtually all of them dating after the mid-fifteenth century. Accounts are arranged in bilateral form, according to the Venetian method (*alla veneziana*), presumably introduced into Florence in the late fourteenth century, so that debit and credit entries in any one account are placed on the separate folio sides laterally opposite one another as the book lies open to the account. Each entry has a brief description in the vernacular and a proper cross-reference indication. Units of money are uniform, figures are Arabic numerals and arranged in columns at the right; and closed accounts are balanced, totaled and lined once diagonally. Accounts are organized into various categories but these are in no particular order and were added according to need until the book was filled. Books were supplied with detachable alphabetical indices of accounts they contained; and books belonging to a series are clearly identified, usually by a letter and the color of the binding (thus, *libro verde B*) as to their place in the series. In all these respects, the accounting techniques used in private administration are familiar enough to historians of Italian business practice.

For a bibliography on the history of accounting, see Federigo Melis, *Aspetti della vita economica medievale (studi nell'archivio Datini di Prato)*, I (Siena, 1962), 339 n.1. Melis, pp. 379-452, discusses Italian accounting practice in the Renaissance; cf. Lane, *Barbarigo*, pp. 153-81; and Heers, *Piccamiglio*. Accounting methods in the Florentine books generally follow the model set down in the manual of Pacioli at the end of the fifteenth century. The only published account book I have seen which closely resembles the kind of book used in this study is that of Giovanni Piccamiglio published by Heers.

[2] AG, Libri 1 and 2.

are not account books properly speaking—that is to say, they do not contain accounts in which credits and debits are enumerated, they do not show income or expenditures, and they reveal nothing about the administration of invested capital. These Guicciardini books are really *ricordanze* of property acquisitions and business contracts. As a kind of running inventory of their capital investments, they reveal a good deal about the composition and extent of the family's wealth; but on the other hand, they hardly permit the drawing up of a financial statement of the family's position at any one time. Although accounting techniques were well known in business practice—and the Guicciardini undoubtedly employed them in their several business enterprises, the records of which have not survived—neither Piero nor Luigi apparently felt a need to utilize complex business procedures in maintaining their private records.

At the very end of the fourteenth century, at about the time the Guicciardini records leave off, Simone Strozzi, then at the beginning of his career, began to keep records of his wealth. With some gaps Simone's records survive for his entire life up to his death in 1424; and along with those of his son Matteo, which extend the record for another decade (to 1434), the Strozzi books form a chronological sequel to the Guicciardini records and take us through the economic careers of two generations of a Florentine patrician family during the early Renaissance.[3] The Strozzi, however, went about the matter of keeping track of their wealth in a way essentially different from that of the Guicciardini; and in a sense that difference reflects something of the mentality with which their generations inaugurated a new era in Florentine culture.

The Strozzi books, unlike those of the Guicciardini, are not just inventories of capital investments but genuine account books, an organized record of credits and debits involving their financial affairs of all kinds. In these books the

[3] See App. I.

The Administration

Strozzi incorporated the rational techniques of accounting long associated with the capitalistic activities of Florentine businessmen; but whereas accounting methods had in the fourteenth century been used primarily for purposes of organizing the financial record of specific capitalistic enterprises, in the Strozzi books it is applied to the general administration of the family's entire wealth apart from any business operation. Thus there are accounts for the commune of Florence (for *prestanze* and Monte credits), for their dealings in marine insurance, for land purchases, for capital improvements of their property (*murare* accounts), for various employees (personal servants, farm workers, and other men under temporary contract, such as painters or woodworkers), and for numerous personal expenditures. There are also company accounts, of course, but it must be emphasized that these books are not primarily company books and the company accounts reflect not the internal operation of the family business (in this case, wool manufactories) but the state of the capital investment in that business. Thus on these accounts the assets are credits extended by the company for personal expenditures of the owners, and these are balanced by periodic assignments of profits made by the company to the owners. For the internal operations of the Strozzi companies there were undoubtedly sets of account books apart, but none of these have survived. The Strozzi books, therefore, are of little interest for the history of their business, but they do reveal a good deal about the financial status of their authors—and that will be discussed below.

As accounts, the Strozzi books employ the format associated with Florentine business records: accounts are categorized, entries are kept in bilateral form, and there is extensive use of double-entry. Nevertheless, the accounting system is far from flawless, and the books are not without serious deficiencies in presenting a comprehensive record of the Strozzi estate. In the first place, there are neither capital accounts nor summary opening or closing accounts, which usually served the function of a capital account in Italian business ledgers; and hence it is not possible to "read" at a glance a financial statement of the Strozzi fortune. Furthermore, although double-entry is used in many of the accounts, the rules of this procedure are not adhered to strictly. Thus some entries have references to others in the same books; but some cross-references are to entries in other books now lost, and some have no cross-reference at all and are in fact single entries. These latter appear to be merely listings for the purpose of a record rather than an integral part of a set of accounts. Finally, there is some information which is missing altogether from these books: for example, there are no accounts for income from farm lands, although some was acquired by both Simone and Matteo; there is no profit-loss account nor is there a cash account. In some important respects, therefore, these books are incomplete as well as unsatisfactory as administrative records; and they cannot be relied upon to yield a fully composed picture of the Strozzi fortune. Nevertheless, in the history of the administrative records of family wealth the Strozzi books mark an advance over fourteenth century procedures in the separation of general estate administration from company accounts and the use of accounting techniques in organizing the records of that administration.

In the course of the Renaissance the quality of private accounts improved markedly. When we proceed to the next generation of Strozzi, for example, and to the books of Matteo's son Filippo (1428-91), we find a considerably more sophisticated system of record-keeping—one, in fact, impressive even by modern standards. Besides the various sets of books kept for his far-flung business interests, Filippo maintained a private ledger in which he summarized all of his economic activities and maintained a record of his over-all financial position.[4] In this book kept for his personal record

[4] CS-V, 22 (and its sequel, CS-V, 41).

alone, Filippo, unlike his father and grandfather, employed flawless double-entry techniques, but even more impressive is the systematic categorization of his accounts so that a neat and ordered schematization of his financial activities was readily available. The key account is one entitled "sustanzia mia." It is the opening account and includes an inventory of personal property, real estate, investments in businesses, and cash-on-hand; from that point it becomes a running account in which are included profits and expenses, so that at any time a balance of this account would reveal his over-all net worth in very general terms. Other accounts fill in the details. There are separate company accounts, summarizing the articles of organization so that even in the absence of a copy of the contract we can know all we need to know about that company as an investment. These accounts record the original investment and profits and are balanced by the disposition of these credits. Other accounts include dowries for his daughters, tax payments to the city, donations to charity, and administration of real estate. These latter include not only accounts of acquisition but also capital expenditures, and they are broken down into a number of accounts each for a particular property or group of holdings. Thus, for example, shortly after he opened an account of his "palagio per mio abitare," on which he wished to include all the expenses involved for this great undertaking, he transferred to it the values represented by all the purchases he had made over the preceding years to acquire its site so that ultimately the account of his palace accurately reflected its total cost to him, including construction as well as the site; meanwhile, the value of this property appears as a debit on the account of his real estate. Another key account is the profit-loss account, on which he includes not his profits in business (which are transferred to his capital account) but a running account of his miscellaneous income, mostly from real estate, and his household expenses. Altogether, Filippo's accounts tell an accurate and detailed story of his wealth and its vicissitudes; and even though his second ledger, opened in 1483, is incomplete because of his death in 1491, it was nevertheless so well maintained that it can be accepted as a reliable record even when accounts have not been balanced and closed out.

Filippo's private ledgers were not books of first entry, for their entries are for the most part summary figures taken from more detailed accounts. Thus behind each major account in the ledger there was likely to be a separate set of accounts, some of which have also survived to make the record of Filippo's income and expenditures virtually complete in many areas. There were, of course, sets of books for the operation of his various businesses; but there are also separate books for expenses of some of his major building projects—those for a chapel, two villas, and the palace have survived—and these would only be summarized periodically in the master book. Although none are extant, we can assume that books were also kept for the administration of his farms. As for his basic living expenses (*spese* accounts), they were enumerated in detail in the main ledger until 1483; thereafter they are recorded in the book of his company in Florence and only annually were total figures transferred to the master book. Filippo thus kept precise and detailed records of all his financial transactions in a variety of books, but his main ledger represented a careful distillation of all these so that the total picture of his financial position was not blurred by an excessive mass of detail.

Filippo's bookkeeping practices represent a degree of organization unknown in the fourteenth century; and yet most of the books from the early sixteenth century show the same degree of detail and the same meticulous organization even though the wealth of their owners may have been quite modest compared to Filippo's. In this study we shall be using the accounts of the heirs of Antonio Gondi, of Alessandro Gondi, of Jacopo Guicciardini, of Niccolò and Giuliano Capponi; and in each the same general characteristics can be found to a greater or lesser degree. This included above all the practice of keeping a main ledger of the general administration of one's fortune. There might be a raft of account books under a man's supervision, but there was always one in which he attempted to give a summary statement of his financial affairs. The ledger capped a hierarchy of subordinate books which can, generally speaking, be categorized into kinds: books of first entry, waste books, and work books in which the minutiae of daily business were recorded; and books —and sets of books—of particular activities. Certainly by the sixteenth century company accounts were kept separate from accounts of the general administration of an estate since companies were by that time themselves separate legal entities; but if the complexity or size of an estate demanded it, there would be other specialized books in which all accounts were relevant to one activity alone. This would be particularly true for the administration of real estate in cases where holdings were sizeable. Jacopo Guicciardini (1480-1552), for example, kept separate sets of books for his silk company, his various farms (*possessioni*), his wife's large estate (which consisted mostly of farms)—and possibly also for his interest in the Antwerp company, although no such books survive— but there was his main ledger as well in which all these activities were summarized. It is the fortunate survival of these books, obviously the most important in any library of account books, which makes it possible to learn so much about private wealth in Renaissance Florence.

Within the ledger the various accounts were likewise specialized to a remarkable degree. Whereas in fourteenth century books all living expenses might be included on one account, and business and private affairs confused, there is in these later books a neat categorization of accounts. Separate accounts were generally kept for food, clothing, household furnishings, major expenses of any one member of the family, and other expenses which occur regularly in a household although these might all be merged in the closing account or, anywhere along the way, into an account of general expenditures. In the course of his ledger, Jacopo Guicciardini, to cite an example of this refinement of specialization of accounts, opened new accounts in which he began to categorize his income according to its source—rents, salaries, profits, and other miscellaneous kinds.

Another improvement in organization was the use of the periodic entry. Although periodic balances were not included in Renaissance account books, entries representing periodic expenditures and income are found in some sixteenth century books, whereas in earlier books entries were not made with periodic regularity. Giuliano Capponi (1476-1565) maintained a profit-loss account on which regular annual entries were made for his income from real estate and for his expenditures for clothes, taxes, charity, food, etc. In his last book his *spese* accounts have a single entry for each month; and there are entries recording annual living expenditures as well as annual income from real estate. Such figures were transferred from work books to the master book with periodic regularity. The concept of the regular, periodic entry added a principle of organization to the dimension of time that is completely missing in earlier books.[5]

By the early sixteenth century the use of accounting techniques in the administration of private fortunes was impressively thorough. With a set of subordinate and specialized books capped by the main ledger, which was kept in correct double-entry and in which accounts were neatly categorized and entries made with periodic regularity, a Florentine patrician had the complete picture of his fortune at his finger tips. This remarkable extension of the original use of accounting techniques introduced an element of rational control over

[5] Giuliano's last book AC (BNF), 21 (1553-68), shows a marked improvement in this respect over an earlier extant book, AC (BNF), 9 (1532-44).

complex business activities. In business the technique had an immediate and practical value, but in the administration of private wealth, especially considering the minute detail found in these books and the modest size of some of the fortunes, its practical value is not so apparent. One can say, perhaps, that the business technique was so deeply ingrained in the Florentine mentality that it had become second nature to apply it wherever figures were involved, even in purely personal and private records. At any rate, in the course of the fifteenth century there was a noticeable improvement in the technique of keeping the written record of private wealth—one can see an impressive difference in going from the books of Simone and Matteo Strozzi to those of Filippo; and by the beginning of the sixteenth century, these techniques had been further refined, especially as regards the principle of organization. The overwhelming abundance of account books from subsequent generations supplies the evidence that the habit had caught on and was widely practiced throughout patrician society.

The one modern feature that never seems to have been incorporated into Florentine private accounts is the periodic balance. In Renaissance Florence there was no need for a periodic accounting of a man's private affairs; and given the protracted nature of Renaissance business operations, profits came in so irregularly that periodic statements of income and expenditure would have made little sense. For business records the periodic balance served a legal and practical function but it was not a feature of a set of books kept for the administration of patrimonial wealth. One cannot, therefore, expect to find in the estate records of the Florentine patrician anything like a periodic statement of his affairs. The use of the periodic entry for more regular income and expenditures enabled him to have a fairly good idea of his basic financial position for all practical purposes; and of course the use of double entry made it possible at any time to draw up a balance for his estate—and there is little doubt that this was done, even though such balances were not incorporated into the ledger and have therefore not survived. In the absence of periodic balances, many accounts remained opened as long as a man maintained his records, and the only balances found in these main ledgers come when the book had been filled up and it was necessary to transfer all open accounts to a new book. Such a balance would be for the duration of their author's economic career up to that point. Theoretically, at the end of his life he could present a financial statement of his lifetime accomplishment as an economic agent. Unfortunately, that final balance was likely never to be made; death precluded that possibility, and it was not customary for a man's heirs to close out his accounts since it was irrelevant to the settlement of his estate. Consequently, most of the extant account books are incomplete, and therefore they contain no balances whatsoever.

It is this absence of balances which, more than anything else, raises serious problems in the use of these records for one can never know what is missing from unbalanced accounts. This is especially true of the main ledgers: because they contain less detail, they usually span a longer period than other ledgers—perhaps a decade or even longer—and since by their nature as main ledgers entries in them were not made with any regularity, the investigator can never be sure that an incomplete ledger has been kept up to date. It is virtually impossible, therefore, to draw up a balance for many estates even when ledgers survive. For certain activities where the periodic entry was used, such as regular income and expenditures, and for capital accounts of real estate and other investments, incomplete ledgers can yield a fairly comprehensive picture of a man's financial position. What is most likely to be overlooked in an incomplete set of accounts are profits from investments in business, since these were assigned very infrequently, usually at the termination of the company contract every three to five years. And since this was a major item of any Florentine's income, any analysis of records which have lacunae in this area proceeds on very shaky grounds—and unfortunately there are sometimes no complementary materials from other sources to fill in the gaps.

There are problems, then, in using Florentine account books, and they are sometimes of such magnitude as to render the documents virtually worthless. These difficulties, however, arise from the state of incompleteness of many extant books and not from an inherent deficiency in the techniques of accounting. On the contrary, as we have seen, by the sixteenth century those techniques were highly refined and their use in the administration of private fortunes, impressively thorough. When one casts his eye abroad to see how the bourgeoisie elsewhere in Europe was handling its affairs, one cannot but be impressed by the Florentine accomplishment—and by something particular in the mentality behind that accomplishment. The very fact that for Florence alone of all Italian cities account books have survived in such great quantity is surely indicative of the greater zeal of Florentines for keeping books in the first place; and even though the techniques of double-entry accounting were most assuredly well known throughout Renaissance Italy, it is doubtful that the degree of organization characteristic of Florentine ledgers can be equaled. The one fifteenth century book which survives from the mercantile republic of Genoa, that of Giovanni Piccamiglio, shows a knowledge of the same techniques used in Florence but is much less refined in the practice; and the scholar who has edited it had to conclude that the procedure imposed too severe an obligation on Piccamiglio for him to carry it out systematically throughout the book.[6] But compared to poor Piccamiglio in the mid-fifteenth century, mer-

---

[6] Heers, *Piccamiglio*, p. 14. Not only was Piccamiglio careless in his use of double entry, but he kept his book in Latin and failed to use a uniform monetary unit.

chants north of the Alps even a century later pale to insignificance in their feeble efforts to keep track of their wealth. The most basic technique, double-entry, was itself probably not known at all until the sixteenth century. Following the publication of the first manual on it by Luca Pacioli in 1494 there were certainly enough tracts that came out on the subject in northern Europe, but there are pitifully few examples of its use before the mid-sixteenth century; and even thereafter to the end of the century, when there is enough evidence that businessmen finally knew something about it, it was not widely used.[7] The great Spanish merchant and banking family of the second half of the sixteenth century, the Ruiz, kept their books in double-entry, but many of their countrymen did not.[8] In England there are only four examples of ledgers kept in double-entry for the entire century, and they are only half-hearted attempts.[9] In one of the better of these, a book by a man as prominent as Sir Thomas Gresham (1519-79), Roman numerals are still used, entries are in chronological order without there having been much of an effort to categorize them, and apparently no books of first entry were used.[10] A generation later another English merchant, Sir Arthur Ingram (ca. 1565-1642), did

[7] For a survey of the history of double entry up to ca. 1500, with bibliographical notes, see two articles by Raymond de Roover: "Aux origines d'une technique intellectuelle: la formation et l'expansion de la comptabilité à partie double," *Annales d'histoire économique et sociale*, IX (1937), 171-93, 270-98; and "The Development of Accounting Prior to Luca Pacioli according to the Account-Books of Medieval Merchants," in *Studies in the History of Accounting*, eds. A. C. Littleton and B. S. Yamey (London, 1956), pp. 114-74. Especially for the sixteenth century, see Henri Lapeyre, *Une famille de marchands: les Ruiz* (Paris, 1955), pp. 339-41.

[8] *Ibid.*, pp. 342-44.

[9] Peter Ramsey, "Some Tudor Merchants' Accounts," in *Studies in the History of Accounting*, eds. Littleton and Yamey, pp. 185-87. Ramsey has published two of these books: *John Isham, Mercer and Merchant Adventurer: Two Account Books of a London Merchant in the Reign of Elizabeth I* (Durham, 1962).

[10] Ramsey, "Some Tudor Merchants' Accounts," pp. 188-91.

not have any system of comprehensive accounts at all.[11] And to continue this survey to the end of the seventeenth century, the books of Sir John Banks (1627-99), one of the richest businessmen in England, although in many respects very similar to Florentine books of two centuries earlier, follow practices which present serious obstacles to a clear reconstruction of his financial position.[12] Finally, on learning that English aristocrats even as late as the seventeenth century were still keeping their estate accounts in Latin and on parchment rolls,[13] one must conclude not simply that Florence was ahead of the times but that there was something exceptional about the Florentine mentality, something that lies beyond the relatively superficial evidence of account books.

It is difficult to explain this Florentine turn of mind which insisted on such complete records of financial activities. Obviously it is something which goes much deeper than "the capitalistic spirit." The capitalists of the rest of Europe during the era were not the less imbued with the spirit of capitalism—nor any less successful—for all their crudities in keeping their records straight; and it is perhaps not going too far to suggest that even today in the United States with the requirements of the Department of Internal Revenue there are not many men who could give as complete an accounting of their affairs as could a Florentine patrician in the Renaissance. Ultimately, perhaps, we have to come back to the master himself, Burckhardt, who has little enough to say about the republics of the Italian Renaissance but, as usual, what he does say is significant: it was there, in Venice and Florence, but above all in Florence, where men cultivated a statistical view of things in their attempt to systematize all forms of outward life. In their account books, no less than in their

[11] Anthony F. Upton, *Sir Arthur Ingram, c. 1565-1642: A Study of the Origins of the English Landed Family* (Oxford, 1961), p. 172.

[12] D. C. Coleman, *Sir John Banks, Baronet and Businessman* (Oxford, 1963), pp. 201-5.

[13] Lawrence Stone, *The Crisis of the Aristocracy, 1558-1641* (Oxford, 1965), pp. 277-78.

art, their historical writings, and their manuals on all aspects of life from the family to the state, the Florentine attempted to impose on his affairs a kind of geometrical schema.[14] Perhaps it satisfied a subconscious aesthetic sense, or perhaps it fulfilled a psychological need for a sense of order in the confused and precarious world in which he had to conduct his affairs. Or perhaps again, as Burckhardt concluded, it was simply his inborn talent as a Florentine. At any rate, even in these hopelessly dull account books breathes something of the spirit of the Florentine Renaissance.

[14] *The Civilization of the Renaissance in Italy* (London, 1951), pp. 51-52.

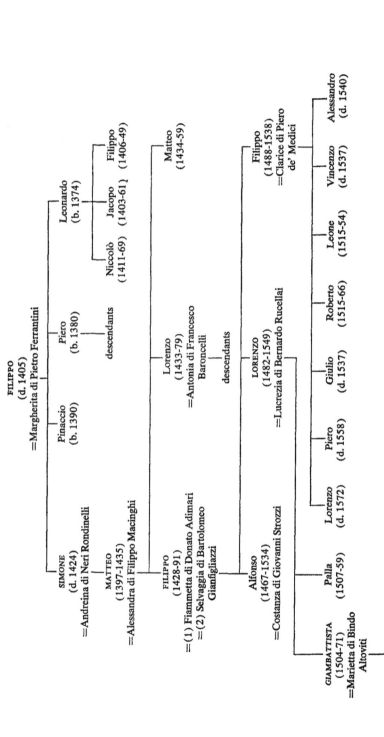

GENEALOGICAL CHART 1. THE STROZZI

A Selective Genealogy

FILIPPO
(d. 1405)
=Margherita di Pietro Ferrantini

SIMONE
(d. 1424)
=Andreina di Neri Rondinelli

Pinaccio
(b. 1390)

Piero
(b. 1380)

descendants

Leonardo
(b. 1374)

Niccolò
(1411-69)

Jacopo
(1403-61)

Filippo
(1406-49)

MATTEO
(1397-1435)
=Alessandra di Filippo Macinghi

Lorenzo
(1433-79)
=Antonia di Francesco
Baroncelli

descendants

Matteo
(1434-59)

FILIPPO
(1428-91)
=(1) Fiammetta di Donato Adimari
=(2) Selvaggia di Bartolomeo
Gianfigliazzi

Alfonso
(1467-1534)
=Costanza di Giovanni Strozzi

LORENZO
(1482-1549)
=Lucrezia di Bernardo Rucellai

Filippo
(1488-1538)
=Clarice di Piero
de' Medici

GIAMBATTISTA
(1504-71)
=Marietta di Bindo
Altoviti

descendants

Palla
(1507-59)

Lorenzo
(d. 1572)

Piero
(d. 1558)

Giulio
(d. 1537)

Roberto
(1515-66)

Leone
(1515-54)

Vincenzo
(d. 1537)

Alessandro
(d. 1540)

Chapter ii

THE STROZZI IN THE FIFTEENTH

CENTURY

AMONG the great patrician families with long and noble traditions within Florence, the Strozzi enjoyed a splendor overshadowed only by the Medici. Their presence in Florentine affairs long antedated the appearance of the Medici; the prestige and power of their wealth and influence throughout Italy and Europe earned them a reputation second only to that of the Medici; and during the Renaissance they presented themselves, for a moment at least, as the only serious rival to the Medici. They far outlasted the Medici, and it has been only in our own time that the family has disappeared forever from the Florentine scene.[1]

[1] The standard genealogy is, as always, Litta, v, *Strozzi di Firenze*. There are also two collections of lives of various Strozzi—one from the sixteenth century: Lorenzo Strozzi, *Le vite degli uomini illustri della casa Strozzi* (Florence, 1892); and one from the eighteenth century: Luigi Strozzi, *Vite degli huomini illustri della famiglia degli Strozzi*, 2 vols. in mss. (1740), CS-III, 75. A sketchy history of the family up to the early fifteenth century can be found in Jones, pp. 183-205; thereafter, there is nothing except biographical material. The collection of family documents, the *Carte strozziane*, is one of the richest mines in Florentine archives. It is composed of five series, with published inventories for the first (2 vols.; Florence, 1884) and the second plus part of the third (1 vol.; n.p., n.d.). The financial records are found mostly in the fourth and fifth series. There is also a very large collection of Strozzi documents in the Folger Shakespeare Library: *The Folger Strozzi Transcript*; but this contains mostly political and religious material in seventeenth and eighteenth century copies, and there is almost nothing relevant to the history of the family. Finally, another collection of papers belonging to a branch of the family exiled from Florence in the early fifteenth century is in Ferrara and has recently been described by Cecil H. Clough, "The Archivio Bentivoglio in Ferrara," *Renaissance News*, XVIII (1965), 12-19.

THE FOURTEENTH CENTURY

In the absence of any family documents it is difficult to reconstruct a coherent history of the Strozzi much before the end of the fourteenth century. From the numerous references to various Strozzi scattered throughout public documents it is possible to delineate a rough genealogy and to make a few observations about certain individual Strozzi, but only the broadest generalizations can be proffered about the internal history of the family. Their origins, like that of the other great Florentine families whose roots were not feudal, are completely obscured; but their name is encountered as early as any other in the annals of the medieval commune. Their rise to prominence accompanied their good fortune as entrepreneurs in the business enterprises which were the foundation of Florentine greatness. At the end of the thirteenth century, as members of the *arte del cambio*, they were conducting banking operations on a scale large enough to be able to advance credit to various nearby communes.[2] By the early fourteenth century they had extended their banking activities into France and England, and at Avignon they were long one of the leading firms at the papal court.[3] Not only did they do business in the international market but their financial position was solid enough to withstand the repercussions of the mid-fourteenth century disasters which threw so many other Florentine firms into bankruptcy.[4]

The Strozzi were just one of the many new Florentine families accumulating fortunes throughout Europe at the time and so laying the foundations of a great international commercial, industrial, and financial center; and along with the

[2] Robert Davidsohn, *Geschichte von Florenz* (4 vols.; Berlin, 1896-1927), II, 466; IV, Pt. II, 139, 226; Nicola Ottokar, *Il Comune di Firenze alla fine del Dugento* (Florence, 1926), pp. 97-98.

[3] Yves Renouard, *Les relations des papes d'Avignon et des compagnies commerciales et bancaires de 1316 à 1378* (Paris, 1941), pp. 113 n. 82, 362-64.

[4] Jones, p. 187.

others, they were deeply committed to the political destiny of the city and vitally involved in the rapid political transformations which the growing commune was undergoing. The Strozzi numbered among the strong *popolani* houses who participated in the Guelf oligarchy after 1302.[5] The head of the clan, Lapo degli Strozzi, was prior in 1302 and 1305 and Gonfaloniere in 1309; his son, Loso, was Gonfaloniere in 1312, and Lapo was again prior in 1315. Throughout the fourteenth century their many descendants continued to figure prominently in all aspects of Florentine political life.

The Strozzi family not only attained wealth and position, it also greatly increased in size. It was the Florentine custom that once a family possessed property in a quarter of the city, their descendants, however numerous, continued to reside there throughout the centuries. The Strozzi had since the early thirteenth century resided in the parish of S. Pancrazio, in the quarter of *Leon rosso*, and it is here that we find the evidence of the family's growth. By 1351 there were twenty-eight Strozzi households; and in the records of the first *catasto*, in 1427, the index lists thirty-one returns from *Leon rosso*. This very fact of so many separate *catasto* returns indicates that along with the increase in size of the family there was a fragmentation of the Strozzi into separate lines or households. Separate returns in the 1427 *catasto* mean separate family groups, separate ownership and patrimonies, and different financial interests all within the Strozzi clan.[6] Likewise their political interests often diverged, and individuals of Strozzi descent can be found on all sides in the tumultuous politics of the late fourteenth century.[7] At least

[5] Davidsohn, *Geschichte von Florenz*, III, 223, 277.

[6] In the fourteenth century the Strozzi matriculated in several major guilds, including most frequently the cloth importers' guild (*Calimala*), the money changers' guild, and the wool guild; ASF, *Carte dell'-Ancisa*, AA, ff. 321r, 322v, 323r, 326v, 338r.

[7] Gene Brucker, *Florentine Politics and Society, 1343-1378* (Princeton, 1962), p. 32; consult the index for numerous other references throughout Brucker's narrative to various Strozzi.

some of them, fortified now with great wealth and desiring to rid themselves of the stigma of their bourgeois origins, attempted to join the ranks of the older nobility by assuming their aristocratic attitudes and unruly way of life. In 1378 many of these were actually declared *magnati* by the state.[8]

What happened to the Strozzi in the course of the fourteenth century was a fundamental transformation characteristic of Florentine society as it outgrew its communal origins. The family, in short, had ceased to be a clan, losing that tribal instinct which had been a basic force of social cohesion in the corporate society of the early commune. This is particularly evident in the case of the Strozzi because, having become so numerous by the latter half of the fourteenth century, their separate interests had become very diverse. Strozzi are to be found on all social levels and in different economic and political groups; and it is difficult to say that all these men had anything more in common than their family name.

THE SONS OF FILIPPO
DI LEONARDO (d. 1405)

To confirm the impression that family groups were undergoing a process of fission which at the same time reduced the size of individual units, one would want to determine the bonds which tied the immediate family of one man together and the extent to which these bonds remained secure, or were loosened, as the family descended in time generation by generation. Such an examination requires family documents, for no amount of searching in the official sources will likely yield the key to the inner life of a man's household. In the case of the Strozzi, the archives of the family contain an abundance of materials dating from the fifteenth century and documenting the history of several branches over enough generations to permit close observation of the internal process of a fam-

[8] Jones, p. 187.

ily history. Fortunately, as a point of additional interest, one of these branches includes two of the most prominent Strozzi in Renaissance Florence: Filippo, called *il vecchio*, who in the later fifteenth century accumulated one of the great fortunes of Renaissance Europe, and his son, also Filippo, called *il giovane*, who in the early decades of the following century played the antagonist in the drama marking the demise of the city's republican tradition and the elevation of the Medici to princely power.[9]

Through its own records this line of the family can be traced back to Simone di Filippo di Leonardo Strozzi, who was active at the very beginning of the fifteenth century. Simone was a great-grandson of the above-mentioned Loso Strozzi. Of his father and grandfather, Filippo and Leonardo, little can be said either of their political activities or of their personal fortunes. Both held numerous political offices; and Filippo, at least, had substantial wealth although his was not one of the great fortunes of the day.[10] Filippo had four sons—Leonardo, Simone, Piero, and Pinaccio; and although Simone's birth date is not known, it is very likely that he was the second of these, having probably been born between 1374 and 1380.[11] In 1395 he opened a book of personal accounts which, with its sequel, survives. These give a fairly clear impression of the wealth of a typical Florentine patrician

[9] For this branch of the Strozzi, see Litta, *Strozzi*, Tavole XVII, XVIII, XX, XXII; the "Proemio" and notes in Alessandra Macinghi negli Strozzi; Alfred von Reumont, *Beiträge zur italienischen Geschichte* (6 vols.; Berlin, 1853-57), V, 173-241; and the appropriate biographies by Lorenzo Strozzi, *Le vite.* . . . The documents of these Strozzi are listed in App. I. Other branches of the Strozzi for which there are series of account books dating from the late fourteenth century include those of Onofrio di Palla (1345-1417) and of his nephew, Palla di Francesco (d. 1377), in CS-III and CS-IV; and that of Marco di Uberto (d. 1408) in CS-IV.

[10] In the *prestanze* of 1403 there were only sixty-seven assessments higher than Filippo's of 31 florins. There were nine over 100 florins. Martines, *The Social World* . . . , App. II.

[11] The birth dates of the three brothers of Simone are known from the 1427 *catasto* records, but by that time Simone was dead. See Genealogical Chart 1.

family during the early Renaissance; and they further suggest something about the material bonds which held the family together.

Filippo had a wool company which was very likely his chief source of income and into which he brought his sons as shareholders. In 1398 Simone, just matriculated in the guild and therefore probably for the first time brought into the company, had a share of 1,000 florins in its capital. In 1404 Simone's records reveal that his brother Leonardo was also a shareholder; and in 1406, a year after their father's death, the company bore the name of three of the brothers, Leonardo, Simone, and Piero. The company, in short, had become a family company in which the brothers shared the capital. Because of a gap in Simone's records, it cannot be known if the company thereafter had an uninterrupted continuity; but the brothers continued to invest jointly in the wool business.[12] In 1422 the same three brothers, Leonardo, Simone, and Piero, were parties to a new contract; and although Simone died two years later, in 1424, the contract was renewed in 1427 with his only son Matteo taking his place alongside his two uncles in the ownership of the company, which thereby entered its third generation as a family investment. Pinaccio, who was not included in these arrangements, had gone abroad sometime before 1422 to establish a wool company in London; but he had dealings with the Florentine company of his brothers, and so there can be little doubt that the capital of these four brothers remained tied up in common business interests.[13]

[12] In his *catasto* report in 1427 Piero refers to outstanding credits with a defunct company of Simone and Piero; and there are also references to a company carrying these names in Simone's books. At the same time Pinaccio in his report lists a credit with a company carrying only the name of Leonardo in 1422. This suggests that the brothers might have organized separate companies for a while; but, at any rate, by 1427 they were back together again.

[13] CS-v, 8, f. 52; 11, f. 62. In 1428 Pinaccio was the "conductor" for three great galleys sent to Flanders and England, and he was most

It is not apparent, however, that the brothers possessed any other property in common apart from the company, and they certainly did not live under one roof. The 1427 *catasto* returns of the three brothers who were still alive in that year reveal that Leonardo and Piero each had his own private residence; Pinaccio, in England, declared only land holdings; and no property is listed by the brothers as being held in common.[14] Earlier, in 1416, Simone had bought his own house, which was inherited by his son;[15] and the surviving records of both father and son contain the accounts of only their own households. Furthermore, in their testaments neither Simone nor his son Matteo showed any concern with preservation of inalienable family property. Simone used the standard brief formula in leaving his estate to his "universal heir" without further ado;[16] and although Matteo stipulated that his house was not to be alienated by his descendants, he further provided that in the absence of these, the property was to go to the monks of S. Maria Novella and not to a collateral line of Strozzi.[17]

Although Filippo's sons continued to invest jointly, they were in fact living separately; and with the maturing of his sons, Filippo's family had branched into four separate lines. Pinaccio apparently had no descendants; but Piero's line continued in Florence; Leonardo's three sons ventured abroad and met with considerable success in business; and Simone's son Matteo, reduced by political adversities, died in exile, leaving three small sons who had to fend for themselves. The affection which may have linked together these various Strozzi

---

likely chosen by the investors who had the contract for this mission to supervise the operation; see Michael E. Mallett, *The Florentine Galleys in the Fifteenth Century* (Oxford, 1967), p. 155.

[14] *Catasto*, 76, ff. 154r-57r (Piero), 213r-213v (Pinaccio), 415r-17r (Leonardo).

[15] CS-v, 12, f. 27. He paid 650 florins for this house which by 1425 was worth 1,200 florins.

[16] See Simone's will: CS-v, 1162.

[17] CS-v, 12, f. 25.

can hardly be assessed, but the concrete bonds of common property and mutual legal obligation had been shattered.

SIMONE DI FILIPPO (d. 1424) AND HIS SON MATTEO (1397-1435)[18]

In important respects Simone and Matteo Strozzi appear as typical Florentine patricians. They were both active in political life at a time when republican sentiments and patriotic loyalties ran high and the responsibility for the well-being of the state was entirely in the hands of men of their kind. Simone held a number of positions which involved his full-time attention, including in 1421 the highest office of the state, the priorate; and on occasion an administrative post in the countryside took him away from the city for long periods of time.[19] Matteo served less in an administrative capacity than his father and was more involved in the various councils which determined policy and directed the affairs of the city, although he too was at least three times absent from the city on diplomatic missions elsewhere in Italy.[20] Vespasiano singles him out as one of the leading statesmen of his day, and his importance in the Albizzi regime can be inferred

[18] On Matteo, see besides the works cited above: Vespasiano da Bisticci, *Vite di uomini illustri del secolo XV*, eds., Paolo d'Ancona and Erhard Aeschlimann (Milan, 1951), pp. 403-4; Martines, *The Social World . . .* , pp. 334-35; Macinghi negli Strozzi, pp. xv-xix; Arnaldo Della Torre, *Storia dell'accademia platonica di Firenze* (Florence, 1902), pp. 287-91; Mario Emilio Cosenza, *Biographical and Bibliographical Dictionary of the Italian Humanists and of the World of Classical Scholarship in Italy, 1300-1800* (Boston, 1962), IV, 3335-36.

It is interesting to note that Matteo was not sure of his own birth date and that there had been no official or private family documents recording the event. The baptistry records list only the number of baptisms; names are not included until later in the fifteenth century. In his *ricordanze* Matteo estimates his birth year to be 1397; CS-v, 12, f. 23. He was matriculated in the wool guild in 1417.

[19] Litta, *Strozzi*, Tavola XVII. Two account books survive of his administration as treasurer at Arezzo, where he was for six months, from September 1409 to March 1410: CS-v, 3 and 4.

[20] Macinghi negli Strozzi, p. x.

from the exile imposed on him in 1434 when the returning Medici considered him dangerous because of his relationship to their enemy, Palla Strozzi. Matteo also had an avid interest in the humanist learning which had penetrated deeply into patrician society of his day. He had all the accouterments of a humanist: not only could he write classical Latin in a fine humanist hand but he was deeply interested in classical learning and numbered among his friends some of the leading humanists of the city.

The fortunate survival of the account books of Simone and Matteo supplies a dimension to our knowledge of Florentine society which is otherwise difficult to perceive, for these documents can provide, as no other kind of document can, a glimpse into the private wealth of early fifteenth century patricians. The Strozzi books are not those of the family wool business but the records of the personal financial interests of their authors, containing the sources and uses of their capital along with all kinds of personal expenditures. Of the three books of Simone, the first, with accounts running from 1395 to 1410, is by far the most useful, for the others—one opened in 1410 and the other in 1420—are incomplete. The picture of Simone's finances is, therefore, fairly clear for the first half of his career. After 1410, however, it fades away as the documentation becomes more meager; but in 1424, the year of his death, his only son Matteo opened his own account book, and in it a running account of credits and debits of his father's estate brings Simone's financial position again into sharp focus, this time at the very end of his career (Table 1).

The only business account in Simone's book is that of the family wool shop already mentioned. Since the surviving books are not the company accounts, they tell us nothing about the internal operation of the Strozzi business; but they do reveal something of the worth of that investment to Simone personally (Table 2). His original investment of 1,000

TABLE 1. THE ESTATE OF SIMONE DI FILIPPO STROZZI IN 1425
(All figures are in florins)

Assets		
Business investment		1650
Real property		4500
House in Florence	1200	
Household goods	800	
Real estate	2500	
State funds		521
Miscellaneous		393
	Total	7064
Liabilities		
Wife's dowry		1600
Miscellaneous		800
	Total	2400
Balance: Simone's net worth		4664

Source: CS-v, 11, ff. 10, 31 (a running account entitled "Estate of Simone," 1425).

florins at the time his account was opened in 1398 had probably been assigned to him by his father from his own capital when Simone matriculated in the guild. After eight years, in 1406 this investment yielded 1,406 florins, an average annual return of 17.6 percent. By this time, also, his capital rose to 1,640 florins, an increase which likely represents an inheritance from his father, who had died the preceding year. Simone kept his capital in the company, now organized with his brothers, but its subsequent vicissitudes are unknown since the incomplete accounts of the later books neither indicate his share in the company whenever it was reformed nor list any profits. There are, however, records of his share in three dissolutions of the company, and these total 1,618 florins to the beginning of 1415. If these figures represent profits, as they most likely do, then Simone continued to earn from his investment in the wool shop at approximately the same rate as in the earlier years. In his last book, opened in 1420 and incomplete owing to his death three years later, Simone's investment in the company was still 1,650

TABLE 2. INVESTMENTS IN WOOL MANUFACTORIES BY
SIMONE STROZZI AND HIS SON MATTEO, 1398 TO 1427
(All figures are in florins)

Date	Company	Total capital	Simone's investment	Simone's profits
1398	Filippo di Messer Leonardo degli Strozzi & Co.	4000	1000	730
1404	Filippo di Messer Leonardo degli Strozzi & Co. (with Leonardo and Simone di Filippo Strozzi, and Antonio di Giovanni Bartolo)	4800	1200	676
1406	Leonardo, Simone, and Piero di Filippo degli Strozzi & Co. (with Antonio Bartolo)	unknown	1640	unknown
1408-1415	.. . .	unknown	unknown	1618
1415	Simone and Piero Strozzi & Co.	unknown	unknown	unknown
1422	Leonardo and Simone di Filippo degli Strozzi & Co.	unknown	1650	unknown
1427	Leonardo and Piero di Filippo degli Strozzi & Co. (with Matteo Strozzi and Daddo d'Antonio di Nanni)	4800	1600	unknown

Sources: CS-v, 2, ff. 13, 20, 26, 29; 5, ff. 10, 67; 8, f. 30; 10, f. 10; 12, ff. 15-16.

florins;[21] and when his son inherited his father's estate in 1424, the value of the share had not changed. This company was Simone's only business investment; and with a total capital of between 4,000 and 5,000 florins and a return on the

[21] In addition he had a deposit of 1,300 florins, on which 7 percent was being paid, but the payments do not extend beyond a year; CS-v, 8, f. 2.

investment of somewhat over 10 percent, the Strozzi firm appears to have been a typical Florentine wool manufactory of the fifteenth century.[22] Simone's profits, averaging perhaps a couple of hundred florins annually, undoubtedly constituted the major part of his cash income.

Although he had no further business investments, Simone supplemented his income by underwriting marine insurance contracts. The second half of his first book consists chiefly of insurance accounts, including a running account in which the profits of these transactions are tabulated.[23] The great majority of these accounts are for insurance of 100 florins on shipments between Italian and various western Mediterranean ports; and the premiums charged varied from 2 to 5 percent. For the years 1408 and 1409 there are eighty separate insurance entries, and Simone's income from this source might have amounted to as much as several hundred florins. One loss necessitating a payment, however, would have offset the income from a number of such fees, although the rate charged would indicate that losses were not very frequent. Unfortunately, Simone's total net income from these profits cannot be calculated because the profit-loss account has an incomplete debit side and no final balance. Although Simone's second book contains no insurance accounts, it is so incomplete that a discontinuance of his insurance ventures cannot be assumed; and we can conclude that private insurance transactions of modest size provided a handsome supplementary income for men like Simone who had the financial security to back up occasional losses.[24]

Another investment was, of course, land. Both books

[22] Compare, for example, the size and earnings of the Medici firms of the same period. One of these was established in 1402 with a capital of 3,000 florins; another, established in 1408, had a capital of 4,000 florins and paid a return which averaged 14 percent annually. Raymond de Roover, *The Rise and Decline of the Medici Bank* (Cambridge, Mass., 1963), pp. 42 and 47.

[23] CS-v, 2, ff. 58, 61, 83.

[24] On marine insurance in fifteenth century Florence, see Florence

have a large number of accounts relating to small land purchases and capital improvements on possessions (*murare* accounts); and there is no doubt that he was steadily, if slowly, accumulating land holdings. Yet there was never a complete inventory of his possessions at any one time, nor are there any accounts that reveal income from this investment. The only sizeable purchase was the 650 florins he paid for a house in the Corso degli Strozzi, which was to become the site for the residence of his descendants until the end of his line centuries later.[25] The value of his real estate in 1425, a year after his death, was 4,500 florins, including, beyond whatever he inherited from his father, not only values of his purchases but also capital improvements as well as 800 florins of household goods (*masserizia*).[26] Of this, almost a half—2,000 florins—represented the value of his home with its furnishings; the remainder—2,500 florins—included four farms (*poderi*), miscellaneous parcels of land, and vineyards, the greatest concentration being in the vicinity of S. Piero at Quaracchi, where he also owned a tavern.

Finally, Simone had investments in state funds. In the early decades of the fifteenth century the city enormously increased the state debt by borrowing heavily at sufficiently high rates of interest to make government bonds a profitable investment; and many of the city's wealthiest men had a considerable portion of their wealth in such funds.[27] When in 1410 Simone transferred accounts to his new book, he recorded his investments in state funds to be worth 1,446 florins, the bulk of this in the *monte comune* yielding a 5 percent return.[28] The new book, as in other cases, does not clearly

---

Edler de Roover, "Early Examples of Marine Insurance," *Journal of Economic History*, v (1945), 172-200.

[25] CS-v, 12, f. 27.   [26] CS-v, 11, f. 10.

[27] Jones, pp. 197-98, 199 n. 130.

[28] CS-v, 2, f. 92. Simone's Monte holdings and the rates of interest they paid are as follows:

Monte comune, 5%	1080 florins
Monte di Pisa, 10%	290 florins
Forced loans inscribed in the *Monte*, 8%	76 florins

record the vicissitudes of Simone's credits with the state, although there are entries recording credit accumulation of unpaid interest. At the time of his death in 1424 his state funds had shrunk to 521 florins, mostly in the *monte comune* and the *monte di Pisa*,[29] and it would not be surprising if by this time these values represented forced loans to the state rather than true investments.

In 1420, after a gap of some eight years in the extant record, Simone opened his last book, and although it is incomplete owing to his death in 1424 (some accounts are closed in a different hand, others remain open), it indicates little change in the composition and size of Simone's fortune. His net worth at the time of his death was just over 6,000 florins. Of this estate the share in the family company, or about one-fourth of his total worth, had presumably been inherited from his father; and so Simone himself had not enlarged his mobile property at all. He had received 1,600 florins as his wife's dowry—and hence it was legally a debit on his accounts—but in what ways this may have been transmuted into state funds, real estate, or liquid capital is not known. In short, at least one-half of Simone's estate came to him by no efforts of his own; and considering that he probably received some real estate and state funds as heir to one-fourth his father's estate, one has to conclude that Simone had not impressively enlarged his fortune by the fruits of his own labor. He must have earned several hundred florins in cash annually, mostly from the wool shop, though partly also from his insurance ventures; and the income from his real estate was not considerable although his income in kind from his rural properties would have helped defray household expenditures. Whatever his income might have been, much of it went into real estate acquisitions; and although

[29] This is the figure used in Matteo's inventory of his father's estate and therefore apparently the market value of bonds which on the Monte books would have a considerably higher value; CS-v, 11, f. 31.

this may have given him security, it did not greatly increase the earning capacity of his capital. One-third of his total worth, after all, represented a non-income investment in his house in Florence; and the cash return on his rural properties —even the rent from his tavern—was not impressive.

Simone's estate passed intact to his one son, Matteo, in 1424.[30] In that year Matteo opened his own book of accounts; and these records, along with the *catasto* reports of 1427, 1431, and 1433, continue the story of that estate through another decade, up to 1434 when this line of the family was suddenly uprooted from its native Florence by the political exile of Matteo. From the summary of information from these sources in Table 3, it is apparent that the only appreciable change in the composition of Matteo's estate from the time of his father's death was the divestment of his business interest. In 1427 Matteo renewed the articles of association for five years with his two uncles, Leonardo and Piero,[31] but subsequently the history of the company is lost.

TABLE 3. THE ESTATE OF MATTEO DI SIMONE STROZZI,
1425 TO 1433 (All figures are in florins)

Description	1425	1427	1431	1433
Real Estate	4500	4492	4718	4511
State funds	521	1024	1100	680
Wool manufactory .	1650	1650	1200	. . . . .
Miscellaneous: balance of debits and credits	—407	30	.	—843
Total	6264	7196	7018	4348

Note: The totals for 1427, 1431, and 1433 are not the same as those which appear on the *catasto* returns. Those records include deductions for dependents and do not include the value of the family residence, which was not income property. The 1425 value of 2,000 florins has therefore been added to the real estate holdings listed on these returns.
Source: 1425: see Table 1. 1427: CS-v, 12, ff. 10-13, 24; *Catasto*, 76, ff. 137v-140v. 1431: CS-v, 12, ff. 28-31. 1433: CS-v, 12, ff. 34-37.

[30] A copy of Simone's will survives; CS-v, 1162, No. 3. His wife had predeceased him by a month.
[31] A copy of the contract survives: CS-v, 12, ff. 15-16. In this part-

Whether the contract was allowed to lapse in 1432, when it would have come up for renewal, cannot be determined although the *ricordanze*, which go to 1434, include no notice of an additional extension of the contract. We know that Matteo had an active political career and considerable literary interests and talent, but to conclude that he withdrew from the company or that the company failed because he had little taste for business or little business acumen is to assume that the company had been dependent on his active management, which is not necessarily the case. It does appear, however, that Matteo may have been living beyond his means during these last years, for, along with the reduction of his capital investment, there is an increase in his indebtedness. Otherwise, at the time he left Florence never to return, his estate seems to be essentially the patrimony handed over to him by Simone.

There is no doubt that Simone and Matteo had sufficient wealth to number among those men who formed the solid core of the Florentine patriciate of the early Renaissance. Although in the *catasto* of 1427 Matteo, with a taxable net-worth of 4,396 florins, ranked far below the eighty-six patricians who claimed a fortune of over 10,000 florins, he was nevertheless one of the 247 men in the city who at that time declared more than 4,000 florins of taxable property after deductions. In other words, he was in the upper two and one-half percent of the population.[32] And yet the Strozzi fortune was not an impressive one: a share in one of the city's wool

---

nership, the *persona* of the manager was not capitalized as usual; instead, he was to receive an outright payment of 900 florins.

[32] These figures are derived from the table of *catasto* returns in Martines (*The Social World* . . . , App. II, pp. 365-78) and calculated on the basis of about 10,000 returns for the city (*ibid.*, p. 106). The largest declaration was 101,422 florins and was made by Palla Strozzi. Matteo was considerably wealthier than his three uncles. Before deductions, and not including residences, the values are: Matteo—5,196 florins, Piero—3,630 florins, Leonardo—3,089 florins, and Pinaccio—2,892 florins.

manufactories and a few holdings of real estate was all it took
to assure men like Simone and Matteo Strozzi not only substantial financial security but a high rank in Florentine patrician society as well. The portfolios of many of their friends
were probably not very different.

The income of the Strozzi came primarily from their investment in a wool company, although the profits were not spectacular and certainly not sufficient to allow a rapid capital
accumulation with which the family might have expanded
its financial interests. A fifteenth century wool manufactory
was by its very nature a limited operation. It was an establishment employing a manager and several workers who were
engaged in only a small part of the process of finishing wool
cloth; most of the labor was done outside the shop and inde-
pendently of the shop management. A wool company's assets consisted of very little equipment and represented mostly
materials; and therefore the capital investment required for
such a company was not very considerable, usually between
4,000 and 5,000 florins, and much of this was necessary to
cover commercial rather than industrial costs.[33] Because of
the nature of its organization, a wool company also represented a limited capital investment, for further investment in the
wool industry would have necessitated organization of another
company rather than further enlargement of an existing one.
Nevertheless, as long as the guild within Florence limited
competition among cloth manufacturers, a wool manufactory
was at least a secure investment for those who had some capital and yet preferred not to make the effort or to take the

[33] The very limited organization of the production of wool has been
established by Raymond de Roover, "A Florentine Firm of Cloth
Manufacturers—Management and Organization of a Sixteenth-Century
Business," *Speculum*, XVI (1941), 3-30. See also F. Melis, "La formazione dei costi nell'industria laniera alla fine del Trecento,"
Economia e storia, I (1954), 31-60, 150-90. For a brief summary of
the operations of a wool manufactory, see de Roover, *The Rise and
Decline . . .* , pp. 171-86. The Medici wool manufactories of the same
period all had a capital of about 4,000 to 5,000 florins; *ibid.*, p. 42.

risks required in reaching out for the greater profits to be had in international commerce and banking. To men like the Strozzi, an investment in a wool company was probably the chief source of a steady cash income.[34]

In fifteenth century Florence the greatest fortunes were made not in small local establishments like the wool company of the Strozzi but in international business—in commerce and, above all, in banking.[35] Had the Strozzi wanted to make a great fortune, they would have had to push their business beyond the confines of their wool shop into the international market. This required, besides capital and a willingness to take risks, trusted agents—usually members of one's family—to represent the business abroad. There is some evidence that Simone's brother were groping in this direction. In 1422 their wool company put 1,200 florins into an *accomanda* with a firm engaged in commercial and banking activities in the city of Aquila.[36] Furthermore, one of the brothers, Pinaccio, established a wool company in London, with which the Florentine company had dealings. A network of such international contacts was the necessary foundation for a great commercial and banking house in the Renaissance; and it was in this way that later the three sons of Leonardo, themselves having ventured abroad to Naples, Spain, and the Lowlands, built up an extensive and lucrative international operation. It was in their organization, in fact, that Matteo's orphaned sons eventually got their start to fortune and to fame despite the political adversities following their father's exile. There is no evidence, however, that either Simone or Matteo took any initiative in this kind of expansion, and certainly neither of them enjoyed any profits from such ventures.

[34] Even the Medici during the most dynamic period of the growth of their bank had investments in wool and silk manufactories on the side, from which profits were much lower than from their other investments; *ibid.*, pp. 47 (Table 8), 55 (Table 11), 172, 193.

[35] *Ibid.*, pp. 171-76.   [36] CS-v, 12, ff. 22-23.

Along with a steady and comfortable income, a wool manufactory provided the possibility of considerable leisure. The
supervision of the few workers in the manufactory as well
as the responsibility for consigning the wool to the various
workmen outside the establishment was usually attended to
not by the major partners in the business but by a full-time
manager, who was salaried or who shared in the profits
according to a capital evaluation put on his *persona* in the
articles of association. The owners would concern themselves with policy, certainly, and generally kept the main
ledger—although not the daily accounts of first entry—
but a shop was not a large operation involving the owners
in a daily routine. Investment in a manufactory, in short, did
not entail full-time employment. It was an ideal investment
for patricians like the Strozzi who had political and intellectual interests which consumed their time.

Land was likewise a secure investment which provided a
modest return without making considerable demands on the
investor's time. Usually land was leased out to tenants on
a profit-sharing basis, called in Tuscany *mezzadria*.[37] Administration of such investments involved the keeping of accounts of rents and contracts, and this task would be time-
consuming only if the land holdings were extensive—much
more extensive than those of the Strozzi. Returns from investment in land, furthermore, were not high, and for the Strozzi
the income from this source took the form less of cash than
of produce which was used in their own household. Land,
therefore, even though it did not return large profits, offered
the Strozzi some security as well as being an investment
which did not require the constant attention of its owner.

As businessmen these Strozzi appear to be rentiers rather
than entrepreneurs. To be sure, they had capital and they

[37] Examples of *mezzadria* contracts can be found in Simone's
account books: CS-v, 7, ff. 97-98. Matteo rented some of his land
for outright payments, usually in kind; CS-v, 12, f. 34.

carefully supervised its investment; but those investments—primarily in land and in the wool industry—were so secure that they can be considered to have composed a very conservative portfolio. Furthermore, a considerable portion of the Strozzi estate—as much as a third—was their nonproductive investment in their Florentine palace. The Strozzi obviously were not men who were primarily interested in the business of making money. Although they did not have the enormous wealth of their cousin Palla Strozzi and other great financiers of equal fame, they nevertheless were comfortably well off by the standards of their day and enjoyed a secure niche in the upper ranks of their society. But above all, these men had leisure; and without the kind of economic base which assured them of some freedom from the counting houses, men like the Strozzi could not have had the time for the intellectual pursuits and the political activities which were so important a part of patrician life in early fifteenth century Florence.

If the history of the Strozzi descending from Filippo through Simone and Matteo has some interest as the story of a typical patrician family of early Renaissance Florence, it suffers from the interruption of its continuity by the exile of Matteo as a result of the political revolution following the return of Cosimo de' Medici in 1434. Thereafter, not only are the financial records of the family less complete, but their history was diverted from the natural course it might have followed had the Strozzi remained residents of Florence. According to the terms of the ban, Matteo was confined to Pesaro and he was not allowed to liquidate his land holdings in Florence in order to acquire capital. In Pesaro he lived frugally, having nothing more than his inheritance which barely reached 4,000 florins;[38] and there is no indication that he pursued any business interests there.[39] He was in high favor

[38] Strozzi, *Le vite* . . . , p. 49.
[39] Neither the biography of Matteo by Lorenzo Strozzi nor Matteo's

at the provincial court of the Malatesta, probably because of his humanist interests: he was given one of the best houses in Pesaro and was frequently and handsomely entertained by the Archbishop Pandolfo Malatesta, one of the three brothers who shared the *signoria* of the city.[40] But his residence there was brief, for his exile was cut short by his death in 1435.[41]

Matteo's widow returned with her small children to live in Florence, but shortly thereafter her sons were brought under the ban against their father and were also compelled to leave Florence. In their adversity, however, the sons of Matteo founded the fortune of their line, and their many years of exile spent in the pursuit of that fortune were never regarded as anything other than a prolonged interval to be ended when the family again could take up its residence in its native city. Impatiently waiting out that interval in Florence was their mother, Alessandra, Matteo's widow, who had been left alone in the city. Her subsistence was the small amount of real estate left by her husband, and slowly most of this was liquidated to provide capital for her sons in their attempt to make their fortune abroad.[42]

---

own *ricordanze* reveal any business activities; and on his death his widow and children in Florence came into no wealth beyond the real estate in Florence which had constituted his own patrimony.

[40] CS-v, 12, f. 41.

[41] His testament survives, along with a number of documents regarding the settlement of his estate in Florence by his widow: CS-v, 1250.

[42] Her extensive correspondence with her sons also survives as a singular document of social life in mid-fifteenth century Florence: Macinghi negli Strozzi, *Lettere*. . . . Alessandra kept her own accounts (see her references, *ibid.*, pp. 117 and 152) and one of her books has also survived: CS-v, 15. By 1459 she had sold all of the property inherited from her husband except the town house, which had fewer than ten rooms, and a very small farm at Pozzolatico; Macinghi negli Strozzi, p. 164. In addition to this, in 1470, one year before her death, her only credits were with her sons' business in Naples and Monte holdings worth 499 florins, and there is no evidence that she was receiving income other than tax credits from this latter source; CS-v, 15, ff. 102-4. Her letters reveal a continual concern about money matters, especially tax payments. Her will survives: CS-v, 1162, No. 6.

Despite the fall of her fortune, Alessandra, without either political influence or wealth, maintained her status in Florentine society. Her two daughters, for instance, married into old patrician families, Caterina's marriage to a fairly wealthy man in Florence, Marco Parenti, being particularly notable. Nevertheless, the fortunes of the Strozzi lay momentarily at least outside Florence in the hands of Matteo's three sons, who entered their majority long after their father's death. Banished from their homeland and with no working capital to assist them, they were forced to make their own way. Yet they climbed to the highest level of international finance and political influence and finally returned home, where they moved into the very center of life in Medicean Florence and for a moment even threatened to eclipse the Medici themselves.

FILIPPO DI MATTEO (1428-91) [43]

Founding a family fortune. The attainment of wealth and prestige by Matteo's sons is a story which is known only in its broad outline; the precise details of the growth have remained obscure despite the survival of a remarkable variety and quantity of family documents. As the story of the building of a great fortune, it has considerable importance in the history of a family which, after a generation of exile, was able to reëstablish its foundations in Florence for four centuries to come. [44]

[43] The collection of family lives by Lorenzo Strozzi contains a biography of Filippo di Matteo, his father; it has been published separately, with documents, by Giuseppe Bini and Pietro Bigazzi, eds., *Vita di Filippo Strozzi il Vecchio scritta da Lorenzo suo figlio* (Florence, 1851).

[44] It is a story that has interested historians too little, despite its climax in Filippo's construction of the great family palace, which is about the only "document" referred to by historians in their reference to the Strozzi fortune; see, for example, Richard Ehrenberg, *Capital and Finance in the Age of the Renaissance (A Study of the Fuggers and Their Connections)*, trans. H. M. Lucas (New York, n.d.), pp. 195-96. The letters to and from Alessandra Macinghi negli Strozzi

At a time when there were many Florentines everywhere throughout Italy and Europe active in all kinds of business enterprises, Matteo's three exiled sons had no difficulty finding relatives and friends who could harbor them and assist their efforts to find firm anchorage in the world of business. Among these were three cousins of Matteo, the sons of Leonardo di Filippo, Simone's brother, who, scattered throughout Europe, had laid an international commercial network of offices in Rome, Naples, Barcelona, Valencia, and Bruges. They were reputed to be very rich, and none had any desire to return to their native city.[45] Before they had reached the age of twenty, Matteo's two youngest sons were taken in by these cousins, and they initiated their apprenticeship by making the rounds of the various branch offices of the family firm. They started their tour in Spain—Lorenzo in 1446, and Matteo in 1450—but soon both moved on to Bruges, perhaps shortly after the death in Barcelona of Filippo di Leonardo in 1449. The youngest, Matteo, continued his journey to Naples, where he died in 1459 at the age of twenty-five. Lorenzo, the second brother, was still in Bruges in 1461 when his cousin, Jacopo di Leonardo, the head of the Bruges branch, died. The oldest brother, Filippo, had left Florence much earlier, in 1441, starting his apprenticeship in Palermo in the business of an old family friend; but he, too, was in his cousins' office in Spain by 1446.[46] The next year, however, he moved to

contain most of the information we have about the earliest stages of the growth of the Strozzi fortune, but by 1470 the documentation extends to numerous extant account books of the brothers; see App. I.

[45] Macinghi negli Strozzi, pp. 25-26. The sons of Leonardo were: Jacopo, 1403-61 (died in Bruges); Filippo, 1406-49 (died in Barcelona); and Niccolò (died 1468 or 1469 in Rome). Two company books of these brothers survive: that of Filippo in Avignon, 1423-26 (CS-v, 9), and that of Jacopo in Bruges, 1450-57 (CS-v, 14). A student of Federigo Melis has done a study of the book of Jacopo but it has not been published; see Melis, *Aspetti* . . . , I, 126 n.1. The notice of the sons of Leonardo in Litta, *Strozzi*, Tavola xvii, is completely inaccurate.

[46] Strozzi, *Le vite* . . . , p. 64.

Naples, where he was associated with Niccolò di Leonardo, the oldest of the three cousins, in the head office of their family business. Filippo very soon was well established in Naples; and by 1455 he was one of the correspondents of the Medici bank there,[47] although he was not yet completely independent of his cousins' firm.

As the oldest of the brothers Filippo was responsible for founding the family's fortune, and he was eager to set himself to that task. The brothers' apprenticeship and association with their cousins, however, was slow in leading them into the inner councils of the firm. Lorenzo, in Bruges, was little more than a functionary, a poor relation, and felt he had little chance, after the death of Jacopo di Leonardo in 1461, of edging out the heirs for a place of his own in the business; and Filippo, in Naples, at this time was not yet in the confidence of his cousin Niccolò. For these two men, now in their thirties and impatient to make their own way in the world, it may well have been the frustration of their hopes and efforts to win over the confidence of their cousins which turned them to an urgent consideration of establishing a completely independent business. Their correspondence during the years from 1459 to 1461 reveals their eagerness to start on their own but still inhibited by their uncertainty about their prospects.

What was required above all else was capital, and that they did not have. It is not possible to trace the capital accumulation of the brothers with any precision although it is certain that they had very little at the start. While Filippo was still in Palermo serving his apprenticeship, he received his mother's dowry, which he invested with the business of his master and friend there, Matteo Brandolini. Thereafter, Alessandra occasionally sold off real estate in Florence in order to advance sums to Filippo in Naples.[48] But by 1459,

---

[47] De Roover, *The Rise and Decline* . . . , p. 257.

[48] Strozzi, *Le vite* . . . , p. 64; Macinghi negli Strozzi, pp. 128, 144, 164. At least one document survives which acknowledges receipt of 1,450 florins by Filippo in 1455—100 for Matteo, 200 for Lorenzo

when Filippo's letters begin to betray an urgency for independence, there still was not enough capital;[49] and he was in correspondence with his brother in Bruges about the prospect of obtaining capital from further sales of the family possessions in Florence. Matteo, the youngest brother, died that year, leaving an estate, worth scarcely more than 500 florins.[50]

Another problem which concerned them was the matter of a location for a permanent business. The strategic importance of this consideration in the highly competitive business world of the fifteenth century necessitated the use of coded references in their correspondence whenever they discussed likely locations.[51] On this point they were especially anxious to take advantage of their association with the already well-established firm of their cousins.

The death of Jacopo di Leonardo in Bruges in 1461 may have been the moment when good fortune finally responded to the brothers' impatience. Lorenzo felt suddenly released from his bonds; and although he had certain responsibilities in ordering the confused affairs of his cousin for the heirs, he was nevertheless ready to join his brother in Naples. There Niccolò, the last of three sons of Leonardo and without any heirs of his own, was now alone with the family business. He may henceforth have become more generous in extending to his young cousins the advantages of his good name and business organization for in the next few years the brothers began to see a rise in their fortune and then were able to establish themselves much more securely in Naples.[52]

The oldest extant documents with which we can begin to

---

and 1,150 for Filippo: CS-v, 1250, document dated 10 January 1454/55.

[49] *Macinghi negli Strozzi*, pp. 170-72.

[50] *Ibid.*, p. 212.   [51] *Ibid.*, pp. 215-16.

[52] One document survives, dated 28 January 1462/63, in which King Ferdinand concedes to Filippo and his agents the privilege of conducting business in his kingdom: CS-v, 1087, No. 12.

chart the history of the Strozzi business date from 1466; and they indicate that by that time, with both a bank and a *fondaco* in operation with a sizeable capital investment, the Strozzi were already well under way toward building their own business organization.[53] At this time their mother, busy in Florence trying to find a bride for her oldest son, considered Filippo to be one of the most eligible bachelors among the large group of Florentine exiles.[54] Furthermore, their reputation was sufficiently exalted among the Florentine merchants in Naples that, despite the ban of exile, Lorenzo was chosen as consul of the Florentine nation there in 1465.

Filippo also gained considerable influence at the court of King Ferdinand I, and, in fact, this alone may ultimately be the key to the brothers' success. In the war of the barons' revolt, Ferdinand borrowed heavily from Filippo and later made him a councillor of state.[55] Filippo's personal influence with the King gave him hope that he would interfere in behalf of the brothers' repatriation to their native city.[56] Even after he had left Naples for good, Filippo continued to enjoy the King's favor, while in Naples his brother Lorenzo replaced him as one of the King's councillors.[57] In 1478 after the Pazzi conspiracy, when Lorenzo the Magnificent was hav-

[53] CS-v, 22, f. 90. The capital was 16,000 *monete di Napoli*, 12,000 from Filippo, who was to manage the bank, and 4,000 from Lorenzo, who was to manage the *fondaco*. The earliest extant book of this company is a book of *ricordanze* dated 1466-67 (CS-v, 18) and identified as book "I," presumably the ninth book in the series; so the company must have been in operation for a number of years.

[54] Macinghi negli Strozzi, p. 542.

[55] Luigi Strozzi, f. 114r. There is documentary evidence for one loan of 2,000 ducats made by Filippo and Lorenzo to Alfonso, Duke of Calabria and oldest son of King Ferdinand: CS-v, 1249, document dated 5 August 1468.

[56] Macinghi negli Strozzi, p. 542.

[57] When Alessandra died in 1471, Filippo received a letter of consolation from the King's son Alfonso, Duke of Calabria; Strozzi, *Vita di Filippo* . . . , p. 33 n. 3. Throughout the Strozzi papers there are a number of documents regarding relations between King Ferdinand and Filippo, some of them concerning loans.

ing his difficulties with the King, he could find no better man to go to Naples to deal with him than Filippo.

In 1466 the ban of exile was finally lifted; and Filippo returned to reëstablish his residence in Florence and to take a Florentine wife although business soon called him back to Naples. Then in 1468 or 1469, another stroke of good fortune occurred with the death of Niccolò in Rome and the inheritance by Filippo of half his large estate.[58] Not only did the additional wealth permit a considerable expansion of the business the two brothers had already initiated, but they fell heir to the good name and international contacts of a well-established business. In 1470 Filippo returned permanently to Florence and opened up a branch office which he directed personally, but Naples continued to be the center of the Strozzi business even after the death in 1479 of Lorenzo, who had stayed on in Naples after the ban was lifted in order to direct the parent organization.[59] In 1482 Filippo opened a third branch in Rome; and until his death in 1491, the branches of the Strozzi business empire were located in these three Italian cities—Florence, Rome, and Naples.[60]

There was nothing unusual about the Strozzi businesses: they were organized like most international commercial and banking firms of the fifteenth century, and the contracts which form the articles of association follow the standard form of the period. The company engaged in whatever venture the manager considered profitable, whether mercantile or financial. The *fondaco* at Naples was, of course, a commercial en-

---

[58] Macinghi negli Strozzi, pp. XXXI-XXXII. His will survives: CS-v, 1162, No. 8.

[59] Lorenzo had two sons and his line was very prolific; see Litta, *Strozzi*, Tavole XVIII, XIX, XXI. His son Matteo, as we shall see, handled investments for Filippo's sons while they were still minors; but thereafter the financial interests of the cousins diverged, as did their political allegiances, for Matteo was a very close personal associate of the Medici dukes, Alessandro and Cosimo. There are a few extant account books of Lorenzo and his descendants: see App. I, D.

[60] The extant account books of Filippo Strozzi are listed in App. I, E.

terprise whereas the banks at Naples, Rome, and Florence engaged primarily in exchange transactions and loans throughout Italy and, outside Italy, especially in Lyons. Although some of the Strozzi clients were from the most elevated ranks, such as the Pope and the King of Naples, Filippo did not encounter those political snares which caught all too many of his compatriots in their money-making ventures abroad, not least of all the Medici.[61] As a private family without the political position of the Medici, the Strozzi were not lured into the disastrous quicksand of financial involvements with foreign princes; nor were their business interests plagued like those of the Medici by political vicissitudes, for example in Rome, where both families had important investments. Furthermore, because the Strozzi were not directly engaged in operations outside Italy, the unfavorable balance of payments which, according to de Roover, may have adversely affected Italian financial interests in northern Europe, was hardly an immediate problem for them, as it most likely was for the Medici.[62] Finally, as we shall see, Filippo had an extraordinarily large cash reserve to cushion any setback he might suffer.

Private wealth. The concern here is less with the history of the Strozzi business than with the private uses of the rewards of their enterprise. Filippo's estate falls into a different category from that of his father and grandfather, for, unlike them, he was an entrepreneur and an international banker and as a result his enormous wealth boosted the family fortunes to the very highest level of Florentine society. His portfolio re-

[61] Lacking *libri segreti* for the companies of Rome and Naples, we have only the word of his son that he loaned to princes: *Le vite . . .*, p. 66. In the family papers there are only three documents that pertain to a loan to King Ferdinand of Naples ca. 1486-87: CS-v, 1154, "Contratti dal 1400 al 1499," No. 29; 1249, document dated 30 March 1487; 1250, document dated 20 November 1487.

[62] De Roover, *The Rise and Decline . . .*, pp. 195-96, 373-74.

veals the investment habits of one of the few men in Florence who was almost as rich as the Medici themselves, which is to say about as rich as any merchant in all of Renaissance Europe.

The records of Filippo's private wealth are reasonably complete, the major item being his ledgers, two books of *debitori e creditori* extending from 1471, shortly after his return to Florence, to his death twenty years later, in 1491. Here are found accounts of the administration of his private wealth neatly organized under a host of categories, including income from business investments, rents from real estate, interest payments from private loans, real estate purchases, expenditures for property improvements, household expenditures of all kinds, dowry payments, and others. Accounts are kept according to a proper double-entry method. The first of these two books is complete—all accounts are balanced and transfers are made to the second—so that it yields up a very precise record of Filippo's wealth from 1471 to 1483. Unfortunately, the second book, which was opened in 1483, was still in use when Filippo died in 1491 and was never completely balanced. Since any ledger is not a book of first entry but consists of accounts which were transferred only sporadically from other work books now discarded, it must be used with great care if it is incomplete, for there is no way of knowing what the missing items might be in any open account. In exploring Filippo's private wealth we are on firm ground as long as we can proceed with balanced accounts, but there were many open accounts at the time of his death and they are all pitfalls for any kind of exact knowledge. Nevertheless, there are other sources for an evaluation of his estate at the time of his death for although his accounts were never balanced, his heirs drew up inventories; and with the records of their division of his estate along with the account books, it is in fact possible to survey the growth of Filippo's fortune over the last twenty years of his life, from 1471 to 1491, and to determine the uses to which he put his considerable wealth (Table 4).

TABLE 4. THE ESTATE OF FILIPPO STROZZI IN 1471, 1483, AND 1491
(All figures are in florins *larghi di grossi*)

	1471	
Naples, old account		3,667
Naples, new account		16,500
Account of Florence		8,250
State funds		384
Cash		60
Miscellaneous		2,788
	Total	31,649
	1483	
Investments		83,635
Real Estate		8,205
Cash (inventory made Sept., 1482)		20,441
	Total	112,281
	1491-92	
Real estate (September, 1491)		16,429
Palace (prop. and bldg. costs to 1491)	8,197	
Other properties	8,232	
Personal property (June, 1491)		12,203
Household furnishings	6,621	
Gold, silver, jewels	5,582	
Cash (June, 1491)		52,428
Business investments (June, 1492)		35,195
Naples: Filippo's account	7,483	
Naples: Alfonso's account	8,685	
Florence	6,843	
Rome	12,184	
	Total	116,255

Source: 1471: CS-v, 22, f. 4. 1483: CS-v, 22, ff. 118, 195. 1491-92: CS-v, 44, f. 265; 51, ff. 105, 187; 54, f. 5; 65, ff. 5, 13-15, 73, 82-83; 67, ff. 47, 51, 52, 54, 58, 59, 61, 62.

In 1471, shortly after his return to Florence from his long exile in Naples, Filippo was worth just over 31,000 florins. From his very modest beginnings, in exile and with very little capital, he had accumulated in the course of over twenty years a very handsome estate indeed. It represented, however, not only the fruits of his own efforts but also, of course, the undoubtedly considerable inheritance from his cousin in Naples; and in 1471 most of this wealth was still invested in Naples, the Florentine company having just been opened the preceding year. For the next dozen years, up to 1483, the account books tell the story of his fortune, as rapid in its growth as it was to be singular in size (Table 5). His private

TABLE 5. INCOME OF FILIPPO STROZZI, 1471 TO 1483
(All figures are in florins *larghi di grossi*)

Company in Naples		77,861
Old account	1,466	
Bank	47,105	
Fondaco	29,290	
Company in Florence		9,118
Interest on personal loans		2,160
Real estate (Nov. 1479-Dec. 1483)		1,040
	Total	90,179

Source: CS-v, 22, ff. 4, 20, 36, 60, 165, 199.

income during these dozen years amounted to 90,000 florins (and this did not include any return on his Roman investment made in 1482 with the accumulation of profits from Florence and Naples); and his net worth in 1483, when he transferred his accounts to a new book, had grown to over 112,000 florins, a four-fold increase in twelve years. Because his second book of *debitori e creditori* is incomplete, the further vicissitudes of his estate after 1483 cannot be exactly recorded. In the key accounts, entitled "sustanzie mie mobili e immobili," credit entries running from 1484 to 1489 total 31,550 florins over the transfer figure, and this represents mostly returns from investments, the largest amount, 14,525 florins, coming from the Roman company. This account, however, is incomplete: there are obviously credit entries missing, such as income from real estate, and there are no debit entries except a couple of dowry expenses, so it is not possible to ascertain the growth of Filippo's estate from this source. Nevertheless, the estate inventories put a value of 116,255 florins on Filippo's fortune, so that despite the opening of the branch in Rome, which at the time of his death carried his largest investments, there was hardly any further enlargement of his estate in the last eight years, although there was some shifting of investments (Table 4).

Table 4 summarizes that inventory of Filippo's estate upon his death in May 1491. Slightly less than a third of his wealth is invested in business—in his own companies in Florence, Rome, and Naples, and in a company of his son Alfonso, whom he had established in Naples earlier that year.[63] The size of these companies was about that of the various Medici companies of the same period, although the Medici had a great many more branch organizations.[64] The Strozzi banks, it should also be noted, undoubtedly received deposits of cash which increased the financial power in the hands of Filippo beyond that of his own capital investment. There are no other business assets—curiously, no manufactory on the side—and no assets in state securities. The balance of the estate was in real property and in cash.

Filippo's land holdings were not large, especially in view of the land-buying habits of many of his contemporaries and our general impression that there was a return to the land by the rich at this time. Filippo's mother had just about divested herself of her husband's legacy in real estate, and when Filippo returned from exile the only possessions of the family was the farm at Pozzolatico and the town house. Filippo showed no great hurry to buy land and he never acquired very much by the standards of his day. He purchased a number of shops and small houses in the vicinity of his

[63] ASF, *Mercanzia*, 10831, f. 104r. This is a record of 5750 Neapolitan ducats given *in accomandita* to Alfonso and Filippo di Lorenzo Buoni in Naples, 18 January 1490/91.

[64] See, for example, de Roover, *The Rise and Decline* . . . , pp. 61 (Table 13) and 67 (Table 15).

own residence, much of it in anticipation of his need for a site for the palace which he was to begin constructing shortly before his death.[65] His rural properties, concentrated in the valley of the Bisenzio just west of Florence on the right bank of the Arno, represented a total outlay of 8,232 florins over the next twenty years, and from these he earned a net income of about 300 to 400 florins annually.[66] His personal property comprised household effects, jewels, and gold, and silver objects worth altogether 12,203 florins. This was, of course, non-income property, although the jewels had perhaps been purchased as a security investment. Finally, there is the great palace itself. Work began on it in 1489 and by the time of Filippo's death it had consumed over 8,000 florins (including property acquisitions for its site) and still was far from completed.

It is curious that almost half of Filippos' estate—52,428 florins—was in cash. This cash fund had grown steadily since 1471 (Table 4), and such moneys were stored in bags and apparently kept in his house.[67] There is no indication that keeping such enormous sums of cash on hand was the usual practice of his contemporaries, and we can only surmise the reasons for it.[68] Perhaps it represents accumulated savings in

[65] Not included in his real estate acquisitions in Table 4 is the amount paid for the property on which the palace was later built; by 1490 this was equal to 6,259 florins; CS-v, 41, ff. 179-80.

[66] Some of the purchase documents survive: CS-v, 1154, "contratti dal 1400 al 1499"; 1250, various unnumbered documents.

[67] There is no doubt on the matter of such large quantities of cash kept on hand. A *ricordanze* entry on 26 September 1482 contains an inventory of cash-on-hand, including foreign moneys, amounting to 20,441 florins; CS-v, 22, f. 118. The inventory of Filippo's estate used in Table 4 lists "la chassa di contanti in mano di Filippo"; CS-v, 65, f. 73. Finally, Selvaggia's accounts refer to her share of the cash found "in più sachetti"; CS-v, 54, f. 71.

[68] I have seen no other indication of such a practice in any of the account books used in this study, nor have I seen references elsewhere to such practices. On the contrary, de Roover claims that it was the usual practice of the time to operate on very slight cash reserves; de Roover, *The Rise and Decline* . . . , p. 228.

preparation for the heavy expenditures anticipated in the building projects upon which he had just embarked at the time of his death, although his son later claimed that these building costs were to be defrayed from annual income and were not to deplete capital resources.[69] Or perhaps it was only for purposes of security in an era when financial difficulties were harassing Florentine houses and lack of cash reserves often meant failure on very short notice. On the other hand, despite Filippo's rapid accumulation of wealth, one suspects that having secured his fortune he became less adventurous in efforts to increase it and so allowed his profits to accumulate instead of committing them to new ventures. Certainly the last decade of his career witnessed no further expansion of his business other than the establishment of the company for his son in Naples the year of his death.

Although Filippo Strozzi started out on his career as a political exile, orphaned and very short of funds, he was nonetheless able to accumulate one of the great fortunes of his day. His family's reputation, which extended throughout the Florentine nation abroad, had been invaluable: it had been in the business of a friend of his father's that he had taken his apprenticeship, and the generosity extended to him by his own more happily situated relatives brought him and his brother into an already prosperous business house and eventually into a handsome inheritance. Yet it goes without saying that this singularly good fortune would have come to nothing—or would not have happened at all—had there not been alive in Filippo the spirit of an entrepreneur. The restless dependence on his cousins, so clear in his early letters to his mother, is as much a proof of his ambitions as his impressive success, once he had declared his independence, is a monument to his talents. At a time when most business operations were contracting and new fortunes seemed to be a thing of the past, Filippo Strozzi had forged ahead, clearing

[69] Strozzi, *Le vite . . .* , p. 72.

the way for one of the great financial houses of the Renaissance.[70]

Public life. Despite his many years of exile and the success he encountered abroad, Filippo had never abandoned his loyalty to Florence. His continual concern in his letters to his mother for a pardon and his hopeful anticipation of his return were not just sentiments of filial piety. His immediate return once the ban had been lifted and the establishment in Florence of his permanent residence, away from the center of his business interests, are evidence enough of that. Once back, he easily reëstablished the preëminence of his family in the life of the city. As one of the city's wealthiest citizens, he was closely associated with Lorenzo de' Medici;[71] and later his children were to marry into precisely those families that were at the very core of the Medicean oligarchy—the Soderini, the Capponi, the Ridolfi, the Rucellai.

How active Filippo was in the private inner circle of the Medici prince-in-disguise, one hardly knows; but his official role in the political life of the city was a very slight one. In 1478 he was the city's envoy in Naples, where at the time of the Pazzi conspiracy his personal acquaintance with the King was of inestimable value to Lorenzo; in 1485 he was on the Signoria but with the Medici behind the scene this post was largely honorific; and in 1486 he was on the board of the Mercanzia. His only other public position was official of the *banco* in 1478, an appointment generally made to raise large sums of money quickly by requiring loans from the officials.

---

[70] De Roover, *The Rise and Decline* . . . , p. 374. De Roover cites the Strozzi as the one exception to the "dismal picture" of the history of Florentine banking in the late fifteenth century.

[71] In 1484 he used his personal influence with Lorenzo to have his sons and nephews included in the new *borsa*; CS-v, 41, f. 154. In 1486 the marriage of his daughter to a Ridolfi was arranged through the service of Lorenzo; *ibid.*, f. 160. And in 1489, at the age of seven, his son Lorenzo appeared in the performance of Lorenzo de' Medici's "Rappresentazione dei SS. Giovanni e Paolo" along with the Magnificent's own children.

With his great wealth it is surprising that he did not appear more frequently on the rosters of this office, although in 1487 he advanced credit of over 21,000 florins to men—including 9,000 to Lorenzo de' Medici himself—who were appointed to the Monte but who were apparently unable to come up with the necessary cash loans immediately (Table 6).[72]

TABLE 6. PERSONAL LOANS MADE BY FILIPPO STROZZI
(All figures are in florins)

Date	Loan	Rate of Interest	Interest Paid	Borrower
1475-78	10,000	6%	2,160	Unknown[a]
1487-88	5,600	14%	762	Bernardo di Giovanni Rucellai[b]
1487-89	5,000	14%	996	Pagolantonio Soderini[c]
1487-89	1,500	14%	435	Antonio di Bernardo di Miniato[d]
1487-89	9,000	12½%-13%	1,443	Lorenzo de' Medici[e]

Sources: [a] CS-v, 22, ff. 36, 60.
　　　　　[b] CS-v, 44, ff. 7, 71, 148.
　　　　　[c] *Ibid.*, ff. 148, 239.
　　　　　[d] *Ibid.*, ff. 71, 239.
　　　　　[e] *Ibid.*, ff. 7, 173, 197, 246; CS-v, 41, ff. 66, 93. Interest payments are not shown in the profit-loss account, as for the others, but in current accounts.

[72] These are the only private loans found in Filippo's books, but of course through his companies he undoubtedly loaned in his capacity as a banker. The interest payments on these loans were entered on a "discrezione" account—the word refers to the "discretion" used by the borrower in giving a free gift to the lender for the use of his money and was hence the thinnest veil for interest charges. On the use of this word, see Florence Edler de Roover, "Restitution in Renaissance Florence," in *Studi in onore di Armando Sapori* (Milan, 1957), II, 782-83. Despite the vigorous objections to this kind of subterfuge by church savants, such as St. Antonino, there is little doubt that such loans were generally not considered usurious in the late fifteenth century. Filippo himself shows no concern with restitution in his testament; and furthermore the interest rates on these loans—no higher than 14 percent—hardly reach the usurious heights that aroused the indignation of churchmen. See Armando Sapori, "L'interesse del denaro a Firenze nel Trecento," *Studi* . . . , I, 223-43. Cf. Heers, in *Piccamiglio*, p. 14, for the kind of subterfuges a near contemporary Genovese merchant had to devise in order to completely disguise interest charges.

Filippo does not appear on the rosters of the several *balìe* with extraordinary powers which Lorenzo organized to effect important political reforms by sidestepping the machinery of the republic, nor on the important Otto di Pratica, where foreign policy was formulated.

History has given us only imperfect hints of the personality of Filippo Strozzi. We have no personal documents from his later years, other than his financial records, and no contemporary accounts reveal any familiarity with him. The restlessness, determination, and independence of his youth were capped with early business successes, themselves a tribute to his talents. And yet his ambitions were not inordinate; the retardation of his accumulation of wealth in the last decade of his life suggests that his desire for wealth was not without its bounds; and politics did not lure him into public life. We have the word of his son that Filippo admired men of letters and scholars, and he saw to it that his sons were given the kind of humanist education which was fashionable in his day;[73] but any enthusiasm he himself had for these pursuits remains unrecorded.

Nevertheless, one cannot but suspect that Filippo Strozzi possessed a sense of grandeur which went beyond the bounds to which most Florentine patricians confined themselves. His wealth alone undoubtedly elevated him well above the lot of most of his patrician friends, and his many years of residence at a princely capital where he was associated with royalty may well have left its mark on the style of his own life. His absence from those innumerable offices in which most patricians were forever involved can perhaps best be explained by the lordly indifference of the returned exile, a realist of the business world who was not to be fooled by the republican façade disguising the Medicean oligarchy, a man whose wealth and hauteur naturally detached him from most of his fellow citizens.

[73] Strozzi, *Le vite . . .* , p. 65.

Grandeur certainly characterized his ambitious project to build a great family palace. The plan called not only for the building of the palace itself but extensive rebuilding of the entire vicinity, including enlargement of the street, the addition of a garden and a new façade for the parish church in the area.[74] The project was so grandiose that there was some concern that Lorenzo de' Medici might be offended by the pretentiousness of it, and only after considerable efforts to allay Lorenzo's suspicions did Filippo feel free to begin construction.[75] This was in 1489, and when Filippo died two years later the project had already cost more than 8,000 florins and was far from being completed. Work on the palace, which was the only part of the original plan to materialize, continued for some time thereafter, and contemporary chronicles reveal how this great structure, conceived on a scale heretofore unknown in Florence, captured the public's attention almost stone by stone as it went up over the years.[76] With this palace Filippo Strozzi left his personal mark not only on his family's history but on his city, where it still stands as one of the grandest architectural monuments of an age of architectural splendor.

[74] Filippo's various building projects are listed in Litta, *Strozzi*, Tavola XVIII; other projects which he had in mind but which were never undertaken because of his death are mentioned in Strozzi, *Le vite . . .* , p. 73. The parish church, S. Maria degli Ughi, no longer stands.

[75] Alfred von Reumont, *Lorenzo de' Medici the Magnificent*, trans. Robert Harrison (London, 1876), II, 149-52; E. H. Gombrich, "The Early Medici as Patrons of Art," *Italian Renaissance Studies: A Tribute to the Late Cecelia M. Ady*, ed. E. F. Jacob (New York, 1960), pp. 307-8.

[76] Tribaldo de' Rossi, *Ricordanze tratte da un libro originale*, Vol. XXIII of *Delizie degli eruditi toscani*, ed. Ildefonso di San Luigi (Florence, 1785), pp. 248-58 *passim*; Luca Landucci, *A Florentine Diary from 1450 to 1516; Continued by an Anonymous Writer Till 1542*, ed. Iodoco Del Badia, trans. Alice de Rosen Jervis (London, 1927), pp. 48-52 *passim*. Some of the account books regarding the building expenses of the palace survive: CS-v, 49, 57, 62, 63, 64, 104. A detailed history of the building of the palace has been extracted from the documents by Guido Pampaloni, *Palazzo Strozzi* (Rome, 1963).

Filippo was a builder on a grand scale, and the palace was not his only project. He remodeled several parish and monastic churches in the vicinity of his estates outside the city and built at least two country houses.[77] In Florence he intended to have a façade constructed for the church of S. Trinita near his palace, but this plan was unfulfilled at his death. In 1486 he purchased the chapel of St. John the Evangelist in S. Maria Novella—formerly not a Strozzi chapel although the Strozzi had long been associated with this church. The chapel was remodeled and Filippino Lippi commissioned to do the famous frescoes which can still be seen there.[78] In an era that is hailed for the enlightened patronage of art by the bourgeoisie, Filippo Strozzi is one of the very few men about whose patronage something fairly definite can be said;[79] yet, to judge from the surviving evidence, he had no interest in the very fashionable pursuit of collecting antiquities, and the only painting commissioned by him was the chapel fresco. His patronage was limited to architectural projects, and there can be little doubt that he considered them public monuments to a man and his family.

Founder of a dynasty. Filippo's building projects were under-

[77] Near his farm in the valley of the Arno northwest of the city, Filippo built a villa and had work done on the oratory of Santuccio, which had been under Strozzi patronage since the fourteenth century; Macinghi negli Strozzi, p. 340 n. A. Also from 1480 up to his death he paid out 1,561 florins for work on the Dominican church of Lecceto; CS-v, 36, f. 390. He erected a villa (*il corno*) in the valley of the Pesa, southwest of the city, and built chapels in a Carmelite church, S. Maria delle Selve, near Lecceto. Some of the accounts for these projects survive: see App. I, E.

[78] Walter and Elizabeth Paatz, *Die Kirchen von Florenz* (6 vols.; Frankfort, 1952-55), III, 708. The contract with Lippi survives: CS-v, 1249, document dated 21 April 1487. This chapel was not completed at the time of his death, and in his will he authorized further expenditures up to 1,000 florins on it; CS-v, 1221.

[79] See Martin Wackernagel, *Der Lebensraum des Künstlers in der florentinischen Renaissance* (Leipzig, 1938), pp. 271-83. All works of art even remotely associated with Filippo are discussed by Mario Salmi in his introduction to Pampaloni, *Palazzo Strozzi*, pp. 11-17.

taken not merely to erect monuments to his own memory; they were his bequest to his descendants, and with them he endowed the Strozzi with the visible symbols, for all Florence to see, of the prominence to which he had elevated his family. Family pride had always been deeply embedded in the Florentine mentality; but Filippo's sense of family was far removed from the clan-like loyalties which had been such a cohesive social force in the medieval commune. His family pride only incidentally reached out laterally to embrace all Strozzi; it was, rather, sharply focused on his own lineal descendants and extended vertically, so to speak, through time to bind them into a single line. There is here something of that sense of dynasty which was to become increasingly evident among the Florentine patriciate in the course of the following century.

Nevertheless, if the grandeur which so much marks Filippo's last years was as much as anything directed to the illumination of the honor of his family, it is not surprising that some remotely related Strozzi came to bask in that glory. His son tells us that Filippo was beneficent toward his relatives and employed some as his household servants.[80] There were others with less menial positions whose names are found throughout Filippo's records. Marco di Benedetto was apparently a financial administrator for Filippo, for in 1482 he was charged with administering the expenses for the building of the villa at Santuccio, and again in 1489 he undertook the supervision of expenditures for the great palace.[81] Filippo's books during the late 1480's record the salaries of three other Strozzi—Palla, Michele, and Lorenzo, all "di Carlo" and therefore most likely brothers—for services as *giovani* and cashiers.[82] Perhaps a fourth brother was Andrea di Carlo,

[80] Strozzi, *Le vite* . . . , p. 67. Nevertheless, on the household accounts of his widow the only Strozzi listed among her eight salaried servants was Piero di Michele, who supervised her real estate.

[81] Marco kept the books of these accounts; see App. I.

[82] CS-v, 44, ff. 148, 239; 51, ff. 48, 184.

who much earlier, in 1472, appears as a small shareholder in the *fondaco* in Naples (perhaps he was a resident manager) and who in 1484 made a business loan for Filippo, possibly acting as his general procurator in business matters at the time.[83] These Strozzi, however, were dependents and not associates of Filippo, but on the other hand they were most certainly not members of his household. He offered them employment, probably relying somewhat on the confidence he could expect from relatives; but it should also be observed that Filippo did not confine himself to relatives in choosing his agents. The family name was no magic password to the back door of his establishment.

Toward his brother's family Filippo was quite naturally more indulgent. Lorenzo had been his associate from the very beginning during the hard days in exile; and after Lorenzo's death in 1479 Filippo brought his brother's family into his own household, although his estate remained a distinct entity. Lorenzo's sons remained associated with Filippo in business, and after Filippo's death his widow allowed them to supervise her two sons' share of the liquid assets of their estate. When these two sons reached maturity, however, and turned to the active employment of their wealth, the ties with their cousins, the descendants of Lorenzo, were for the most part severed and each line went its own way.[84]

Filippo's family pride and his incipient dynasticism did not influence the legal disposition of his estate. Immediately following his death, his estate was divided among his three sons, one-third going to Alfonso, his only son by his first marriage, and two-thirds going to his widow as guardian of her own two sons, who were still minors. Personal property and the cash reserves were actually divided at that time; but whereas divisions of investment credits and the real estate were assigned, these properties continued to be jointly ad-

[83] CS-v, 22, f. 25; 41, f. 151.
[84] See App. I, D, for the books of this branch stemming from Lorenzo di Matteo.

ministered until the younger sons reached their majority some ten years later. Other than the fideicommissum involving the great family palace, which was to be enjoyed by all of his descendants until the extinction of the line, Filippo had no concept of a patrimony to include indivisible and inalienable properties to be kept intact from generation to generation for the benefit of the entire family; nor did he assign a particular status to the oldest son as an heir either to an estate or to the responsibilities toward the family. The family was not yet considered an entity apart from its individual members, with an acknowledged head and possessing the material substance for its well-being.

For his contemporaries, nothing in Filippo's life must have been quite as grand as his exit from it; his funeral was one of the most elaborate that the city had ever witnessed. The pageantry with which his body was conducted through the streets to his chapel in S. Maria Novella, accompanied by mourners, friends, and relatives, armed attendants, and finally by the entire hoard of workers employed at the time on his palace, had a style that befitted a public figure, even a prince. The cost of the affair was over 3,000 florins.[85] And the testament he left behind bespeaks the egocentrism of his ideal of the family. In it he not only expresses considerable concern that the family palace be completed at all costs but goes on to make the most elaborate provisions governing the subsequent inheritance of that family monument to the very extinction of the line. The will itself, with its many folio pages (and index) of details regarding mourning, masses, charitable bequests, provisions for completion of the palace, the dowries of his daughters, and above all the procedures

---

[85] For all this, see Strozzi, *Le vite . . .* , p. 75. The only other contemporary descriptions are brief references to the funeral in Bartolomeo Masi, *Ricordanze*, ed. Gius. Odoardo Corazzini (Florence, 1906), p. 14; and Rossi, *Ricordanze . . .* , pp. 256-57. Filippo's tomb in S. Maria Novella was done by Benedetto da Maiano; the bust of him done for this monument is now in the Louvre.

for the inheritance of the palace in the generations to follow, is a document far different from the brief and highly formalized testament of an earlier generation—for example, that of his grandfather, Simone. It is a personal document, one that expresses the concern of a proud man who is disposing of his effects with a careful regard for the fame of his dynasty.[86]

[86] There are several copies of this testament, some of them dated long after Filippo's death. This fact itself indicates the importance of dynastic thinking in the disposal of property in contrast to the earlier practice of leaving the disposition to customary procedures as it passed to a man's "universal" heirs. Two original copies—one on parchment —along with two later copies are in CS-v, 1162, No. 12. A more readable copy, dated 1535, can be found in CS-v, 1221; it has fifty-three folios. Cf. Simone's testament of 1424: CS-v, 1162, No. 3.

Chapter iii

THE STROZZI IN THE EARLY

SIXTEENTH CENTURY

In some respects, the Strozzi in the fifteenth century appear to be a typical Florentine family. Individually, they tell us a good deal about the economic foundations of their class. Simone and Matteo, whose wealth put them at the upper level of their society but whose economic sphere did not extend much beyond the confines of the city walls, represent probably as well as any men of their class the solid core of the Florentine patriciate. Filippo, on the other hand, as an international financier and a man of enormous wealth, brings us into the much more rarefied atmosphere of the uppermost range of that same patriciate. In a study of the "natural history" of a Florentine family, however, the Strozzi in the fifteenth century present a special case because of the interruption of their continuity in Florence by the exile imposed on Matteo and Filippo. Taking a general view of the history of the family over the entire century, one might be inclined to say that the Strozzi were on the "rise," and that with the wealth and cosmopolitan status of Filippo, with the new style of life he gave the family, with the incipient dynasticism which seems to mark his attitude toward his family, the Strozzi appear to be undergoing a "natural" process of transformation from a bourgeois to an aristocratic family. The Strozzi, therefore, might be cited as an example of a social phenomenon which most Florentine historians have assumed was occurring during this period of the city's history. In the absence of personal documents, such as correspondence and diaries, it is difficult to test the validity of this theory by searching for the psychological implications of this phenomenon. Already we have seen that what is usually considered to be an economic feature of this social process—withdrawal of capital from an active investment market in order to secure it in more conservative ways, above all in land—is not found in the case of Filippo Strozzi. It remains now to take the story of the Strozzi into another generation to see whether Filippo's sons betray any characteristics which might be considered departures from their burgher traditions and whether a dynastic ideal lived on in another generation of a family that now had three branches in the three sons of Filippo.

THE HEIRS OF FILIPPO IL VECCHIO

Alfonso (1467-1534). Little is known of Filippo's son by his first marriage; none of Alfonso's records survive and there are only scattered references to him in the papers of the other Strozzi. He was born about 1467 in Naples while his father was still in exile and was emancipated on 3 May 1489. Thereafter there are references to him in Naples, where by the time of his father's death he had his own company.[1] It is very likely that there was some ill will between him and Selvaggia, Filippo's widow and the mother of his other two sons; for when his father died, Alfonso detached his financial interest from hers and the estate was hence not kept intact. Later, in fact, there was a good deal of animosity between these half-brothers, some of which even took them into the courts.[2] Lorenzo di Filippo, in the biography of his father, accused Alfonso of unnecessarily disposing of some Neapolitan

---

[1] CS-v, 41, ff. 111, 157, 169, 175.

[2] Strozzi, in Niccolini, p. xiii. Some documents survive concerning a dispute in 1503 over Alfonso's debt to his half-brothers arising out of settlement of their father's estate; this amounted to 7,235 florins, including his unpaid share in the building expenses of the palace: CS-v, 1088, document dated 11 August 1503; 1154, "Contratti dal 1500 al 1540," Nos. 3, 5, and 6.

property which his father had intended to be enjoyed by all of his descendants. After 1498 Alfonso failed to keep up in his share of the building costs of the palace; and although the palace was held in common ownership, Alfonso's half remained unfinished to his death. When the palace reverted to his two half-brothers, they were involved in considerable additional litigation over the obligations of Alfonso's estate to settle the arrears in payments for the continuing building costs.[3]

Besides these personal differences, the brothers were also opposed in the political arena; and their personal feuds and different political allegiances came together in Alfonso's opposition to the politically controversial marriage of Filippo *il giovane* to the daughter of Piero de' Medici.[4] Alfonso was a good friend of Piero Soderini and a vigorous partisan of the popular government, and he belonged to that faction which was bitterly opposed to a patrician oligarchy as well as to restoration of the Medici. During the three years of the last Florentine Republic, he was especially prominent as an agitator of republicanism among the people; and when it finally fell in 1530, he was exiled from Florence and confined to the countryside, where he died still under the ban in 1534.[5] He was survived by two daughters.

Although his father had boosted the family fortunes to an unprecedented level in the history of the family, Alfonso seems not to have radically departed from his burgher traditions. He was prepared for a business career and his political interest involved him deeply in public life. On the other hand, his personal squabbles with his half-brothers and his

[3] CS-v, 1091, No. 4; 1221, No. 2. See also Pampaloni, pp. 114-15.
[4] Strozzi, in Niccolini, pp. XII and XXIII.
[5] During the last period of the republic, Alfonso was an Official of the Monte (1528) and one of the Ten of Liberty (1529). The modern historian of this period calls Alfonso a "hot democrat" and a "demagogue" known for his "notoriously hot republicanism"; Cecil Roth, *The Last Florentine Republic* (London, 1925), pp. 51, 91, 233.

disinterest in the family palace despite the injunctions in his father's will indicate that whatever dynastic ambitions Filippo *il vecchio* had had, they hardly lived on in his eldest son. It was perhaps just as well for Filippo's heritage that Alfonso had no male issue.

Selvaggia. Filippo's widow was left with six small children and the task of administering their share of her husband's large estate. In the name of her two sons, Lorenzo and Filippo, both still minors, she made an immediate division of the cash reserves and personal property with Alfonso. The real estate was also nominally divided but kept under the single administration of a relative, Piero di Messer Michele Strozzi; and Selvaggia had the income from her share until 1501 when the property was at last divided among the three brothers. Finally, Filippo's business investments were divided in 1491 and over the next decade his companies in Naples, Rome, and Florence were liquidated. In 1493 she invested in a wool manufactory of Giovacchino Guasconi, whose association with her husband went back as far as 1478 in Naples. The remainder of her liquid assets were managed by her husband's nephews, Carlo and Matteo Strozzi, who used her capital in their own enterprises.[6] In 1493 they organized a *battiloro* manufactory under the name of Lorenzo di Filippo, then of course still a child; but the greater part of Selvaggia's capital they had put in their own mercantile and banking houses, one under their own name in Florence, and the other, with Piero di Girolamo Corboli in Venice.[7]

[6] Her accounts show assignments of credits from Carlo di Lorenzo Strozzi and Company, Carlo and Matteo di Lorenzo Strozzi and Company, and Matteo di Lorenzo Strozzi and Company. These were the various names of the companies of the two sons of Filippo's brother, Lorenzo: Carlo (1473-97) and Matteo (1474-1541). Cf. above, Ch. II n. 59.
[7] The information regarding these companies is widely scattered throughout the Strozzi papers. All the references are cited in Tables 9 and 10 (see pp. 87, 88).

The major portion of the estate of Filippo's heirs was managed by relatives—the real estate by Piero Strozzi, the investments by the sons of Lorenzo di Matteo Strozzi. Alfonso kept
his own accounts separately and he played no role in the administration of Selvaggia's finances. By the time her sons came
into their inheritance, she had divested herself of any interest
in Alfonso's businesses although she still had some credits
on his accounts.[8] Selvaggia assumed the management of her
own household, and her books survive providing a clear picture of her expenses during the decade that she was still responsible for the property of her two sons (Table 7). After
1501, when she turned the estate over to her sons, she continued to keep accounts of her own living expenses up to her
death in 1524. Besides payments from her sons, she had her
dowry of 1,000 florins and, after 1503, property inherited

TABLE 7. INCOME AND SELECTED EXPENDITURES OF
SELVAGGIA STROZZI, 1492 TO 1502
(All figures are in florins *larghi di grossi*)

Income	
Profits from company in Rome	3,834
Profits from other investments	3,140
Earnings from real estate	5,611
Depletion of cash reserves	18,299
Total	30,884
Selected Expenditures	
Living expenses	2,815
Taxes	7,812
One Dowry	1,622
Expenses of two sons	790
Filippino Lippi, painter	103
Payments stipulated in husband's will	633
Real estate purchases	2,161
Purchases of personal property	1,150
Building expenses of palace	13,601
Total	30,687

Source: CS-v, 54, ff. 52, 86, 100, 169, 201.

[8] An open account of the three brothers was maintained until as
late as 1530, but by that time the amounts were very small; CS-v,
105, ff. 146-47.

from her mother, which was valued at 1,709 florins.⁹ In 1518 she evaluated her real estate at 4,638 florins.¹⁰

Her sons' share of their father's estate had been worth just over 76,000 florins; and when a decade later they came into their inheritance, the estate handed over to them by their mother had the same value although there had been some shifting of investments (Table 8). During this period the

TABLE 8. THE PATRIMONY OF FILIPPO AND LORENZO STROZZI
IN 1491 AND 1501
(All figures are in florins *larghi di grossi*)

Assets	*1491*	*1501*
Cash	35,045	16,746
Personal property	6,703	7,853
Real estate	5,488	12,711
Palace	5,465	19,066
Investments	23,463	20,201
Total	76,164	76,577

Source: CS-v, 54, ff. 201-202; 65, ff. 82-83; 67, f. 62.

cash reserves had been considerably reduced—by more than one-half—but this was balanced by an increase in the value of personal property and real estate, including the expenses of the palace.

*Lorenzo and Filippo.*¹¹ Selvaggia was responsible for the edu-

⁹ CS-v, 60, f. 94 (figure is in *fiorini larghi di grossi*).
¹⁰ CS-v, 61, f. 33 (figure is in *fiorini larghi d'oro in oro*).
¹¹ There are no good studies of either of these sons of Filippo *il vecchio*. The best biography of Filippo is the one in the collection of family lives by his brother Lorenzo; and the best edition of it is that of Pietro Bigazzi, which appears in G.-B. Niccolini, *Filippo Strozzi, tragedia* (Florence, 1847), pp. IX-CXXIII. This volume also includes a number of documents, mostly letters, relevant to Filippo's life, pp. 177-359. See also: Alessandro Bardi, "Filippo Strozzi (da nuovi documenti)," *ASI*, Ser. V: XIV (1894), 3-78; Carlo Capasso, *Firenze, Filippo Strozzi, i fuorusciti e la corte pontificia* (Camerino, 1901); Luigi Alberto Ferrai, *Filippo Strozzi, prigioniero degli Spagnuoli* (Padua, 1880). The concern with all these is, of course, the political events of the last phase of Filippo's life. This is also true of the general account of Leopold von Ranke, "Filippo Strozzi und Cosimo

cation of her small sons. With the prominence of the immense wealth and prestige left by her husband, she must have moved in the very highest circles of Florentine society and was naturally anxious that her sons enjoy the full measure of their father's heritage. Lorenzo especially, the older of the brothers, figured prominently as a patrician youth in the spectacles which colored the scene in Florence before the debacle of the Savonarolan era. Already before his father's death, in 1489 at the age of seven, he appeared along with the sons of Lorenzo the Magnificent in the famous "Rappresentazione dei SS. Giovanni e Paolo" written by the Magnificent himself; and in 1494 he participated in the festive entrance of Charles VIII as one of the young patrician sons who carried the rich baldacchino made for the occasion. Selvaggia also saw to it that they had a proper education by Florentine standards of the time, which of course included humanistic studies;[12] and she sent them to the school of the prominent Neoplatonist, Francesco Cattani da Diacceto. Selvaggia, how-

---

Medici, der erste Grossherzog von Toskana," in *Sämmtliche Werke* (54 vols.; Leipzig, 1875-1900), XL-XLI, 361-445. Of slight value are the popular biographies: Angelo Maria Bandini, "Vita di Filippo Strozzi," *Magazzeno toscano d'istruzione e di piacere*, II (1755-56), 17-33, 49-66; T. Adolphus Trollope, *Filippo Strozzi: A History of the Last Days of the Old Italian Liberty* (London, 1860), a judicious and critical view; and Luigi Limongelli, *Filippo Strozzi, primo cittadino d'Italia* (Milan, 1963), a laudatory and superficial treatment.

There is a contemporary biography of Lorenzo by Francesco Zeffi, a canon of San Lorenzo and member of the Florentine Academy, who was a tutor in the Strozzi household: "Di Lorenzo Strozzi autore di queste vite," in Strozzi, *Le vite . . .* , pp. VII-XXVI. See also the "avvertimento" by P. Bigazzi in the edition by Bigazzi and Bini of Lorenzo's biography of his father, Filippo, pp. XI-XXIV. Lorenzo's literary work has been studied by Pio Ferrieri, "Lorenzo di Filippo Strozzi e un codice ashburnhamiano," in his *Studi di storia e di critica letteraria* (Milan, 1892), pp. 221-332; and the same scholar has edited some of Lorenzo's poetry, *Rime inedite di un cinquecentista* (Pavia, 1885).

Numerous letters to and from both Lorenzo and Filippo survive in Florentine archives; consult Paul O. Kristeller, *Iter italicum* (London, 1963).

[12] Their tutors included Messer Antonio da Milano, Messer Niccolò da Bucine, and Bartolomeo Fonzio; Ferrieri, p. 235.

ever, had less interest in giving them the erudition of scholars than in rearing them as gentlemen who would be able to move easily in the fashionable society of their time; and she certainly had no interest in preparing them for business careers.[13]

Despite their mother, both Lorenzo and Filippo developed literary and scholarly tastes; and throughout their lives the brothers continued to have more than just a passing interest in letters. Lorenzo numbered among his friends most of the literary figures of prominence in Florence at the time; and he himself wrote a good deal, including poems, a tragedy on Brutus, and other theatrical pieces. Filippo, for his part, continued to dabble in philosophy, astrology, and literary studies; and his zeal for learning brought him solace in prison, where he spent his last days translating selections of Polybius into Tuscan.[14] Their education also included music, both instrumental and vocal; and both of them performed their own compositions before friends. Lorenzo especially was noted for his musical talents and gained some distinction when he introduced music in the performance of his comedies before Duke Lorenzo de' Medici, an innovation at the time.[15]

With the leisure afforded by their wealth and with the taste of educated dilettantes, Lorenzo and Filippo lived in a style which had for some time been cultivated by those patricians who had frequented the circle of Lorenzo the Magnificent, a style which was effective in detaching from the general body of patricians a small elite who formed among themselves something of a social and cultural aristocracy within Florentine society. This elite, having politically languished in the Medicean splendor, found itself in difficult straits once the

[13] Strozzi, in Niccolini, pp. x-xi; Zeffi, in Strozzi, *Le vite* . . . , pp. xii-xiii.

[14] For Filippo's dabblings in translation, see Giulio Negri, *Istoria degli scrittori fiorentini* (Ferrara, 1722), p. 177. There is also a volume of bound "fragmenti diversi di composizioni e opere di Filippo di Filippo Strozzi," in CS-v, 1221, No. 1.

[15] Zeffi, in Strozzi, *Le vite* . . . , pp. xii-xiv.

Medici were gone. It was henceforth on its own, forced into the political arena of the republic where it naturally hoped to maintain its preëminence, now as a political elite. On the one hand its members had misgivings about any republican government broadly based in the Florentine populace, in which their role would be minimal; and, on the other hand, as attuned as they had been to the life of the Medicean court, they were nevertheless not yet so politically enervated that they were prepared to relinquish their power by supporting an outright Medicean principate. They hoped, once the Medici were gone, to find a middle ground between principate and republic, to establish themselves as a political elite by organizing some form of oligarchic government. The very existence of this group of powerful patricians throughout this period, from 1494 to 1537, contributed to the general political confusion and considerably complicated the business of giving the city a stable regime. Furthermore, the desperation with which they faced successive crises and the ambiguity of their changing position evoked among them considerable intellectual speculation about possible political solutions and enlivened their interest in constitutional studies and in political theory in general.[16]

Filippo and Lorenzo numbered among these *ottimati*. One of their leaders, Bernardo Rucellai—Soderini's most outspoken enemy—was Selvaggia's closest advisor after her husband's death; and his daughter married Lorenzo in 1503. Both the brothers for personal reasons were no friends of Soderini, who championed Alfonso's cause in the litigation involving the brothers; and their marriages—Lorenzo with Rucellai's daughter, Filippo with Clarice de' Medici—further

[16] The political thought of this period has been studied with particular attention to political circumstances in the following works: Rudolf von Albertini, *Das florentinische Staatsbewusstsein in Übergang von der Republik zum Prinzipat* (Bern, 1955); Antonio Anzilotti, *La crisi costituzionale della Repubblica fiorentina* (Florence, 1912); Felix Gilbert, *Machiavelli and Guicciardini: Politics and History in Sixteenth-Century Florence* (Princeton, 1965).

aroused the suspicions of republicans. It is not surprising, therefore, that Lorenzo held no political office before 1512.[17] Nevertheless, their attitude was a correct one, and they did not openly or otherwise oppose the regime.[18]

After the Medici were restored in 1512, the Strozzi enjoyed great favor. Lorenzo held several important public offices; and Filippo, although he held only a couple of positions, was one of the closest advisors of the Medici not only because of his marriage with Clarice but also because of his intimate friendship with Giulio, later Clement VII. In fact, Segni observed that during the stewardship of Duke Lorenzo, Filippo was no less master of the city than the Duke himself.[19] And yet it is important to observe that the brothers were perhaps no more devoted to the Medici as political rulers than they had been opposed to the popular government. Lorenzo ardently opposed the installation of the bastard Ippolito de' Medici as ruler in Florence and was

[17] Lorenzo refused to serve as an Official of the Monte in 1511, preferring to pay a fine instead; Strozzi, *Le vite . . .* , p. xvii. Before 1512 Filippo was too young to hold office.

[18] Filippo refused to be associated with the attempts of Julius II to arouse opposition to Soderini; Strozzi, in Niccolini, pp. xxvi-xxix.

[19] Bernardo Segni, "Vita di Niccolò Capponi," in *Storie fiorentine* (3 vols.; Florence, 1835), iii, 231-32; see also Strozzi, in Niccolini, p. xxxv. The only important office held by Filippo was that of Official of the Monte for two years, 1518 and 1519; *Tratte*, 84, f. 69v. His only other office was Provisor of the Gabella for one year, 1523; *Tratte*, 84, f. 118v. He went to France twice for the Medici: in 1515, for the coronation of Francis I, and in 1518, to accompany Lorenzo for his marriage. Lorenzo, on the other hand, held a number of offices (*Tratte*, 84 *passim*):

1513—Official of the Rivers (five years)
1514—Official of the Monte
1515—Otto di Custodia
1516—Prison official
1520—Prison official
1521—Prior
1522—Official of the Monte; prison official; *balìa*
1523—Ambassador to Clement VII
1524—Prison official
1525—Prison official; Conservator of the Law; *onestatis offitiale*
1526—Prison official

therefore excluded from the higher council of state after 1523.[20] Although Filippo was drawn into the Medici court not only in Florence but also in Rome after the election of Clement VII, he was by no means a courtier and he had no intention of becoming one. He had no taste for such aristocratic pleasures as hunting and jousting, nor was he temperamentally suited to the servile ways of court life. He even refused fiefs and a title which Duke Lorenzo offered him.[21]

Both Lorenzo and Filippo survived remarkably well the vicissitudes of the city's turbulent politics of these years. Both were accepted in Florence during the last republic, from 1527 to 1530, and again by the Medici after their final restoration in 1530.[22] Their commitment to either side was less than complete; they recognized on the one hand that the Medici had enough influence abroad to make the likelihood of their restoration a realistic political consideration, and on the other, that there was in Florence the kind of strong determination for some form of self-government that had to be considered in any evaluation of the city's future. Most patricians found themselves to varying degrees in this position, ready to accommodate themselves to either side whatever their personal preferences might have been. Some, like Lorenzo, simply withdrew from political affairs.[23] Others persisted in the attempt to find a reasonable accommodation of the

---

[20] Zeffi, in Strozzi, *Le vite* . . . , pp. xix-xx.

[21] Strozzi, in Niccolini, pp. xxxiv-xxxvi.

[22] Filippo was hailed as a liberator when in 1527 he arrived in Florence after an absence of several years. Although he had had a serious falling out with Clement that year when the Pope, having put him up as a hostage in agreements with Charles V, broke those agreements and left Filippo stranded in prison in Naples, this alone would not explain the enthusiasm with which the Republic welcomed him as an opponent of the Medici. Filippo, however, held no offices from 1527 to 1530. Lorenzo, on the other hand, in that crucial year 1529, had several embassies as well as commissions to arrange for supplies from the countryside and to fortify key posts in the Arno valley; Zeffi, in Strozzi, *Le vite* . . . , p. xxi.

[23] After 1530, Lorenzo lived a resigned and obscure life until his death in 1549; Strozzi, in Niccolini, p. cxi. The biography by Zeffi leaves off after 1529.

oligarchy with Medicean leadership but eventually had to re-sign themselves to the inevitable and accept their fate.[24] Only a few took to the field to fight the Medici; and although Filippo numbered among these, it was with considerable mis-givings—if we are to believe his brother and biographer.

FILIPPO IL GIOVANE

The business interests and personal finances of the two broth-ers are not as clear as the historian would like, and yet much more is known about these Strozzi than about other mem-bers of the patriciate.[25] Whereas Alfonso had received at least some education for a business career and was early in life engaged in business, it was not so with the other two brothers. Selvaggia was not at all interested in giving them any business training and there is no indication that either brother as youths had any intention of engaging in business. Lorenzo, who, being the elder, came into possession of their patri-mony in 1501, took no initiative in enlarging the family for-tune, although he later had investments in his brother's enter-prises; and his personal records reveal that after 1530, when he retired from an active political life, he had little wealth tied up in business investments. As for Filippo, who was to be the dynamo in the further ascent of the Strozzi fortune, he too showed no interest in business until circum-stances made it advantageous to learn something about it, and this was long after the age when most Florentine mer-

[24] For all this, see the works of von Albertini and Anzilotti.

[25] Although the younger Filippo is more famous than his father even as a financier, his political activities have always overshadowed his business ventures; see, for example, the account of Filippo as a banker in Ehrenberg, pp. 212-16. Not as many books of the younger Filippo survive as of the older, but those that do help clarify the independent growth of the former's own financial empire. See App. I, G. There are numerous other financial documents of Filippo and Lorenzo widely scattered through the *Carte strozziane*. Especially use-ful is a book of *ricordi* of Matteo di Lorenzo Strozzi, the brothers' cousin, who supervised their capital while they were still children and who shared in their enterprises once they struck out on their own: CS-III, 215.

chants and bankers received their training. Except for these circumstances, which will be discussed shortly, it seems that the Strozzi were stepping back from an active involvement in the business world, a withdrawal already indicated by the older Filippo in the last days of his career.

Once in possession of their patrimony, the brothers did not immediately reinvest their wealth. They retained their investments in the manufactories, although they never entered into the active management of any of them (Table 9). They became virtually the sole investors in the wool manufactory after 1503, when the company—perhaps owing to Guasconi's death—assumed the name of the two brothers. It lasted until 1518; but shortly before it was dissolved, they invested in a new wool manufactory with Guasconi's son, and that continued until the mid-1520's. At the same time, the *battiloro* shop continued operations until 1524 without any important changes in its capital investment. By the end of the 1520's all these companies had been dissolved; and there are no indications that Lorenzo, who, unlike his brother, was in continual residence in Florence until his death in 1549, had any further investments of this kind.

Furthermore the brothers did not immediately withdraw their capital from the commercial and banking companies in Venice and Florence operated by their cousin Matteo Strozzi, to whom Selvaggia had entrusted her investments since 1492. The brothers had 6,000 florins with the company of Florence, and as late as 1521 and 1522 there are profits from this company credited to their accounts.[26] The Venetian company was dissolved in 1513; and although Matteo di Lorenzo Strozzi and his former partner, Corboli, organized other companies in Venice, Lorenzo and Filippo did not participate in them, apparently having withdrawn their capital

[26] In 1521-22 this company was apparently in its third *ragione* and the capital which Lorenzo and Filippo had in it was still 6,000 florins. There are no later references to this company. CS-III, 215, ff. 20r, 21r; CS-v, 54, f. 199; 96, ff. 17, 18; 1164, contract dated 23 December 1491.

TABLE 9. INVESTMENTS OF FILIPPO AND LORENZO STROZZI IN
CLOTH MANUFACTORIES, 1493 TO CA. 1530
(All figures up to 1503 are in florins *larghi di grossi*;
those after 1503 are in florins *larghi d'oro in oro*)

Company	1492	1501	1503	1515	1520	1525
Giovacchino Guasconi & Co. (wool), 1493-1503, continued as Lorenzo and Filippo Strozzi & Co., 1503-18.[a]	995	1700	3500	3600	......	....
Raffaello di Giovacchino Guasconi & Co. (wool), 1515 to ca. 1530.[b]	.....	....	......	1680	1680	1680
Company with Carlo di Niccolò Strozzi (wool), 1525-27 (?)[c]	....	....	....	....	....	4500
Lorenzo di Filippo Strozzi & Co. (*battiloro*), 1493-1524.[d]	1500	2000	2000	2500	2350	....
Total	2495	3700	5500	7780	4030	6180

Sources:
[a] CS-v, 54, ff. 81, 162; 89 (account book of the first *ragione*, 1502-1508); 96, ff. 24; 1164, contracts dated 1 Nov. 1498, 27 Jan. 1502/3.

[b] CS-v, 96, ff. 49, 209, 210; 105, ff. 135, 146-47. This company was renewed in 1521 for five years (CS-v, 1164, contract dated 26 March 1521), and at least once again—probably in 1526—because there are references in Lorenzo's accounts of 1532 to profits credited to him from book "C" (the third *ragione*?) of this company. Lorenzo still had outstanding credits with the company in 1536, when Filippo's property was confiscated: CS-v, 105, ff. 146-47.

[c] CS-v, 1164, undated contract between Lorenzo di Filippo Strozzi and Carlo di Niccolò Strozzi.

[d] CS-III, 215, ff. 21r, 22r, 23v, 26r; CS-v, 54, ff. 107, 172, 175; 96, ff. 24, 47, 65, 86, 99; 100 (account book of the sixth *ragione*, 1519-24); 1164, contracts dated 1 Dec. 1506 and 1 Dec. 1510.

in 1513 (Table 10). In conclusion, it does not appear that either of the brothers had a keen interest in immediately enlarging their already considerable fortune through their own efforts as merchants or bankers, not even as investors.

It was not until 1510 that they began to reinvest their wealth. By that time, Lorenzo was twenty-eight, and that

TABLE 10. INVESTMENTS OF FILIPPO AND LORENZO STROZZI WITH
MATTEO DI LORENZO STROZZI AND PIERO DI GIROLAMO CORBOLI
AND COMPANY IN VENICE, 1495 TO 1513

Dates	Total capital (*Venetian* ducats)	Lorenzo and Filippo's share		
		Capital		% of Profits
		ducats	florins	
1495-1497	15,000	4,500	4,839	18-1/3
1498-1502	19,000	5,700	6,156	22-1/2
1503-1505	23,000	6,500	6,990	25
1506-1513	18,000	4,500	4,839	25

Source: CS-III, 215, ff. 21-23; CS-V, 54, f. 198; 1164, contracts dated
1 Oct. 1494, 29 Nov. 1502, 20 Nov. 1505.

he had waited so long is probably best explained by a tem-
perament little suited to business matters. Filippo was twenty-
two, and it was he who undoubtedly took the initiative. For
the preceding few years he had been very much involved in
the political complications accompanying his marriage with
Clarice de' Medici; but in 1510 he had just returned to Florence after a brief exile imposed on him because of his politically suspicious marriage, and he and his bride settled
down as the first residents of the famous palace.[27] Since subsequently it was always to be Filippo who took the initiative
in establishing new companies, it can be assumed that it was
also he who now organized the first independent company of
the brothers. Nevertheless, Filippo himself was never to be an
active partner in any of his companies, and it was not until
a later time that he began to apply himself seriously to learning the ways of the business world.

Their first venture was a company, apparently organized in
1510, to engage in commerce and exchange called "Lorenzo
and Filippo Strozzi and Company," for in that year they
opened a book of "cambi e mercanzia" classified as "libro
verde A." Very little is known about this organization.[28] Its

[27] Clarice brought a dowry of 6,000 florins; CS-V, 1154, "contratti
dal 1500 al 1540," No. 21.
[28] Three books of the company survive: see App. I.

capital, which is not known, presumably came from the patrimony of the two brothers; and its profits derived partly from interest on loans but mostly from exchange operations, especially with the company of Francesco Pitti of Lyons. Profits from 1510 through 1518 amounted to 3,444 florins.[29] It went through several reorganizations, but in 1522 Filippo became the sole owner,[30] although after 1523, when Filippo was absent from Florence, Lorenzo was entrusted with overseeing the books but was not, however, obliged to be responsible for the company.[31] The company maintained operations until the latter part of Filippo's life when he became engulfed in political problems;[32] and the books were still open at the time of his death.[33]

In 1513 Filippo accompanied his close friend Giulio de' Medici to Rome for the funeral of Julius II in order that the Medici cardinal, Giovanni, could take advantage of the Strozzi wealth to promote his own candidacy in the ensuing elections. When those efforts were successful, the new pope, Leo X, made Filippo the Depositary General of his income; and for the first time Filippo considered seriously a business career and began to familiarize himself with business practices.[34] Thus it was to be Filippo, the youngest of the brothers, who followed the course of his father in launching forth in the world of international finance and commerce. Like his father, he had both considerable capital to draw upon and the kind of influence with political figures which could be used to place that capital in lucrative investments.

Filippo, in short, rode the tide carrying the Medici again

---

[29] CS-v, 92, ff. 26, 149; 96, f. 61.

[30] CS-v, 96, f. 212. After Filippo took over, the preceding *ragione* went into dissolution, and from 1523 to 1529 each received 3,921 florins credit from this dissolution; CS-v, 96, ff. 130, 142, 147.

[31] CS-v, 96, f. 213.

[32] Strozzi, in Niccolini, p. LXXIV.

[33] In his testament Filippo refers to accounts of this company.

[34] Strozzi, in Niccolini, p. XXXIV. Ehrenberg, p. 206, mistakenly assumes that Filippo already had banks in both Lyons and Rome when he became Depositary.

to high ground. The Medici financial empire had long before collapsed, but their influence and prestige, though originally built on the success of their financial enterprises, easily survived the loss of that prop. In 1513 when they returned to a position of power with the conquest of the papacy, which was to be theirs for the next two decades, the way was open for others to build their fortunes by providing the banking services that the Medici themselves could not provide, not only because they no longer had any business establishments but also because, no doubt, having outgrown their bourgeois origins, they had advanced into those social realms where business was no longer conducted. Despite his wealth, education, and social status, Filippo Strozzi had no distaste for business, even though he may not originally have had any intention of pursuing a business career. Once the way was open, he took the path. We have the testimony of his brother that he kept his own books, at least in the early years, and that business became one of his major interests; and the fact of his enormous wealth is itself the mark of his talents in his new calling.

The earliest documentation of a Strozzi company in Rome dates from 1514, the date of a surviving contract for a company to begin 25 March 1515.[35] There can be no doubt that the organization of this company was linked with Filippo's appointment the preceding year as Depositary General. To perform that function he needed access to banking facilities, and he himself was certainly in a position to put up capital for a company of his own.[36] This sudden need for capital may explain the withdrawal in that year of the brothers' investment from the Venetian company of their cousins. He also might have been able to tap the wealth of his wife, Clarice de' Medici, who of course enjoyed access to the remnants of

[35] CS-v, 1250, contract dated 1 November 1514.

[36] For a brief explanation of the office of Depositary General, see de Roover, *The Rise and Decline . . . ,* pp. 197ff.

the Medici wealth.[87] Nevertheless, a portion of the capital invested in Filippo's name undoubtedly came from his brother Lorenzo and his half-brother Alfonso, so that Filippo was able to incorporate those funds that were still in the brothers' joint accounts as heirs of the older Filippo.[88] This suggests that his wealth during this early period of his business activity was not sufficient for him initially to undertake such an expensive venture alone (Table 11).

The company was organized to engage in commerce and banking in Rome and elsewhere, and none of the partners was permitted to conduct any business in Rome outside the company. Nevertheless, the stipulation in the articles of association that the company was to handle the affairs of Filippo as Depositary of the papal income clearly indicates what must have been one of the major activities of the company. The contracts also reveal the kind of privileges that Filippo came to enjoy at the papal court, such as collection of customs fees, control of the mint, salaries, salt taxes, and other incomes which were farmed out by governments at this time. The 1514 contract requires Filippo to put at least a third of such financial activities into the hands of the company (in 1516 it went up to one-half) except for the customs

[87] Clarice had an exceptionally large dowry of 6,000 *scudi*; CS-v, 1154, "Contratti dal 1500 al 1540," No. 21. Lorenzo Strozzi claimed that Clarice was to get half of the estate of her mother, Alfonsina de' Medici, who died in 1520 leaving an estate worth 80,000 *scudi*, but that Cardinal Giulio de' Medici prevented her from getting her fair share; in Niccolini, p. xxxvii. In a copy of her will, however, she names Leo as her heir and leaves to Clarice only half the value of her dowry, that is, 6,000 ducats; CS-v, 1221, Vol. ii, f. 52r. In this will Alfonsina roughly estimated the value of her estate to be about 20,000 ducats.

[88] The first contract, dated 1 November 1514, does not list Alfonso and Lorenzo, only Filippo, whose share was to be 21,000 cameral florins; but in the second contract, of 10 November 1516, the same capital sum is broken down into shares as indicated on Table 11. There is every reason to believe that the brothers likewise participated in the earlier company, for it was not unusual for the total capital collected from a number of relatives to be indicated in contracts under only one name.

TABLE 11. CAPITAL INVESTMENT IN THE HEIRS OF FILIPPO DI MATTEO
STROZZI AND COMPANY IN ROME, 1515 TO 1519
(All figures are in cameral florins)

Partnership of 1515		
The Strozzi		21,000
Antonio di Messer Michele Strozzi, manager		4,000
	Total	25,000
Partnership of 1517		
The Strozzi		21,000
Filippo	11,000	
Alfonso	7,000	
Lorenzo	3,000	
Antonio di Messer Michele Strozzi, manager		4,000
	Total	25,000
Partnership of 1519		
The Strozzi		21,000
Filippo	17,000	
Lorenzo	4,000	
Filippo di Simone Ridolfi, manager		3,000
	Total	24,000

Source: Contracts and *ricordi*: CS-v, 96, ff. 200-2 (1517),
204-5 (1519), 212 (1522), 213 (1523); 1164, contract dated 10 Dec. 1516;
1250, contract dated 1 Nov. 1514. Accts.: CS-v, 96, ff. 61, 71, 72,
100, 101; 101 (an account book of the company), ff. 154, 156 and
passim.

privileges, which he could dispose of as he pleased. It is quite
clear that this company took much of its life from the political influence Filippo had at the papal court and that it
was to be the exclusive agency of the vast fortune that Filippo
Strozzi built up in the papal capital.

The company underwent a couple of premature reorganizations over the next few years—in 1519 and 1522; and during this time Filippo's share increased although the total capital of the company does not seem to have changed. The first
manager was Antonio di Messer Michele Strozzi (whose
brother Piero had managed Selvaggia's real estate); but he
was replaced in 1519 by Filippo di Simone Ridolfi, who may
have been a nephew of Filippo.[39] At this time Alfonso with-

[39] Filippo's sister Maria had married a Simone di Jacopo Ridolfi.

drew from the partnership and Filippo's share rose to 17,000 cameral florins. Although the 1519 contract was to run for five years, the death of Ridolfi occasioned another premature reorganization in 1522, and this time Lorenzo withdrew, leaving Filippo apparently the only Strozzi partner. The next year, 1523, with the election of Clement VII, Filippo himself moved to Rome and thereafter took much more direct interest in the company's affairs. The size of the company at this time is unknown, and in fact there is no further documentation of the company until the notice of its liquidation in 1533 in anticipation of the death of Clement VII.

The profits of the company came chiefly from the administration of papal finances in the hands of the Depositary, but there were also credits with the Pope personally as well as with the city of Rome, from which the company had purchased offices and privileges for fixed fees. The company, of course, performed the usual banking services, including the acceptance of deposits, which greatly enlarge its working capital. No evaluation of Filippo's wealth in Rome can be determined in the absence of records, but the company was dealing at the highest level of international finance at the time. In 1523 the assets of the company including capital, profits, and all credits, amounted to 82,140 florins. Three years later we have his own word that he had 103,000 florins in credits with the Pope alone.[40]

Despite his awakened interest in business, Filippo was not able to manage directly the affairs of the company in Rome. After 1513 his presence was demanded in Florence as an advisor of Cardinal Giulio and Lorenzo de' Medici. There, he was very much involved in the affairs of the Medici court, including social activities that were little to his pleasure. In 1521, while back in Rome for the funeral of Leo X, he found the company in dire straits owing to losses in Naples and to an overextension of credits by the manager,

---

[40] Letter of Vettori, 30 June 1526; in Bardi, pp. 46-49.

Ridolfi, who was now harassed by the company's creditors.
Filippo was able to restore the confidence of these creditors
with jewels he had on deposit as security from the papacy,
and in short time he put the company back in shape and its
books in order. In 1523, with the election of Clement VII,
Filippo removed himself permanently to the papal court,
following his old friend and patron; but once again the demands of that court on his services and attentions precluded a dedicated involvement in his business, and according to his brother, he perforce lived a life much more that
of a courtier than of a merchant and banker.[41]

Meanwhile, Filippo extended his financial operations to
Lyons, which under royal patronage had become one of the
great financial centers of Europe in the Renaissance and a
city where many Florentines had business establishments.
Much of the papal income directed to Filippo's bank in
Rome undoubtedly was channeled through this important
banking center, and his private financial interest would quite
naturally have led him to open a banking house there. The
first organization for which we have documentation dates
from 1517 (Table 12).[42] It was a family enterprise, involving
not only Alfonso but also the brothers' cousin Matteo di Lorenzo Strozzi; and the manager was also a distant relative.
Filippo's share in the capital was originally very small. In
1521, however, at about the same time that he was increasing
his share in the company in Rome, there was a reorganization of the company in Lyons making Filippo the major
shareholder and bringing in two important new partners.
These were the brothers Giovanfrancesco and Piero Bini, who
formerly had been associated with Francesco di Carlo Pitti in
a company that had engaged primarily in the transmission of

[41] Strozzi, in Niccolini, pp. XXVIII-XXXIX.

[42] The history of the Lyons company is very obscure. No accounts
survive in the *Carte strozziane* and there is no information about the
company in the Lyons documents regarding the Strozzi there; Comte
de Charpin-Feugerolles, *Les florentins à Lyon* (Lyons, 1893), pp.
184-90.

TABLE 12. CAPITAL INVESTMENT IN THE STROZZI COMPANY OF LYONS,
1517 TO 1532
(All figures are in écus)

Partnership of 1517		
The Strozzi		7,000
Lorenzo and Filippo	2,000	
Matteo di Lorenzo	2,000	
Alfonso	3,000	
Carlo d'Andrea di Carlo Strozzi (including		
800 écus for his *persona*)		2,800
Total		9,800
Partnership of 1521		
The Strozzi		12,000[a]
Lorenzo and Filippo	7,333	
Matteo di Lorenzo	3,667	
Francesco di Piero del Nero[b]	1,000	
Piero and Giovanfrancesco Bini, managers		8,000
Total		20,000
Partnership of 1532		
The Strozzi		16,400
Filippo	10,400	
Lorenzo	3,000	
Lorenzo di Piero Ridolfi[b]	3,000	
Neri Capponi (including 1750 écus for his *persona*)		3,200
Giovanfrancesco Bini (including 1750 écus		
for his *persona*)		4,400
Total		24,000

[a] This includes 2,000 écus loaned to Piero Bini for his *persona* and to be paid back before division of the profits.

[b] Del Nero and Ridolfi participated in the Strozzi interest through separate arrangements not included in the company contracts.

Source: Contracts and *ricordi*: CS-III, 215, ff. 25r, 26v; CS-v, 96, ff. 203, 206-14; 105, ff. 132-33; 106, four unnumbered folios at end of volume; 1164, contracts dated 2 Sept. 1517, 1 Aug. 1522, and 1531; 1250, contract dated 2 March 1531/32. Accts.: CS-v, 96, ff. 78, 112-13.

benefice fees to Rome and in the considerable business related to that lucrative privilege. That company was in the process of dissolution when in 1521 Filippo and the Bini drew up the articles of organization for their new company. The contract explicitly declared that the new company of Strozzi and Bini was to replace the defunct one of Bini and

Pitti, but Bini was given the privilege of continuing to conduct business in his own name if he wished. The company was to engage in commerce and exchange transactions as well as transmission of benefice fees, and it was to be the only company in Lyons with which Filippo was to be associated. Filippo, in short, was using this new company to control one of the major channels through which funds traveled to Rome from northern Europe.

In 1528 Filippo himself was in Lyons to take up temporary residence following his self-imposed political exile from Florence. Although we have no records of his involvements in his company there, he was very popular with the large community of Florentine merchants and bankers in Lyons and took an active interest in their affairs.[43] Lyons was, of course, much more important as an international commercial and financial center than Rome, and at least two documents survive which make it quite clear that Filippo used his new base and his close association with other Florentines to extend his own network of business contacts even farther afield, to Spain and the Lowlands.[44] In 1532 there was another reorganization—probably the fourth[45]—and Neri di Gino Capponi, a member of another prominent Florentine family of long standing in Lyons, was brought into the company as one of the managers. Capponi became one of Filippo's closest

[43] Strozzi, in Niccolini, pp. LIV-LV.

[44] *Mercanzia*, 10832, f. 6. These are two *accomande* made in 1533, one for 5,500 écus for commerce in Antwerp; the other for 11,960 florins from Filippo and Giuliano Capponi together, for business in Seville. For the latter company, the contract survives in two copies: CS-v, 106, five pages among unnumbered folios at end of volume; and 1090, No. 3, contract dated 8 May 1532.

[45] The company of 1521 was to last three years, until 1524, but there are records of three one-year extensions to 1527. Thereafter documentation is lacking until 1532, except for a balance, dated 1 September 1532, of "libro azurro C," showing profits of 11,600 écus to be equally divided between the Bini and the Strozzi. Presumably book "C" was that of the third *ragione*, ending with the new company of 1532. CS-v, 105, ff. 132-33 (a *ricordo* of Lorenzo); 1089, No. 2, balance dated 1 September 1532.

and most trusted associates, and in his testament Filippo named him as one of his executors and charged him with the responsibility of administering all his liquid assets for the benefit of his sons.[46]

It is not possible to be exact in estimating the wealth of Filippo Strozzi since none of the *libri segreti* of his companies are known to survive. The capital investments of his companies in Lyons and Rome are known from the existing contracts, and they are not extraordinarily large.[47] Nevertheless, with this capital considerably increased by deposits and channeled through an international network of business organizations with offices in Rome, Florence, and Lyons, Filippo was able to wield considerable financial power. We have his own statement that in 1526 he had credits of 103,000 ducats with the Pope, but only 60,000 ducats were secured.[48] In 1533 he was able to guarantee the 130,000 ducats of Catherine de' Medici's dowry, and the following year he stood a judgment against him for 175,000 ducats in favor of the municipality of Rome. Furthermore, his political activities during the last year of his life necessitated large outlays of capital. The credits advanced to the exiles were considerable; and the cost to him of the battle of Montemurlo alone amounted to over 25,000 *scudi*. In his testament he anticipated an estate of at least 60,000 *scudi*, for his executors were charged with converting this amount into real estate in Rome for his six sons;[49] but there is no inventory of his possessions. In prison he jotted down a tabulation of his expenses of all kinds from 1526 up to his imprisonment, and his

[46] Niccolini, p. 327.

[47] In an earlier testament, dated sometime after 1534, he estimated the total capital of the three companies in Lyons, Rome, and Venice as between 25,000 and 30,000 *scudi*; CS-v, 1162, No. 31.

[48] Letter to Francesco Vettori, 30 June 1526, in Bardi, pp. 46-49. Machiavelli, writing in 1525, claimed that Filippo had made 150,000 ducats in profits from the popes alone; *Lettere*, ed. Franco Gaeta (Milan, 1961), p. 441.

[49] The testament is printed in Niccolini, pp. 323-31.

own total was just under 300,000 florins.[50] Segni calls him
the richest man in Italy, and assessed his estate as worth
300,000 *scudi* in cash and 200,000 *scudi* in jewels, property,
and income from official positions he still held.[51]

If influence at the court of a prince could mean access to
wealth for a merchant and banker, it could as well be a road
to ruin. The rise and decline of many Florentine houses
throughout the history of the city's role in European finance
illustrates that point clearly enough. Filippo Strozzi had gone
to the top under the protection of a patron, but his very involvement with a prince of the Pope's political stature exposed the foundations of his financial empire to forces far
beyond his control; and a banker such as he had to be
prepared for any contingency.[52] Much of this involvement
was through direct loans to the papacy, and Filippo must
have found these ties almost inextricable. In 1526 he com-
plained that "io sono exhausto talmente che più sangue non
ho adesso," and goes on to explain that he had 43,000 ducats in unsecured credits with the Pope which "sono in sul
fiato di Sua Stà."[53]

Filippo was fully aware that once Clement was gone he
would lose his protector and very likely become the object of
efforts to unseat him from his favorable position in Rome,
where he had come in for his share of the resentment directed
against the Medici Pope. It was this—and especially his fear

[50] *Ibid.*, pp. 336-38.

[51] Segni, *Storie . . .* , II, 246. There are inventories of Filippo's
real estate in Florence. One, drawn up in 1526, lists twenty-two
poderi and other miscellaneous rural properties belonging to the two
brothers worth 32,970 florins; CS-v, 1221, Vol. III, No. 1. There is
also the inventory of Filippo's properties seized by the Ufficio dei
Ribelli in 1539; it contains twenty items (including eleven *poderi*)
and indicates their disposition; CS-v, 1221, Vol. II, ff. 303r-315r.

[52] See, for example, the 1522 provision in the Lyons company
contracts allowing for temporary deletion of Filippo's name from
company documents in case of "guerre et altre cose"; CS-v, 96, f. 211.
Likewise in the contract of 1532: CS-v, 1164.

[53] Letter to Vettori, 30 June 1526, in Bardi, pp. 46-49.

of recriminatory actions against him from the Medici themselves—that prompted him to order the liquidation of his
assets in Rome and the closing of his accounts with the Holy
See in 1533. This, unfortunately, was not quite soon enough,
for the Pope died the next year, and the immediate consequences of that event on the fortunes of Filippo more than
justified his fears. In Rome his position was endangered by
immense unpopularity and suspicion directed against him
once the Pope was gone. In dealings with the municipal authorities to provide the city with grain, his plans had gone
awry because of political complications. The Neapolitan vice-
roy forbade the exportation of the grain from Sicily which Filippo had counted on, and he was forced to go further afield
to find grain supplies, with the result that prices rose in Rome
and so did public hostility against him. Furthermore, his position at the Vatican was tenuous because of the inordinate
quantity of papal jewels, taxes, incomes, and privileges which
Clement had consigned to him as security for putting up the
dowry of 130,000 *scudi* for Catherine de' Medici in her
marriage with the son of the King of France. Fortunately,
Filippo was able to establish himself on good terms with Clement's successor and so emerged from the difficulties of that
year with only slight losses from his papal accounts, although
his settlement with the municipal authorities cost him 175,000
scudi (if we are to believe his brother).[54]

Nothing more than the events in Florence after 1530, however, made Filippo realize how much he depended on papal
support. There Duke Alessandro, who had been established
as Medici representative following the fall of the last republic,
became increasingly hostile toward Filippo. Filippo himself
had returned to Florence in 1530 and for the first time in his
life had entered actively into the political life of the city as,

[54] For all this, see Strozzi, in Niccolini, pp. LXVI-LXXIX, and letters
of Filippo in Rome to Francesco Vettori in Florence dated 5 December 1534, 12 December 1534 and 29 April 1535, published by Bardi,
pp. 68-78.

of course, a close friend and advisor to Clement, who pulled all the strings of power in the city from the Vatican in Rome.[55] The Duke resented Filippo as Clement's close friend, but even more because he was jealous of Filippo's immense wealth; and he may have suspected Filippo of political ambitions in Florence. The hostility between the two was intense and open; and as soon as Clement was dead, Filippo, fearing the consequence of the hostility, ordered his Florentine agent, Francesco Dini, to close out his company there.

In 1534, while Filippo was in Rome trying to bring some order to his affairs there following the Pope's death, an attempt was made on his life at the instigation of Duke Alessandro de' Medici, now free from his uncle's tutelage. This was enough to bring Filippo around to a more sympathetic attitude toward the many political exiles from Florence who were engaged in building up what they hoped would be a successful opposition to the Medici power there and the reëstablishment of patrician government. Filippo advanced them funds in their efforts to win the support of the Emperor although he remained as yet aloof from any close association with them. Nevertheless, the exiles drew him into the maelstrom of international power politics. When they appealed to Charles in Naples for assistance, Francis, who had just renewed hostilities against the Emperor, imprisoned Filippo's manager and partner in Lyons, Giovanfrancesco Bini, fearing that an association of Filippo with the exiles and the Emperor might endanger payments of the last 30,000 *scudi* still owed on the dowry of Catherine de' Medici. Following the refusal of the Emperor to support them, the exiles turned instead to

[55] For the first time Filippo became a holder of political offices (*Tratte*, 85 *passim*):

1530—Official of the *monte di pietà* (three years); Twelve procurators of the Republic

1531—Otto di Custodia; Official of the Abbondanza; Otto di Pratica; Official of the Merchants' Guild.

1532—Council of Forty-eight (senate); Official of the Monte; Councilor of the Duke

Francis; and so Filippo was able to make his peace with the King, who now had access to the resources of the Strozzi bank in Lyons to outfit troops in Italy to be used against the Emperor. Filippo's involvement became even more complicated when, against his wishes, his son Piero accepted a commission from Francis and was soon leading troops against imperial forces. The consequence of this was retaliation by the Emperor, who ordered Filippo's property in Naples and Sicily confiscated. This, however, was not a considerable loss; and furthermore, Filippo suffered no interference in his business affairs elsewhere in imperial territory, either in Flanders or in Spain. In Florence, meanwhile, he had been declared a rebel for his association with the exiles and his property there was seized.[56]

By 1536, having closed shop in Florence, suffered setbacks in Rome and losses in the Neapolitan Kingdom, and exposed his entire financial empire to the vagaries of the dynastic power struggle, Filippo, wary of further involvements, abandoned Rome altogether and retired to Venice. Hardly was he settled there, however, than word came of Duke Alessandro's assassination in Florence. This event finally aroused the exiles to action and Filippo now came forward as the protagonist in their efforts to reconquer Florence. From that time on, Filippo poured money into their campaign and took the field himself; and if that last effort of his life reduced him to the indignity of death in prison, it also, at least in the hearts of some, elevated him to the heights of martyrs and patriots in the annals that close the city's long history as a republic.[57]

Filippo *il giovane* had attained heights that surpassed those reached by his father; his ambitions went beyond the doors of his palace and even the gates of his city. That climb, however, arose on the foundation laid by Filippo *il vecchio*,

---

[56] CS-v, 105, ff. 146-47.
[57] For this episode in the life of Filippo, see especially Ferrai, *Filippo Strozzi* . . . , and von Albertini, pp. 212-21.

and the son made every effort to buttress the dynastic tradition passed on to him by a father whom he had never known. Throughout his life he had continued the work on the great family palace, and in his last testament, drawn up in the final hopeless hours in prison, he is quite explicit in obligating his heirs to complete the task.[58] Likewise his various real estate holdings were to compose a great patrimony on which he placed a fideicommissum so that they could never be alienated.[59] And finally, he instructs his brother to have a marble monument built for him in the family chapel of S. Maria Novella, "without respect for the painting that is there now, which will perhaps be destroyed because by its nature it is not very durable."[60]

Filippo's progeny were barred from taking up residence in their native city. None of them ever returned; and furthermore, none of them carried on their father's business. With their wealth and their international prestige, it is not surprising that they were attracted away from their bourgeois origins to the glamor of the courtly world which their father had entered but never wholeheartedly accepted. Filippo himself seems not to have pushed any of them into business careers.[61] In fact, he had hopes that the eldest, Piero, would

[58] "E perchè io desidero sopra ogni cosa che il Palazzo di Firenze riceva in qualche tempo la perfezione sua, obligo tutti li beni che al presente posseggo, e li eredi miei a tale fabrica. . . ." The testament is published in Niccolini, pp. 323-31. See also a similar provision in an earlier testament of 1535, also published in Niccolini, pp. 315-22.

[59] This is a stipulation in the earlier testament of 1535. Filippo's real estate in Florence was confiscated and sold; see the inventory, CS-v, 1221, Vol. 2, ff. 303r-15r. His half of the palace was also confiscated but later restored to a grandson of Filippo, from whom it passed to the line of Filippo's brother Lorenzo.

[60] ". . . nè abbia rispetto alla pittura che ve è oggi, quale è forza guastare, conciosia che di sua natura non è molto durabile." The painting was, of course, the famous fresco of Filippino Lippi. The model for the tomb suggested by Filippo was that of Giuliano Gondi in the corresponding chapel on the opposite side of the main altar.

[61] He had high hopes for his son Giulio, one of his three sons still a minor when he made out his testament in 1537. He assigned him a guardian who was to instruct Giulio "nelle cose mercantili," and he

be a priest and earn a high place in the papal curia—hardly the usual prospect for the eldest son of a typical Florentine merchant.[62] Instead, Piero preferred a military career and became one of the great captains of his day. At least three other sons went off to study in the university of Padua. Of the six sons who outlived Filippo, all were knighted and received military commissions. They were all at one time or another in the service of Francis I or Catherine de' Medici and were active in the field in various places during the dynastic struggles of the period. Two died in battle and two others ended their lives as officers in the French army. Another advanced from military commissions to church offices in France and died Archbishop of Sens and a cardinal. Only two of the brothers themselves had sons; one of these died fighting for the Spanish in 1582, and the other lived out his life in Rome. But Filippo's line did not extend beyond this generation.[63]

LORENZO DI FILIPPO

Much of the interest in the history of the Strozzi brothers lies in a consideration of what men who had inherited about as much as anyone could have hoped for in Renaissance Florence did with their lives. Alfonso had been groomed for a business career and Filippo eventually took the same course; and both were active in Florentine politics, although in very different ways. On the other hand the third brother, Lorenzo, was hardly involved in business and politics; and in

was to be released from this tutelage at a much earlier age (eighteen) than his two brothers, who were under the same tutor. Unknown to Filippo, however, Giulio was dead when the testament was drawn up. Niccolini, pp. 326-27.

[62] Throughout the 1520's, when Piero was still under age, his name was included on lists of prospective cardinals although he was never actually elevated to the office; Marino Sanuto, *I diarii* (58 vols.; Venice, 1879-1902), xxxii, col. 188; xxxviii, col. 251; xli, col. 286; xlvi, col. 443.

[63] On Filippo's sons, see Litta, *Strozzi*, Tavola xx; and Émile Picot, *Les italiens en France au XVIe siècle* (Bordeaux, 1902), pp. 43-45.

the history of the family it is his life that suggests the expected transformation from a bourgeois to an aristocratic mentality.

One can only suppose that it was an utter disinterest in the world of commerce and finance which kept him for a while only at the periphery of his brother's financial empire and eventually led him to withdraw altogether. His biographer mentions not the slightest interest in business. When the brothers began to put their capital to work in their own ventures after 1510, it was almost a full decade after Lorenzo had entered his majority, and he undoubtedly was following the lead of Filippo. The brothers owned their property in Florence jointly and Lorenzo's capital was used by Filippo in the early organizations of his businesses, but eventually Lorenzo began to withdraw from his brothers' enterprises despite the highly lucrative investment opportunities they must have offered. In 1522 he pulled out of both the companies of Florence and Rome; and although he retained an interest in the Lyons company, in 1533 he consigned those credits to his son Palla, who established himself there and entered into the management of that business.[64] Meanwhile, the jointly held property of the two brothers had mostly been divided: the cloth manufactories were discontinued (Table 9; see p. 87), and in 1531 their real estate was divided.[65] In 1536, when his brother was declared a rebel and his property in Florence confiscated, Lorenzo claimed outstanding credits with his brother of only 6,982 florins.[66] Lorenzo's own accounts, which are fairly complete, make it quite clear that his wealth in later years was entirely in land.[67] As a business-

[64] CS-v, 106, ff. 181, 222.

[65] The total value before the division was 23,042 florins *larghi d'oro in oro* (compare the value of their real estate in 1501 when they received their share of the patrimony, worth 10,682 florins *larghi d'oro in oro*); CS-v, 106, f. 117.

[66] CS-v, 105, ff. 146-47.

[67] Up to 1535 Lorenzo's records show that his major credits came from the joint investments with his brother. Thereafter, although his last books are incomplete, the only income he lists, besides farm

man Lorenzo represents the most conservative Strozzi in the four generations we have traversed.

Lorenzo, not being so closely associated with the Medici as his brother, was therefore not so devoted to their interest. Like most patricians, as his biographer puts it, he "knew how to stabilize his boat in the tempestuous times of the Florentine Republic so that no change barred him from a safe port."[68] He was thus able to survive the various political vicissitudes which his life spanned, even the bad days of his brother. He participated in the meetings of the Orti Oricellari, where political questions of the day were discussed, and he numbered among those who generally favored an oligarchical form of government;[69] and after the death of Duke Lorenzo, the last of the direct line of Lorenzo the Magnificent, he was outspoken in insisting on a return to the republican traditions of Florence. He was therefore not included in important embassies or in the private councils of state during the government of Ippolito de' Medici, whom he had opposed, unlike his brother. During the revived republic, from 1527 to 1530, he was closer to the center of things, but, again, not so completely committed—like his half-brother Alfonso—that he could not survive its collapse. After the final Medici restora-

---

rents, are 180 florins from the 6 percent Monte, 78 florins in salaries from public office, and 957 florins in credits extended by his son Palla. There are several records of small business investments: CS-v, 1164.

In the division of 1531 Lorenzo received real estate worth 11,521 florins from the patrimony plus 3,000 florins in land from his mother's estate. In 1535 his properties altogether were worth 16,724 florins; CS-v, 106, ff. 117, 223. His income from this source for five years, from 1531 to 1536, was 3,624 florins. His books after 1535 being incomplete, the extent of his acquisitions cannot be determined, but it is perhaps reflected in his *decima* assessments: in 1534 it was 47 florins, 11 *soldi*, 9 *denari*, and in 1560, when his property reverted to his son Giambattista, following Palla's death, it was 57 florins, 14 *soldi*, 3 *denari*; CS-v, 742, ff. 111, 119-32.

Lorenzo's testament also survives: CS-v, 1162, No. 33.

[68] Zeffi, in Strozzi, *Le vite . . .* , p. xv.
[69] Von Albertini, p. 76.

tion he held no major offices; and undoubtedly his brother's activities barred him from the intimate circles of Duke Cosimo, although his own conduct had been such that he was able to end his days in his native city as a respected citizen.[70]

Lorenzo had always been more interested in literary pursuits and aristocratic pleasures. As a youth he had been active in festive celebrations and he had some creative talent for theatrical performances. He was an accomplished musician, both as a performer and a composer, and he had a reputation for his ability to combine his literary and musical talents in entertainments for the high society of Florence. His presence in the Orti Oricellari and the few literary works which survive further attest to the refinement of his education and taste. To a certain extent Lorenzo's life marks a departure from the traditions of his forebears in being removed from the counting house and the public square. It in fact conforms to a pattern one might expect to find in the lives of many patricians at a time when political changes were increasingly dampening their public spirit and compelling them to withdraw to more private pursuits. Furthermore, with substantial wealth in land they could afford a more leisurely way of life. And literary tastes like those of Lorenzo gave a new style to that life of withdrawal and leisure.

Of the three sons of Filippo, only Lorenzo established a branch in Florence which was to bear fruit in future generations. Alfonso had no sons, and Filippo's were barred from the city (and failed to extend their line of the family beyond another generation). Lorenzo had two sons. The oldest, Palla, entered the business world and moved to Lyons, where he assumed responsiblity in 1533 for his father's investments with the company of Strozzi and Bini. He spent the remainder of his life there actively engaged in that company's affairs, which eventually assumed his name. He died in 1559 without

[70] For Lorenzo's offices, see above, notes 19 and 22.

issue.[71] Nothing is more telling about the attitude of the patriciate toward the business world than Palla's very presence in it. Business was still very much a part of Florentine life, and there is no indication that for either economic or social reasons men hesitated to engage in it. Filippo *il vecchio* raised his oldest son to go into business, and the grand style of the youngest, Filippo *il giovane,* did not preclude his entry into it as well. Despite a generation of retirement from the marketplace by Lorenzo, his elder son—and this deserves emphasis—did not hesitate to return.

Lorenzo's younger son, Giambattista, remained in Florence living very much the kind of life his father led in his later years. He was a friend of the Medici and a member of the Senate after 1561, but he preferred to avoid public life; and although he had married the daughter of the prominent papal banker Bindo Altoviti,[72] he himself had no interest in business. Like his father, he was dedicated rather to literary pleasures.[73] He inherited his brother's estate and eventually acquired complete ownership of the family palace from the last heir of Filippo.[74] It was his line which continued to reside there until its extinction in our own century.

[71] Unfortunately we know next to nothing about Palla. Passerini is mistaken in fixing Palla's death in 1514. In 1533 Lorenzo made over credits to Palla, who was with the company of Filippo Strozzi and Capponi in Lyons; CS-v, 106, f. 155. The accounts of Lorenzo's estate in 1548 show credits of 6021 florins, including capital and profits, with the company of Giovanfrancesco Bini and Palla Strozzi in Lyons; CS-v, 134, f. 1; cf. CS-v, 1163, No. 29 (*A saldo* of all accounts of Palla and his father made in December 1546). Palla died in 1559, naming his brother sole heir; CS-v, 740, document containing a family tree. Accounts kept in Palla's name of properties owned in Florence also survive: CS-v, 133-37. There are in addition a number of business papers: CS-v, 1090, packet No. 2; and CS-v, 1282.

[72] The marriage contract survives: CS-v, 1161, No. 12. Her dowry was 4,000 florins.

[73] Litta, *Strozzi,* Tavola xxii; Negri, p. 251; Luigi Strozzi, ff. 168r-69r. There are also extant account books relevant to his real estate: CS-v, 126-32.

[74] CS-v, 1091, No. 4. Filippo's share had been confiscated and held by the government.

GENEALOGICAL CHART 2. THE GUICCIARDINI

A Selective Genealogy

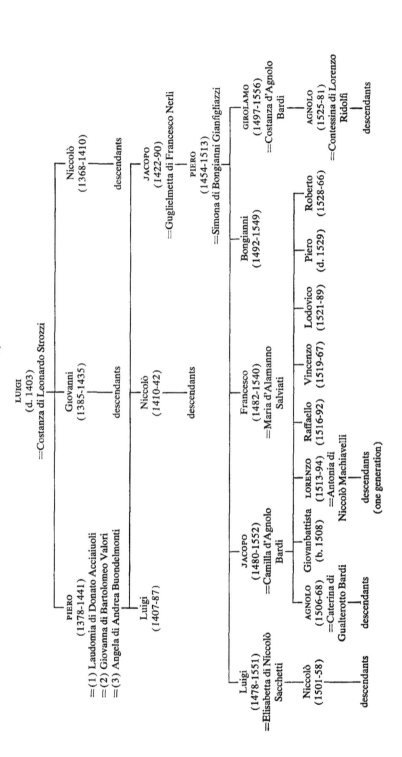

Chapter iv

THE GUICCIARDINI

AFTER the Medici, the Strozzi are probably the best known of Florentine families abroad although their fame arises less from a familial role in the life of the city than from a few grand gestures made by individual Strozzi. The younger Filippo was the protagonist in the dramatic episode that closed the city's honorable republican tradition, and his father made an indelible mark on the city with a palace that is not only a monument to the family's great fortune but even more, for the generations of tourists who have swarmed around its corner and through its courtyard, a symbol of the grandeur and good taste of an entire age. The Guicciardini have known no such glory though they have provided one of the great historians of that epoch. Yet families like the Guicciardini made up the backbone of Florentine patrician society in the Renaissance. They have always been vitally involved in all aspects of the life of the city, and their presence is still very much felt on the Florentine scene. The Guicciardini did not suffer the interruptions and the eccentric behavior which mark the history of the Strozzi, and the very continuity in the roles played by the seven generations we shall follow gives this history the quality of being the story of a much more typical patrician family, however lacking it may be in drama.[1]

---

[1] The Guicciardini family maintains its own archives, located in the family palace in Florence. It is one of the largest collections of family documents in the city. Documents exist in complete series from the latter half of the sixteenth century to the present, and there are numerous miscellaneous documents for the earlier period as far back as the fourteenth century. It is well organized, completely catalogued, spaciously housed, and conveniently accessible to scholars; see the description in Roberto Ridolfi, *Gli archivi delle famiglie fiorentine* (Florence, 1934), pp. 95-210. Especially valuable is the card catalogue

The Guicciardini

Not much more can be said about the origins of the Guicciardini than of any other of the great patrician families of Florence.[2] In the mid-twelfth century a certain Guicciardino was a land owner in the valley of the Pesa, at Poppiano, where the family has continued to own land to this day; and they had the patronage of a church there. The tenacity with which later Guicciardini held to their ownership of the ruins of the fortress at Poppiano hints at possible feudal origins of the clan. At any rate, in the next century their names begin to appear in the city's records. Another Guicciardino, the grandson of the former, matriculated in the silk guild in 1240, and his descendants for many generations were owners of silk manufactories. His son Tuccio laid the foundation of the family's wealth; and Tuccio's sons, in turn, were admitted into the government and enjoyed a role in the ruling oligarchy. Their tower and residence in the *oltr'Arno* section of the city was the nucleus of subsequent Guicciardini residences and the site of the present Guicciardini palace.[3] Their descendants continued to be active in both business and politics. Up to the very end of the republic, the Guicciardini held an extraordinary number of offices at all levels, including all together forty-four priorates and sixteen tenures of the office of Gonfaloniere, and several of them were knighted by the commune.

---

of information on individual members of the family made by the late Conte Paolo Guicciardini. He assembled all the biographical information he could find from the family archives, the state archives, and other sources, and put it on cards (with complete citation of sources), filed chronologically under headings of individuals. It is a remarkable genealogical record, indispensable for the study of any member of the family. It is cited here as AG, *Spogli*. Of great importance also is the family history written by Francesco Guicciardini, "Memorie. . . ." See also *Guicciardini di Firenze* in Litta, III (1834).

[2] For several opinions about the family's origins, see the *Enciclopedia storico-nobiliare italiana*, III, 630-31.

[3] Paolo Guicciardini and Emilio Dori, *Le antiche case ed il palazzo dei Guicciardini in Firenze* (Florence, 1952), p. 20.

The Guicciardini

After the Black Death, the Guicciardini were one of the most prominent *popolani* families in the city.[4] The grandson of Tuccio, Piero (d. 1370), was on the Signoria twice (once as Gonfaloniere) and in 1364 was knighted by the commune. His son Luigi (d. 1403), who was Gonfaloniere in 1378 at the time of the Ciompi revolt, was caught in the vortex of the factionalism which so disturbed the political scene of his day; but, not being strongly partisan, he managed to survive these struggles without great personal losses.[5] Although Luigi's house had been burned in the revolt of 1378, he nevertheless maintained his stature in the state and was knighted by the new government (and so referred to as Messer Luigi by his descendants). Up to the time of his death, he continued to serve the state in a number of capacities, including several important ambassadorial posts and, twice more, the office of Gonfaloniere.[6]

Both Piero and Messer Luigi had large fortunes.[7] Piero was one of the richest men in Florence,[8] but just how he accumulated his wealth is not known. He probably did not inherit much property, for most of the real estate he passed on to his son had been steadily accumulated throughout his own life.[9] Furthermore, his extant accounts do not reveal any association with a family business, although he had several brothers. In the early 1340's, in fact, he was a factor of the

[4] Brucker, *Florentine Politics* . . . , pp. 124-25.
[5] *Ibid.*, p. 375, n. 121; AG, *Spogli.*
[6] For the political offices of both Piero and Luigi, see AG, *Spogli.*
[7] Two books of their accounts survive: AG, Libri 1 (of Piero, 1344-66) and 2 (of Luigi, 1369-1404). These books are not kept in double entry; they contain separate entries of credits, of debts, and especially of land purchases, along with personal *ricordi*. A great deal of their contents is transcribed in AG, *Spogli.*
[8] Brucker, *Florentine Politics* . . . , pp. 30-31, referring to *prestanze.*
[9] Piero recorded land purchases totaling 20,460 florins from 1344 to 1366; AG, Libro, 1, ff. 60r-79r, 90v-92r.

Acciaiuoli in Chiarenza. By 1344, however, he had returned to Florence; and thereafter he accumulated enough capital to buy considerable real estate as well as to undertake extensive building projects for the church. When he died in 1370, his son evaluated his estate at 58,077 florins.[10] His estimate of the real estate was 18,000 florins; the rest was in diverse credits, including a wool manufactory, a *banco* in Florence, and a *fondaco* in Foligno. Piero was clearly an active investor of capital and much of his wealth undoubtedly came from his business ventures. In fact, when Piero died without leaving a testament, Messer Luigi had difficulties with the bishop over the burial because of his father's usurious practices and ill-gotten gains.[11]

Being an only son, Messer Luigi inherited the entire estate and so was able to maintain his father's financial stature. He continued to keep some of his wealth in business, his major investment being 10,000 florins in a company engaged in commerce and banking in Florence and Flanders.[12] At the same time, however, he steadily increased his land holdings.[13] When he died in 1403, Luigi was one of the very richest men in the city.[14] A precise evaluation of his estate cannot be made; but it was large enough that even after division, each

[10] AG, Libro 2, f. 18r.

[11] Unless otherwise indicated, the source for Piero's biography is AG, *Spogli*.

[12] This company is mentioned in entries dated 1378, 1380, and 1397; AG, Libro 2, ff. 53, 54, 70. Besides Luigi's capital of 10,000 florins, the company included the *persone* of Piero d'Antonio Benizi, Duti di Filippo del Popolo di San Lorenzo, and, in 1380, Agostino degli Strozzi.

[13] His purchases from 1381 to 1401 are listed in AG, *Spogli*. No values are listed in Luigi's book, but there were thirty-five *poderi* along with numerous other miscellaneous properties included in these purchases.

[14] Based, again, on *prestanze*: in 1390 he paid the highest in his quarter, 380 florins (Martines, *The Social World* . . . , p. 113 n. 91) and in 1403 he paid the second highest in the city, 240 florins (*ibid.*, p. 362). In 1400 his son Piero, returning from Rome, was taken prisoner and held for a ransom of 10,000 florins; he was not released until 1404, just after his father's death, at a cost of 7,000 florins; AG, *Spogli*.

of his three sons still ranked among the wealthiest patricians. In the 1427 *catasto*, one son, Messer Giovanni, and each of two grandsons by another son, Niccolò, declared estates worth over 10,000 florins, putting all of them in the upper one percent of the taxpayers of that year.[15] The return of the third son, Piero, however, indicated an estate of considerable lower value, owing, as we shall see, to heavy losses.

Luigi having been an only son, there is a certain unity in the history of the Guicciardini over these two generations, at least as regards the family patrimony; but when Luigi died leaving behind three sons, the family's history trifurcates into completely separate lines with the only point in common being their origin. Even in the course of this first generation, his three sons were following their own courses. Their father's property was divided and there is no indication of common investment interests in a family enterprise. Their political allegiances likewise diverged: Messer Giovanni was closely tied to the anti-Medicean forces in 1433 and 1434, while his brother Piero was an ardent supporter of the Medici; and each suffered loss of influence during the eclipse of his political faction.[16] Writing several generations later, Francesco Guicciardini shows hardly any interest in the descent of lines collateral to his own. He completely dismisses Niccolò and discusses Messer Giovanni only because of his political activities, but he is not at all concerned with the branches which stemmed from both these brothers of his great-grandfather, Piero.[17] Like "the Strozzi," "the Guicciardini" had ceased to be a family in any social sense; it was merely a surname.

[15] The declarations were: Messer Giovanni di Messer Luigi, 18,595 florins; Battista di Niccolò di Messer Luigi, 11,045 florins; Giovanni di Niccolò di Messer Luigi, 10,450 florins; Martines, *The Social World . . .* , p. 376.

[16] F. Guicciardini, "Memorie . . . ," pp. 7-15.

[17] *Ibid.*, pp. 7, 13. For the descendants of Niccolò and Giovanni, see Litta, *Guicciardini*, Tavole I and II. On Giovanni, see Margherita Antonelli Moriani, *Giovanni Guicciardini ed un processo politico in Firenze (1431)* (Florence, 1954).

THE FIFTEENTH CENTURY

With the proliferation of branches of the family in the fifteenth century, it is a meaningless and impossible task to follow them all in parallel studies. Moreover, the only branch for which records survive from this period is that of Piero; and fortunately, as in the case of the Strozzi, the best documented line is also the most distinguished.[18]

Piero di Luigi (1378-1441). As heir to one-third of his father's estate, Piero undoubtedly came into a sizeable fortune, much of it securely invested in land.[19] He had been matriculated in both the wool guild (1385) and the money changers' guild (1391) but he had little interest in business. He left his finances in the hands of others with disastrous consequences, for he soon began to suffer losses large enough to devour the bulk of his inheritance. In 1416 he made an official declaration of his financial difficulties in order to gain a reduction in his taxes; and at one point his wealth was so reduced that he was only prevented from selling his house because it involved his wife's dowry and she withheld her consent.[20] Nevertheless, however serious these losses might have been, he was certainly again on solid ground by 1427 and 1433, when he filed *catasto* declarations of credits and property worth over 5,000 florins (Table 13)—a figure, however, still far below the values reported by the other heirs of his father.[21] And yet, a decade later, in 1442, a year after his death, his widow included on her tax declaration, along with farms and other properties, an impassioned plea to the officials. She wrote that because expenses of her sizeable family consumed more than her income she would soon be insolvent, and she

[18] No Guicciardini account books, however, survive for the fifteenth century. The sources for the family's wealth for these generations are chiefly *catasto* returns (copies in AG, *Decimario*), the *Spogli* in the Archivio Guicciardini, and references in F. Guicciardini, "Memorie . . ."

[19] An inventory of his one-third share of the real estate survives: AG, Filza xxxv primo, No. 7.

[20] F. Guicciardini, "Memorie . . . ," p. 9.

[21] See note 15 above.

TABLE 13. THE ESTATE OF PIERO DI MESSER LUIGI GUICCIARDINI
IN 1427 AND 1433
(All figures are in florins)

	1427	1433
Real estate:		
Residence: one-half palace ...		
Unfinished house at Poppiano ...		
Farms and other rural properties	2,312	2,896
Investments		
Monte holdings:[a]		
Daughter's dowry	1,990	2,224
Other credits	184	
Balance of debts and credits	751	—83
Total	5,237	5,037

[a] These figures represent the market value, or 70% of the value on the Monte books in 1427. In the 1433 report, there are a few Monte credits of small value, but their market value cannot be determined and they have not been included here.

Source: 1427: AG, *Decimario*, ff. 75-82 (cf. ASF, *Catasto*, 65, ff. 53-54); *Catasto*, 434, ff. 336r-339r; 488, ff. 319r-22v.

requested that they give her case careful consideration.[22] Writing a century later, Piero's great-grandson tells us that Piero died poor, leaving an estate of around 5,000 florins.[23]

Although Piero had lost his wealth, he did not lose his political influence. On the contrary, a list of the numerous offices he held in the state is impressive. Besides a host of positions on various city councils which met only periodically, he was almost continually involved in major responsibilities for the state in positions which must have demanded little less than his full attention (Table 14). He was often away from the city for months at a time as a regional administrator in the territories ruled by Florence. Moreover, as one of the city's most distinguished diplomats, he was frequently off on missions to the other states of Italy. He died, in fact, while on a mission in Lombardy in 1441. Most of his important offices were held before 1434, when he was instrumental

[22] AG, *Decimario*, 100r-102v. The original return is lacking one folio.
[23] F. Guicciardini, "Memorie . . . ," p. 13.

TABLE 14. Major Administrative Offices held by
Piero di Messer Luigi Guicciardini

1409	Captain of Florentine provinces in the Romagna
1412	Vicar of the Valle dell'Era
1416	Prior
1417	Vicar General of Piombino
1419	Podestà of Perugia
1421	Gonfaloniere
1422	Captain of two Florentine galleys to the Levant
1423	Captain of Arezzo
1424	Podestà of Prato
1425	Ten of Liberty
1425-1433	Numerous embassies to the Emperor, the King of Aragon, the Pope, Milan, Venice
1431	Sea Consul, Ten of Liberty
1433	Podestà of Ghiacceto
1435	Gonfaloniere
1439	Gonfaloniere

Source: AG, Spogli.

in bringing Cosimo back to power.[24] He was one of the all-important *accoppiatori* for the scrutiny of that year, and he was included in both the Medicean *balìe* held before his death.[25] His great-grandson, Francesco, ranked him after Cosimo de' Medici and Neri di Gino Capponi as the most important man in the state.[26]

Service to the state was accepted by most Florentine patricians as their civic obligation; and with their wealth securely invested in land and cloth manufactories, many of them had leisure to devote to political affairs. Furthermore, political life had its own rewards: it opened up the road to power and prestige for patricians who aspired to distinguish themselves among their fellows in ways that money alone could not buy. Ambassadorial posts were especially attractive to men like Messer Luigi and Piero Guicciardini. As representatives of

[24] F. Guicciardini, "Ricordanze," *Scritti autobiografici e rari*, pp. 7-13; G. S. Gutkind, *Cosimo de' Medici* (New York, 1938), p. 92; von Reumont, *Lorenzo de' Medici*, I, 121.

[25] These rosters are published in Nicolai Rubinstein, *The Government of Florence under the Medici, 1434 to 1494* (London, 1966), App. I-III.

[26] "Ricordanze," p. 11.

their state at the courts of princes, the ambassador had that sense of power which some men have always craved. Moreover, the ambassador enjoyed the dignity of being associated with princes and rulers; and a Florentine patrician like Messer Luigi no doubt felt that he was altogether worthy of such company.[27] Hence ambassadorial missions satisfied desires which the walls of Florence could not contain. It must have been a fine moment indeed for the Guicciardini when in 1416 the Emperor Sigismund conferred on Piero the title of count palatine. He did not use it, of course, in bourgeois Florence; but later, when such things were more the fashion, his descendants resurrected it, and they continue to use it to this day.

A post as a regional administrator in the Florentine state also had appeal to the political man seeking the exercise of power, and it was an administrative function commensurate with the dignity of a patrician. But in other respects, such posts were less attractive. They kept him away for longer periods of time—for six months usually, sometimes a year —and confined him to many routine duties in a provincial town. Messer Luigi had been only twice in such a post; and one of these, the vicarate of the lower valley of the Arno in 1393, he may well have accepted because his headquarters at San Miniato was not far from his ancestral lands at Poppiano. Piero, on the other hand, frequently took such positions— even outside Florentine territory—and one wonders whether this might not have been due to his need of income during his financial difficulties, for political positions such as these paid substantial stipends.

The sons of Piero. The next generation of Guicciardini, the sons of Piero, were heirs to a noble name but little wealth, and perhaps because of this heritage they were attracted to

[27] In Francesco Guicciardini's "Memorie . . . ," the biographical sketches include many remarks on personal relations between the Guicciardini and various princes of Italy.

political careers. Most patricians of Florence served on a host of advisory councils during their lifetimes, but there could not have been many like Piero's sons Jacopo and Luigi, who were probably as close to being professional civil servants at the highest level of power outside the Chancellery as can be found in the history of the Florentine republic.[28] From Tables 15 and 16, which summarize their careers as officials of the state, it is apparent that both Luigi and Jacopo dedicated a major portion of their time to the state, and much of that was spent outside Florence as a vicar or captain of one of the provincial centers under Florentine domination or as an ambassador abroad. Moreover, they also received a number of commissions as official representatives of the government with the city's armies in the field during military campaigns, and this, too, demanded their steady attention and time. At the same time, both men were much more than administrators and diplomats in a technical capacity; they also sat on the various citizens' councils concerned with the government within the city. For both Luigi and Jacopo, these included several turns on the Signoria as well as posts on other important policy-making bodies, such as the Monte, the Ten of Liberty, and the Otto di Pratica. They were both regular members of the various Medicean *balìe*, and both numbered among the first forty in the important Council of Seventy in 1480.[29] Jacopo especially was influential with the Medici, and the year of his death he was chosen as a member of the special *balìa* of seventeen organized by Lorenzo for major reforms.[30]

[28] Less is known of the third brother, Niccolò. He died in 1442 and left three sons, who, along with their sons, appear frequently on the rosters of officeholders but rarely appear on any of the important policy-making councils of the city.

[29] Consult the rosters published in Rubinstein, App. II-IX. They were absent from the *balìe* of 1466 and 1471.

[30] There are numerous letters from Lorenzo to Jacopo; consult Nicolai Rubinstein and Pier Giorgio Ricci, eds., *Checklist of Letters of Lorenzo de' Medici* (Paris, 1965). Other letters of both Jacopo and

Luigi and Jacopo had gained a taste for power, both in their official functions and in the councils of the Medicean circle, and they knew the prestige that power in the service of the state brought. Each was several times the official chief-of-state (Gonfaloniere), and Luigi was knighted by the city for his services in 1464—an increasingly rare honor in fifteenth century Florence.[31] They both entered actively into the social life of the Medicean circle, Jacopo especially. He was an equestrian of sufficient skill to be able to joust in the popular mock tournaments of the day and on at least one occasion he came off with the prize.[32] Furthermore, Luigi shared the humanist taste of his times and was included as one of the participants in Matteo Palmieri's dialogue, *Della vita civile*. Jacopo, on the other hand, was a man *senza lettere*,[33] although he was respected enough by Ficino, who dedicated to him a Tuscan translation of some of his moral sermons, "in perpetuo segno della nostra singulare amicitia."[34]

These two generations of Guicciardini—Piero and his two sons—were above all concerned with matters of state, and the use of their time had no better purpose than service to the state. A sense of civic responsibility must have been almost instinctive for the Guicciardini with their long tradition of dedication to the state, if not second nature as Florentine patricians. Moreover, for men with the family pride and social dignity of the Guicciardini living in a state still nominally

Luigi can be found in *Archivio Mediceo avanti il principato. Inventorio* (4 vols.; Rome, 1951-63).

[31] Gaetano Salvemini, *La dignità cavalleresca nel comune di Firenze* (Turin, 1960), pp. 374-75. Salvemini found only fifty names of men knighted in the fifteenth century, whereas from 1320 to the end of the fourteenth century there were more than 150. In 1472 Benedetto Dei listed thirty-five Florentine knights in his chronicle; Pagnini della Ventura, II, 276-77.

[32] F. Guicciardini, "Memorie . . . ," p. 30.

[33] *Ibid.*, p. 42.

[34] P. O. Kristeller, *Supplementum Fincinianum* (Florence, 1937), I, 72. Apparently Jacopo did not know Latin. He is mentioned twice by Ficino in letters; *ibid.*, I, 130.

Table 15. OFFICES HELD BY LUIGI DI PIERO GUICCIARDINI

Year	Regional administration	Embassies and commissions	Internal offices
1436	Podestà of Fermo	...	Gonfaloniere
1437	Captain of Todi	Milan	...
1438	...	...	Balia
1439	Captain of Aquila	...	...
1440	Vicar of the Nievole valley	...	Master of the Mint, Prior
1441	Captain of Volterra	...	Otto di Custodia
1443	Vicar of the Casentino	...	Conservator of the Law
1444	...	Milan	Balia
1445	...	Milan	...
1446	Vicar in the Upper Valdarno Captain of Pisa	...	...
1447	... (3 mos.)	Milan	Master of the Mint, Prior
1448	Vicar in the Nievole valley	Genova, Volterra	...
1449	Podestà of Milan	Pisa, the Maremma	...
1450	Podestà of Milan	...	...
1451	Podestà of Milan	...	...
1452	...	Venice	Balia
1453	...	Upper Valdarno	Gonfaloniere
1454	...	Venice, Rimini	...
1455	Sea Consul	...	...
1457	...	Pope, Naples	Gonfaloniere Official of the Studio (3 yrs.), Balia
1458	...	...	Otto di Custodia
1459	Captain of the mountains of Pistoia	Pope	...
1460	...	...	...

Table 16. OFFICES HELD BY JACOPO DI PIERO GUICCIARDINI

Year	Regional administration	Embassies and Commissions	Internal offices
1452	...	...	Balia
1454	...	...	Prior
1457	Patron of a galley sent to the Levant	...	...
1458	...	...	Provisor, Otto di Custodia, Balia
1459	Captain of Borgo San Sepolcro	...	...
1460	...	...	Conservator of the Law
1461	...	...	Prior
1462	Captain of three galleys sent to Flanders and England	...	...
1464	...	...	Master of the Mint Tower official
1465	Sea Consul	King of Naples	Balia
1466	Vicar of Anghiari	Venice, Milan	Accoppiatore
1467	Captain of Arezzo	...	Otto di Custodia, Conservator of the Law
1468	...	Milan	Gonfaloniere
1469	Sea Consul	Rome, Milan	...
1470	...	Naples, Prato	Accoppiatore, Balia
1471	Captain of Pisa	...	...
1472	Vicar of the upper Valdarno	In field during war against Volterra	...
1473	...	Pistoia	Monte official
1474	...	Milan	Otto di Custodia
1476	...	Milan	...
1477	...	...	Conservator of the Law, Gonfaloniere

1461	...	...	Monte official
1462	...	Mantova	Master of the Mint, Conservator of the Law
1463	...	Mantova	...
1464	...	Piombino, Pope	...
1465	...	Naples, Milan	Otto di Custodia
1466	Vicar of the Val d'Elsa	Milan	Balìa
1467	...	Bologna, Milan	...
1468	...	Siena, the Emperor at Ferrara	
1469	...	Milan, Ferrara	Master of the Mint
1470	Vicar in the Lower Valdarno	...	Master of the Mint
1471	Captain of Arezzo	...	Balìa
1472	Vicar of Certaldo	...	
1473	...	Ferrara	Gonfaloniere
1474	Vicar of the Casentino	Venice	...
1475	...	Venice	Accoppiatore
1476	...	Milan, Pistoia, Venice	...
1477	...	Ferrara, Milan	...
1478	...	Commissioner General in war vs. the Pope	Prior
1479	...	Venice	
1480	...	Rome, Urbino, Venice	Balìa, Council of 70
1481	...	Urbino	Otto di Custodia
1482	...	Urbino, Colle	...
1483	Vicar of Vicopisano	...	...
1484	...	...	...
1485	...	...	Gabelle treasurer
1486	...	...	...
1487	Vicar of the Mugello		

Source: AG. *Spogli*.

1478	...	Lunigiana	Official of the *accatto*
1479	...	...	Otto di Custodia
1480	...	Naples	Otto di Pratica, Balìa, Council of 70
1481	...	...	Otto di Custodia, Prior
1482	...	Cremona-war vs. Venice	Ten of War, Otto di Pratica, Monte treasurer
1483	...	Ferrara, Lombardy	...
1484	...	Ambassador and Commissioner at large in war vs. Genoa	...
1485	...	Milan	...
1486	Vicar of the Val d'Elsa	...	...
1487	...	...	Otto di Pratica
1488	...	War vs. Genoa	Otto di Pratica, Tower official
1489	...	Livorno	Accoppiatore
1490	...	...	Master of the Mint, Balìa of 17 Reformers, Otto di Pratica

Source: AG, *Spogli*.

a republic, prestige and power were found in the offices and councils of state. And what about wealth? Could the state be "used" by such men for their personal financial advantage?

There are almost no financial records extant from the span of the family's history covered by the lives of these two men, and to survey their fortunes we have to approach the gap from either end. The inheritance left them by their father was not large; and once it was divided three ways, there could hardly have been very much for any of them. The figure of 1,500 florins, which Francesco Guicciardini asserted was the value of the inheritance of his grandfather, Piero's son, would not be out of line with the value of the estate in 1433 (Table 13; see p. 115).[35] For this reason, Piero was probably interested in profitable marriages for his sons, preferring not only large dowries but dowries that could be readily converted into cash. His oldest son, Luigi, recieved his wife's dowry in cash and was able to buy land with it. Possibly the same was true of the second son, Niccolò, whose marriage with a non-Florentine—the daughter of Braccio di Fortebraccio, *signore* of Perugia—was most unusual in fifteenth century Florence. Both brothers were obliged to file their own *catasto* returns in 1442 separately from their mother's, which included the as yet undivided patrimony.[36] In 1446 the third son, Jacopo, gained a dowry of 3,500 florins—an exceptionally large one in fifteenth-century Florence—and he was able to use the capital for investments.[37] Although their inheritance was small for men of their standing, all three sons gained

[35] F. Guicciardini, "Memorie . . . ," p. 30. In estimating the value of Piero's estate for purposes of his sons' inheritance, the sizeable dowry of his daughter must be eliminated and the value of his residence added.

[36] AG, *Decimario*, ff. 103r-109r; cf. *Catasto*, 609, ff. 332r-337v. Luigi stated on his return that the property included land purchased with cash from his wife's dowry.

[37] F. Guicciardini, "Memorie . . . ," pp. 28-29.

from dowries additional capital that was at their disposal for whatever use they might have had for it.

Undoubtedly to conserve expenses, the entire family had remained under the same roof. In her report of 1442 Piero's widow included her husband's two natural children, her own three sons, a daughter, the wives of Niccolò and Luigi, and Niccolò's three sons. Ten years later the families of Luigi and Jacopo (now married) were still living together (Niccolò had since died); but sometime between 1451 and 1457 they made a final division of their patrimony and moved into separate quarters. Since Piero's half of the town house went to Luigi alone, for the next twenty-five years Jacopo had to rent quarters for his residence in the city. In 1449, these two brothers had purchased for 2,700 florins one-half of the old family *castello* at Poppiano—which had passed on to a collateral line after the older Luigi's death—and along with it a couple of farms, smaller pieces of land, and cottages; and these properties were added to those of their father in the same area.[38]

The wealth of Luigi (1407-87) in 1457 was modest by the standards of his class,[39] and apparently his many years of service to the state did not give him the opportunity of enlarging it. There is no further documentation of his estate; but the historian Francesco Guicciardini, in his notes on his great-uncle, asserted that Luigi lived primarily off his farm rents, with further assistance from a natural son, a priest who held lucrative church offices, and that he left a very small estate when he died.[40] Although he married four times, Luigi left

[38] This property had been sold by Giovanni di Niccolò di Luigi Guicciardini, a first cousin of Luigi and Jacopo, despite the fidei-commissum of his father's testament. When Luigi and Jacopo bought it, half of it returned to Giovanni; but in 1458 he sold this half to Luigi.

[39] See Table 17. In 1480 he paid a *catasto* of 6 florins, 14 *soldi*, 7 *denari*, which put him among the 543 highest taxpayers (the upper 5.11 percent).

[40] F. Guicciardini, "Memorie . . . ," p. 27. Luigi's natural son

no legitimate sons and no line of Guicciardini descended from him. The second brother, Niccolò (1410-42), had descendants, but hardly anything is known of them.[41]

Jacopo (1422-90) had no more of a patrimony than his brother, but he had the good fortune of marrying a woman who brought him an extraordinarily large dowry for his day —3,500 florins. This capital was available to him, and he was willing to put it to work by investing it in business.[42] What kind of investments he made and their worth cannot be determined, but the growth of his estate can be recorded. When his son Piero married in 1475, Jacopo set him up in a silk company; and, according to Francesco, this brought the family 11,000 florins in profits over the next twenty years.[43] By 1480 the value of Jacopo's property had gone up by more than 50 percent over the 1457 percent evaluation (Table 17), an increase which is entirely represented by additional acquisitions;[44] and in 1482 he finally bought himself a residence in Florence, a "large house" formerly belonging to his cousins, located in the same area in which his family had traditionally resided.[45] The fact that after 1473 he had only

---

Rinieri (1449-1504) became a priest and rector of the Studio at Pisa. Through association with Cardinal Giovanni de' Medici, he accumulated a number of church offices, including the bishopric of Cortona, but he died a poor man, his wealth having been consumed by his ambitions. According to Francesco, he lacked "lettere e virtù." *Ibid.*, pp. 44-48.

[41] Francesco does not mention Niccolò. See AG, *Spogli*; Litta, *Guicciardini*, Tavola II; and note 28 above.

[42] F. Guicciardini, "Memorie . . . ," pp. 28-29, 41. In his tax report of 1457 he listed business investments worth 1,400 florins (Table 17).

[43] *Ibid.*, p. 41. In 1480 Jacopo noted a silk manufactory in the name of his son, but, claiming that it had little business because of shortage of capital, he declined to give the business any value at all; *Catasto*, 995, f. 324r. By this time, however, taxpayers were using any excuse to avoid declaring business investments, and there is no reason to believe that Jacopo was any more honest than his fellows in this respect.

[44] In 1457 he paid a *catasto* of 10 florins, 9 *soldi*, 11 *denari*, which put him among the 227 highest taxpayers (the upper 2.13 percent).

[45] AG, *Spogli*.

TABLE 17. THE ESTATE OF JACOPO DI PIERO GUICCIARDINI
AND HIS SON PIERO, 1451 TO 1498
(All figures are in florins)

Description	1451 Jacopo and Luigi	1457 Luigi	1457 Jacopo	1480 Jacopo	1498 Piero di Jacopo
Real estate (income property)	4,279	2,184	1,978	3,004	5,596
Business investments				1,400	unknown	unknown
Monte credits	unknown	654	441	unknown	unknown
Miscellaneous	unknown	—152	373	unknown	unknown

Source: 1451: *Catasto*, 688, f. 445r. 1457: *Catasto*, 789, ff. 159r-62r, 311r-15v; AG, Filza XLV, No. 4. 1480: *Catasto*, 995, ff. 324r-25r. 1498: AG, Filza XLV, copy of 1498 *decima* declaration.

one regional administrative post may also reflect the relatively greater affluence of his later years and his lesser need for outside income. He certainly did not build up a great fortune —but he established his son in a silk manufactory and on his death handed over to him farms and other country properties which gave Piero much more security than he himself had had.

Piero di Jacopo (1454-1513). Piero was Jacopo's only son and so inherited the entire estate of his father. There is no documentation for a systematic analysis of Piero's financial activities; but he managed to increase his wealth further. He had a continuing interest in the silk industry. Already in 1475, before his father's death, he had used 800 florins of his wife's dowry in a manufactory,[46] and this was probably supplemented with funds from his father to form the capital for his own company. Piero Guicciardini and Company, which is mentioned in Jacopo's *catasto* of 1480. After 1500, as his sons began to mature, he set up new companies for them (Table 18) and at the same time considerably enlarged the

[46] AG, Filza XXVII, No. 7.

TABLE 18. INVESTMENTS OF JACOPO GUICCIARDINI IN
SILK MANUFACTORIES, 1504 TO 1529
(All figures are in florins *larghi d'oro in oro*)

Dates	Company	Total capital	Total profits	Jacopo's capital	Jacopo's profits
1504-1508	Luigi Guicciardini & Co., with Piero, Luigi, and Jacopo Guicciardini, and Gherardo di Giuliano Carnesecchi, manager[a]	——	——	800	164
1507-1511	Giovanfrancesco di Tommaso Benci & Co.[b]	——	——	700	169
1513-1514	Jacopo Guicciardini & Co., with Piero Guicciardini, and Andrea di Tommaso Signorini, manager[c]	2,000	291	1,200	131
1514-1529	Jacopo Guicciardini & Co., with Andrea Signorini, manager[d]	2,000	6,659	2,000	4,995

Source:

[a] AG, Libro 12, f. 53; Libro 13, f. 181 (contract). The company was dissolved because of too little capital.

[b] AG, Libro 12, f. 41; Libro 13, ff. 4, 111.

[c] AG, Libro 13, f. 184 (contract); Libro 16 (ledger); Libro 24 (*giornale e ricordanze*). The company was dissolved following Piero's death.

[d] AG, Libro 13, ff. 44, 59, 186 (contract of 1514); Libro 14, f. 117; Libro 15, f. 169; Libri 17-19 (ledgers, 1514-43); Libro 32 (book of *entrata e uscita*, 1513-20). Profits recorded here are those to 1529. Sometime shortly after that date, the company went into dissolution and the capital was paid back; additional profits amounted to only 366 florins up to 1543.

investment in his own company (Table 19). The company for Luigi yielded very small profits and was dissolved in 1508, after only four years. Another for Jacopo, organized in 1513, was much more successful; and after his father's death that year, when he took over the full capital investment, Jacopo continued for many years to collect impressive returns on his investment.

Besides these business investments, Piero also added to his land holdings although again the record is not at all clear.

TABLE 19. CAPITAL AND PROFITS OF SILK MANUFACTORIES BELONGING
TO PIERO GUICCIARDINI AND HIS SONS, 1502 TO 1523
(All figures are in florins *larghi d'oro in oro*)

Dates	Company	Capital	Profits
1502-1504	Jacopo Guicciardini and Lorenzo Segni & Co.	. ..	837
1506-1509	Jacopo Guicciardini and Lorenzo Segni & Co.	5,600	2,186
1509-1512	Piero Guicciardini & Co. with Segni and Guglielmo di Francesco Nettoli, manager	5,600	.
1512-1514	Unknown[a]	. ...	. . . .
1514-1517	Heirs of Piero Guicciardini & Co., with the five brothers and Nettoli	6,300	2,035
1517-1523	Heirs of Piero Guicciardini & Co., with the five brothers and Nettoli	6,300	. ...[b]

[a] The company was reformed in July 1512, with Jacopo included by his father in the capital, his share being worth 800 florins. When this company dissolved following Piero's death in December 1513, Jacopo's share of the profits up to that time was 86 florins.

[b] Jacopo's share of the profits to 1520 was 100 florins; he had 400 invested in the company.

Source: AG, Libro, 12, ff. 22, 58; Libro 13, ff. 56, 57, 159, 179 (contract of 1518), 181 (contract of 1509), 184 (contract of 1512), 186 (contract of 1514); Filza xxvii, No. 11 (balances of 1504, 1508, and 1515); F. Guicciardini, "Ricordanze," pp. 81, 82, 86-87.

In the 1498 *decima* he declared properties with a total annual income of 326 florins. Although the precise capital value of these properties cannot be determined, the list of them contains more than twice the number of items on his father's *catasto* of 1480. Both Jacopo and Piero steadily added to their ancestral holdings at Poppiano, and it is very likely that from 1480 to 1498 they had in fact doubled their value.[47] To this taxable property there would have to be add-

[47] For the 1480 *catasto*, see *Catasto*, 995, f. 324r. For the 1498 *decima*, see AG, Filza XLV (a copy of 1528). The former includes five

ed the non-income property, namely, the palace in Florence
bought by Jacopo in 1482 and the *castello* at Poppiano. In
1504, when Luigi's natural son Rinieri died, Piero probably
inherited his uncle's properties;[48] but judging from what his
son Jacopo received from the division of the estate in 1514,
it seems that after 1498 until his death in 1513, Piero did not
add appreciably to his land holdings.[49] During this period his
sons were coming of age and all the available capital he then
had probably went into the business ventures already
mentioned.

When Piero died in December 1513, he left a sizeable estate. His son Jacopo in a lengthy note in his *ricordanze* on his
father's estate, estimated it close to 20,000 florins.[50] He placed
a value of 4,593 florins on the liquid wealth, consisting of
credits with the two silk manufactories. This was divided
among the five brothers along with the farms and other properties, which were given no value on Jacopo's inventory but
were probably worth at least 10,000 florins.[51] Besides these
items, 300 florins worth of jewels was also divided. The re-

---

farms, three smaller parcels of land, two cottages, a vineyard, and a
mill; the latter lists ten farms, three smaller parcels, five vineyards,
two cottages, and three mills. These categories by no means represent
uniform values, but at least one can conclude that the Guicciardini
were continually adding to their land holdings. If the income of 326
florins, 9 *soldi*, 7 *denari*, reported in the 1498 *decima* is capitalized
on the basis that it represents a 7 percent return, the total value of
the property becomes 4,664 florins, considerably higher than the
3,004 florins reported as the value in 1480, and this would be a
minimum value.

[48] F. Guicciardini, "Memorie . . . ," p. 46.

[49] Jacopo, in the division of 1514 with his four brothers, received
two farms and miscellaneous parcels of land, which had an estimated
decima value of approximately one-fifth that of the 1498 figure, as far
as the properties can be specifically identified and equated with those
on the *decima* return. Compare the list of Jacopo's inheritance AG,
Libro 13, f. 187, with the list already mentioned in AG, Filza XLV.

[50] AG, Libro 13, f. 185. Francesco, in a *ricordo* of his father's death,
estimated an inheritance of 4,000 florins for each of the five brothers;
"Ricordanze," p. 80.

[51] Francesco's one-fifth share was worth 2,000 florins and had an
income of about 75 florins; "Ricordanze," p. 81.

mainder of the estate remained common property. This comprised small Monte credits and the non-income real estate—the palace in Florence and the country residence at Poppiano along with their furnishings. A final item in the inventory was a 13 percent share in the copper mines of Montecatini at Volterra. What this was worth is not known, but it is certain that the brothers received no income from this source.[52] At any rate, Piero handed over to his sons a patrimony which was somewhat larger than that he had received from Jacopo.[53]

Piero had willingly invested in business enterprises and was happy to establish his sons in business, but he himself had little inclination for business matters and preferred to meet the responsibilities of a large family with frugality rather than apply himself to the business of making money.[54] Like his father and his uncle, Piero was a political man and was almost continually in the service of the state although, with somewhat more financial security than they, he appears less frequently in the rosters of those full-time administrative officials whose remuneration from the state was a living wage.[55] His family had, of course, been on good terms with the Medici, and in 1490 he was on Lorenzo's special *balìa* of seventeen reformers; but even after the expulsion of the Medici in 1494 until his death in 1513, Piero was active at the most important level of government in Florence. He was prior twice; and after the establishment of the Consiglio Maggiore, he was on its directing agency, the Eighty. He also appeared

[52] Jacopo's books from 1503 to 1529 are very complete and they contain no entries regarding copper mines. Luigi Guicciardini had been included in a company organized to exploit the mines at Montecatini and this property may have been part of his estate; Enrico Fiumi, *L'impresa di Lorenzo de' Medici contro Volterra (1472)* (Florence, 1948), p. 64.

[53] So asserted his son, Jacopo; AG, Libro 13, f. 185.

[54] *Ibid.*

[55] An essay by Piero on the scrutiny of 1484 has recently been published by Rubinstein, pp. 318-25.

among the officials of the Monte, who determined financial policy, and in the councils of the Ten of Liberty and Peace, where foreign policy was formulated. Furthermore, he was active as an ambassador and as a commissioner, especially in those years of crisis, 1494 and 1513. Piero, in short, honorably upheld the tradition of his family with his constant attention to civic matters; and for him this was hardly a course taken out of financial necessity, nor is there any evidence that it was one which led to great pecuniary rewards.

As a youth of twenty-one, Piero had participated in the famous joust of Giuliano de' Medici in 1475;[56] but to judge from the comments of his son Francesco, Piero much later in life was a very sober man with a distaste for such frivolous pursuits of the Medicean circle. It is not surprising, therefore, that he came under the influence of Savonarola. Intellectually, Piero was more attuned than his father to the taste of the times for humanism. With an interest in literary and humanistic studies and a creditable knowledge of both Greek and Latin, as well as of philosophy and sacred scriptures, Piero had some standing in the learned circles of his day.[57] He was a student and friend of Marsilio Ficino, who in 1482 witnessed the baptism of his son Francesco;[58] and in 1486 he became an official of the Florentine Studio. Both his sons, Francesco and Jacopo, comment on his taste for the kind of learning popularized by the humanists of his day, and there undoubtedly existed in the Guicciardini household an atmosphere conducive to the cultivation of intellectual interests. Out of his family over the next two generations came a number of Guic-

[56] Paul Oskar Kristeller, "Un documento sconosciuto sulla giostra di Giuliano de' Medici," *Studies in Renaissance Thought and Letters* (Florence, 1956), pp. 437-50. This humanist document is dedicated to Piero.

[57] His sons comment on his father's learning: Francesco, in "Memorie . . . ," p. 49; and Jacopo, in AG, Libro 13, f. 185. See also Della Torre, pp. 727, 802-3; Kristeller, *Studies* . . . , p. 444; and idem, *Supplementum Ficinianum*, II, 344.

[58] F. Guicciardini, "Ricordanze," p. 53.

ciardini who modestly distinguished themselves as men of letters in their own time—and at least two of them for all time: his son Francesco and his grandson Lodovico.

During the span of the fifteenth century the financial fortunes of the Guicciardini family underwent considerable transformation. The great heights of Messer Luigi's vast wealth at the turn of the century were never to be reached again. First, its tripartite division among Luigi's sons, and then very heavy personal losses suffered shortly thereafter, left Piero in considerably reduced circumstances. When his estate in turn was divided three ways, this line of Guicciardini, just two generations after Messer Luigi, found itself almost in the depths of poverty by the standards of their class. Without a family business and with very little real estate, two of Piero's sons sustained themselves partly through political officeholding, but it is clear that neither their salaries nor their political influence led them to great fortune. Jacopo was able to get a start in building the family fortune with a large dowry and a willingness to invest modestly in the cloth business on the side. Since he had only one son, his estate remained intact after his death; and between father and son, there was a slow but steady accumulation of wealth. By the time of his death in 1513, Piero had built up an estate probably worth about 20,000 florins, a handsome fortune, though hardly equal to Messer Luigi's a century earlier. At this point, however, the family estate underwent division among Piero's five sons, and consequently the next generation faced the threat of another plunge in the family's financial fortunes.

THE SONS OF PIERO

Piero had been fortunate that his father's estate underwent no division upon his death and he was thus able to maintain his father's stature and even heighten it. After Piero's death, however, the patrimony had to go five ways; and no one share qualified its holder as very wealthy. Shortly after Piero's death the estate was divided among the sons, both the invested capital and the real estate, with the exception of the town house and the family villa, which were to remain common property. The brothers continued to invest jointly in the family silk business; and in 1519 three of them put capital in the Flemish venture (see below p. 146). By the early 1520's, however, even these weak financial bonds were loosened; the silk company, which had never earned impressive profits, apparently was dissolved after 1523; and the Flemish company soon became the exclusive concern of Jacopo alone. Then, in 1524, with the marriage of Girolamo, the two family residences, the only property still held in common, were divided. Thereafter each brother had his own estate, and they lived apart. Bongianni retired to the country, Francesco lived in his own villa, Jacopo had to buy a residence in the city, and Girolamo alone possessed the family palace of their father. And so with another generation, each took his share and went his own way.

For a Florentine coming of age at the height of the Renaissance shortly after the turn of the century, what were the alternatives for making one's way in the world suitable to the dignity of an old patrician family? Among Piero's five sons we find several paths that could be taken; and their very existence testifies to a society not yet rigidly confined in its behavior, one still open, economically and socially, to various possibilities. Piero's family has been completely overshadowed by Francesco, the famous historian; but the five brothers taken all together represent about as good a cross section of Florentine patrician society as one can hope to find.[59]

Liugi (1478-1551).[60] Piero's oldest son, Luigi, presumably

[59] In his excellent biography of Francesco, Ridolfi has some comments on Luigi but does no more than take note of the other brothers; *Vita di Francesco Guicciardini* (Rome, 1960), p. 26.

[60] For Luigi the chief source is, again, AG, *Spogli*. For his political career and writings, see the editor's introduction in Luigi di Piero

had little interest in business. Although his father had invested in a silk manufactory in Luigi's name, it was not a success;[61] and Luigi's financial difficulties and debts gave his father considerable worry.[62] He continued to hold a share in the family silk business, but he did not participate in the later ventures of his brothers in the Lowlands.[63] Luigi apparently preferred to enjoy the modest financial security of his inheritance rather than to gamble it on greater wealth.

Luigi was very active in political affairs, especially during the Medicean periods, and several surviving documents attest to a serious interest in political ideas. Although he neither went on many embassies abroad nor held many major administrative posts in the state, he was continually in political office on one of the many city councils, including the Signoria five times and the board of directors of the Florentine Studio at Pisa. He shared the oligarchical sympathies of many of the city's leading patricians who were desperate to free themselves from the tightening hold of the Medici after 1512, and even more after 1523, when the city came under the remote control of Clement VII. Luigi was, in fact, Gonfaloniere when the tumult of 26 April 1527 again drove the Medici from Florence; but as it became increasingly obvious during the brief life of the last Florentine republic that the oligarchical alternative was not viable, that republican

---

Guicciardini, *Del Savonarola, ovvero dialogo tra Francesco Zati e Pieradovardo Giachinotti il giorno dopo la battaglia di Gavinana*, ed. Bono Simonetta (Florence, 1959), pp. 5-45; and for his political ideas, von Albertini, pp. 193-97, 260-73. Paolo Guicciardini, *Il ritratto vasariano di Luigi Guicciardini* (Florence, 1942), is of slight biographical value. For letters and other writings in manuscript, consult Kristeller, *Iter italicum*. See also *Lettere di Isabella Guicciardini al marito Luigi, 1535-1542* (Florence, 1883).

[61] See p. 126.

[62] F. Guicciardini, "Ricordanze," p. 71.

[63] Luigi's detachment from his brothers is also indicated by his absence from the list of heirs of the two brothers who predeceased him—Francesco and Bongianni, neither of whom had sons—although his son Niccolò is included along with the other brothers.

government was to become wider than many patricians cared to tolerate, some, like Luigi, prepared themselves to accept a return of the Medici. As one of the consultants of Clement VII on the reorganization of the Florentine state after 1530, Luigi advocated firm control by a Medicean prince and was one of those most willing to abandon the city's republican traditions. He became a member of the new Senate in 1532, and thereafter was frequently on the Duke's Council as well as in a host of minor offices and several regional posts. Although, like his brother Francesco, Luigi supported Medicean absolutism, he does not appear to have been the new kind of professional administrator his brother was. His political career better represents the civic traditions of public service of his forebears, Jacopo and Piero; but his political ideas herald the entrance of the prince and the transition to an absolutist state.

A generation later, Luigi's one son, Niccolò (1501-58), chose another alternative for making his way in the world, one that may have been increasingly popular with young patricians of only modest estate but proud traditions: the professional learned man. Niccolò was a lawyer—he inherited his famous uncle's practice—and although he was a frequent officeholder after 1530 and a member of the Senate after his father's death, he made a scholar's career out of his profession, writing on legal as well as historical matters, and teaching as a professor of law in the university at Pisa.[64]

Francesco (1482-1540).[65] Another son of Piero, the famous

[64] For the descendants of Niccolò, see Litta, *Guicciardini*, Tavola III. Litta, however, hardly mentions Niccolò's grandson, Filippo di Lorenzo, who was a wealthy banker in seventeenth century Rome; see AG, *Spogli*; and Jean Delumeau, *Vie économique et sociale de Rome dans la seconde moitié du XVIe siècle* (2 vols.; Paris, 1957-59), II, 847, 857, 861-62.

[65] The bibliography on Francesco is of course very extensive, and the reader will find good guides to it in the most recent studies: Ridolfi, *Vita di Francesco Guicciardini*; and the work of Gilbert on

historian Francesco, entered the one profession of his day
which the patrician deigned to enter, the legal profession.
Lawyers in fifteenth century Florence did not confine themselves to a private practice, but, in a period when the municipality was outgrowing the medieval tradition of corporative
government and advancing into the modern world of constitu-
tionally centralized sovereignty, specialists in law were increasing their role in public affairs as technicians, even threatening
the deeply entrenched position of the many citizens' councils
in which the patricians had long wielded their power.[66] The
lawyer was therefore a respected person—in Florence, he
shared the honorific title "messer" with those the commune
knighted—and his was a profession which could lead to political power. Law was nonetheless still a profession, requiring
specialized education and consuming time in its practice;
presumably, therefore, despite its prestige, it was not an occupation which an affluent patrician was likely to take up.[67]
Nevertheless, Francesco's career brought him both considerable political influence and a large fortune; and it hardly endangered his social standing, for he married a daughter of
Alamanno Salviati, of one of the grandest families in Flor-

---

his political and historical thought. Only one of his account books
survives, a book of *debitori e creditori* and *ricordanze*, 1527-29 (AG,
Libro 11), dating from the time he was back in Florence following
the sack of Rome. The *ricordanze* from this book have been published
by Paolo Guicciardini, ed., *Ricordanze inedite* (Florence, 1930). This
ricordanze and an earlier collection dating from 1508 to 1515 compose the "Ricordanze," ed. Palmarocchi, pp. 53-98. They are both
now translated into English: Francesco Guicciardini, *Selected Works*,
ed. Cecil Grayson, trans. Margaret Grayson (London, 1965), pp.
129-70.

[66] See, for example, the resentment of them by Benedetto Varchi,
Storia fiorentina (Florence, 1888), Bk. vi, Sec. 5. The political mental-
ity of a lawyer-administrator is illustrated in an interesting study of
Francesco by Alexander George Mylonas, "Francesco Guicciardini:
A Study in the Transition of Florentine and Bolognese Politics, 1530-
1534" (unpublished Ph.D. dissertation, Harvard University, 1960).

[67] Francesco estimated the cost of his legal education to have been
over 500 florins, including books, fees, and expenses; Ridolfi,
Vita . . . , p. 16.

ence,[68] and two of his daughters married Capponi cousins, the sons of Niccolò and Giuliano.

Francesco's career is too well known to require elaboration here. He took his degree in 1505 and then practiced in Florence. Because of his family association with the Medici, he was bound to profit from their accession to power in Florence and in Rome in 1513. In 1516 he became an official in the papal bureaucracy as Governor of Modena; from that post he moved on to be Governor of Reggio and Parma, then to the presidency of the entire Romagna, and finally to the direction of foreign affairs for the Holy See and the lieutenancy general of the papal army in the war of the League against Charles V. In 1527, with the sack of Rome, he returned to private life in Florence, but after 1530 he had official duties in Florence representing Clement's interest in reëstablishing a secure Medicean government. He was again in the papal bureaucracy as Governor of Bologna from 1531 to 1534, and then returned to Florence following the death of his patron, Clement VII. Thereafter, he was closely associated with Duke Alessandro; and after the Duke's assassination, he was instrumental in establishing Cosimo with the patriciate. He finally ended his political life in 1537 because of personal inclinations for a more tranquil existence with time to write.[69] As a lawyer and a bureaucrat long in the service of a prince, Francesco had no qualms about accepting a more authoritarian government for his native city; nor as a member of one of the noblest of patrician families, secure in its long tradition of service to the state, did he have qualms about accepting the Medicean principate. He knew that no prince

[68] F. Guicciardini, "Ricordanze," p. 58.

[69] Mylonas follows Remigio in this judgment and discards Segni's account according to which Francesco retired because of disgust with Cosimo's government; Mylonas, pp. 52-54. Ridolfi suggests that age and ill-health were his reasons for rejecting another papal lieutenancy at the time; Ridolfi, *Vita . . .* , pp. 395-97. For this last phase of his political career, see Roberto Ridolfi, "Francesco Guicciardini e Cosimo I," *ASI*, cxxii (1964), 567-606.

could rule without the support of patricians such as the Guicciardini and that his family could survive political changes without loss of dignity; and the many positions of favor held by members of his family in the following years proved him correct.[70]

Francesco profited handsomely from his employment. As an ambassador to Spain for two years, he earned three florins a day and, in addition, had an outright grant of 300 florins;[71] and he was able to save enough of this to buy a major share (2,400 florins) in the family silk business when he returned in 1514. His salary as Governor of Modena was 100 florins a month and as Governor of Reggio, 160 florins a month;[72] and when he had his highest paying position, as President of the Romagna, he not only had a salary but a share in the revenue as well. In 1526, when he had to absent himself for business in Rome, he arranged for his brother Jacopo to assume his duties. The agreement was that Jacopo would pay Francesco a flat 2,000 florins plus one-half of everything over 4,000 florins which he would have as income.[73] Jacopo for that period, from May 1526 to January 1527, cleared 1,646 florins as net profit.[74] In other words, 4,000 florins was a reasonable estimate of what Francesco himself could hope to earn in a year at a time that he had his most lucrative post.

His earnings as an administrator enabled him to invest in both business and land in Florence. By 1517 his credits in the family silk firm amounted to 3,500 florins;[75] and in 1519 he invested 1,500 florins in the Flemish company of his brothers.[76] Throughout the 1520's he consigned large

---

[70] This is the thesis of Mylonas' study of Guicciardini's political ideas.

[71] F. Guicciardini, "Ricordanze," p. 80.

[72] *Ibid.*, p. 27. When Jacopo on several occasions replaced his brother as governor, his profits were about fifty florins net a month; presumably that was after payment of a fixed sum to Francesco.

[73] *Ibid.*, p. 35.   [74] AG, Libro 15, f. 131.

[75] AG, Libro 11, f. 12.

[76] See below, p. 146. This money was invested with the stipulation

amounts of capital to his brother Girolamo for investing;[77] and in 1526 he anticipated an estate of 13,000 florins in liquid wealth alone.[78] Francesco also bought large amounts of land. His *ricordanze* mention purchases from 1518 to 1528 of a half dozen farms and three villas, representing total expenditures of 9,060 florins;[79] and these properties brought him an annual income of about 400 florins.[80] The opening account of his one extant account book indicates an estate in 1527 of about 15,000 florins not including his share of the patrimony. After that date he did not have the lucrative posts that he had held earlier, and yet his estate apparently continued to grow much larger. He was the first of the five brothers to die; and, leaving no sons, he provided for the division of his lands among his three remaining brothers and a son of the fourth, with the stipulation that they pay each of his three daughters 7,500 florins (including their dowries). When the final division of the properties was made in September 1540, the total value was 8,000 florins.[81] If the 8,000 florins was what was left after the payments to his daughters—and it is not likely that he left such large bequests to them unless he thought his estate could afford them—then the total value of his estate would have been in the vicinity of 30,000 florins.

that Francesco would not be responsible for losses; F. Guicciardini, "Ricordanze," p. 80.

[77] By January 1528 he estimated his credits with Girolamo to be worth 9,437 florins of invested capital plus about 2,000 florins in unassigned profits; *ibid.*, pp. 93-94.

[78] *Ibid.*, p. 91.

[79] *Ibid.*, pp. 83, 85-86, 88-89, 92-93, 94. These figures correspond to accounts in AG, Libro 11.

[80] The account of his income shows 415 florins for 1527, and 380 florins for 1528; AG, Libro 11, f. 18.

[81] AG, Filza xxvii, No. 24 (an assessment for purposes of division of the estate). The inventory there shows a total of 6,500 florins, but to that has to be added 1,500 florins which Girolamo paid the estate for Francesco's country house; *ibid.*, No. 47, f. 109 (record of the property accumulation by Girolamo's descendants).

Bongianni (1492-1549).[82] Bongianni lived a life very different from that of his brothers and yet one probably not so abnormal among patricians with no political ambitions, with modest financial security, and no desire to risk it in efforts to gain more wealth. Bongianni never married and lived a quiet existence in retirement at Poppiano. He persistently refused to accept public office whenever his name came up, and he did not busy himself with efforts to enlarge his wealth.[83] He supervised the family properties at Poppiano, but under the *mezzadria* system that was hardly an occupation. With a smattering of humanist learning, he preferred to use his leisure in the quiet pursuit of his literary and intellectual interests. As a dilettante, he wrote on the usual variety of subjects, from history to science, but achieved no distinction either in his own day or in later times, neither among his contemporaries nor in the eyes of modern scholars with their passion for reviving forgotten figures.

Bongianni qualifies for the kind of patrician many historians would like to find in Florence during the High Renaissance, one who preferred to invest in land and in culture and who withdrew from the life of the city to a villa in the countryside and dedicated himself to a kind of life more characteristic of an aristocrat than of a bourgeois patrician. With their political indifference, such men as Bongianni may have

[82] For Bongianni there are two relevant account books: his own *libro di conti*, 1531-49 (AG, Filza xxvII, No. 22) and a book of *debitori e creditori* of his heirs, Agnolo, Raffaello, and Lorenzo di Jacopo, 1549-51 (AG, Libro 50). Some of his letters have been published by I. Del Lungo in *Almanacco dell'amico del contadino*, 1887, 1889-90, 1891, 1892, 1893.

[83] Bongianni's estate was divided into three parts—one each to his two brothers, Girolamo and Luigi; and one to the three sons of his brother, Jacopo: Agnolo, Raffaello, and Lodovico. The accounts of the latter record the tripartite division in 1549-50; AG, Libro 50, ff. 1, 11. Bongianni's estate was worth 4,821 florins and since this would include his share of Francesco's estate—property worth perhaps 2,000 florins—his own wealth could hardly have been much more than that of his original share of the brothers' patrimony.

paved the way for the Medicean principate, but they were not the nucleus of an aristocracy in the usual sense of the word. When they withdrew from the piazzas of the city, they did not enter the festive court of a prince; rather, they retired to the villa. They were not courtiers and aristocrats, but patricians who found their "aristocracy" in intellectual pleasures, however feeble their efforts may have been. Florentine society was, of course, not "rigidly structured" and clear distinctions cannot be drawn between classes of intellectual patricians and a court aristocracy of the Dukes; but time and time again we encounter men of Bongianni's generation who had similar interests and who must have given to the upper ranks of Florentine society more than a tinge of intellectual refinement and good taste. They were as different from the civic humanists of an earlier era as they were from the rural feudal aristocracy of northern Europe and even from other nobilities of patrician origins, like that of Venice of the same period. It was the growing class of gentlemen intellectuals like Bongianni Guicciardini which prepared the ground for the flourishing life of academies in Florence in the later sixteenth century and throughout the Enlightenment.

Jacopo (1480-1552). The other two sons of Piero took a completely different course from that of their brothers. Both sought wealth in the business world; and although they both found their fortunes by marrying wealthy heiresses (who were sisters), they never withdrew altogether from the world of business. Girolamo was the more successful, but Jacopo, with seven sons to establish in the world, made the more adventurous—if disastrous—effort. Jacopo is a particularly interesting subject of study as a touchstone to his age not only because the documentation is very rich, especially for the years from 1505 to about 1530, but also because the history of his family through the next generation repeats the cycle of disintegration and diversity. And again, the careers of his seven sons reveal the alternatives open to men of high birth but with incommensurate wealth.

Jacopo was from the beginning destined to go into the business world. It was perhaps with this intention that his father had used his son's name in the silk manufactory which he formed in 1502 with Lorenzo Segni (Table 19; see p. 127). After that company was formed in 1506, however, the family firm dropped his name and he invested 700 florins on his own in a company with Giovanfrancesco Benci. This company with Benci earned very little in profits because the capital, despite the addition of 300 florins by Jacopo, was too small to build up the business. In 1513 after its dissolution, Jacopo, with considerable assistance from his father, organized another company with Andrea Signorini. This company assumed the name Jacopo Guicciardini and Company, and unlike his earlier effort, it earned extraordinarily handsome profits, much better than the company of his father, which had almost three times the capital investment of Jacopo's. During these earlier years Jacopo no doubt learned the silk business thoroughly, for although a shop owner of a patrician family usually had as a partner a man of lesser social standing who managed the shop, he himself was not above learning the business by doing work on the premises.[84] It was probably for such services that Jacopo received annually a small

[84] In 1527 the Venetian ambassador reported seeing in Florence "li primi, che gubernano el Stato, vanno alle loro boteghe di seda e, gettati li lembi del mantello sopra le spalle, vanno alla caviglia e lavorano la seda overo lavorano con il rocchello, publice, nella sua bottega, che ognuno li vede; e li figliuoli suoi stanno in bottega con il gremial dinanzi e portano il sacco e la sporta alle maestre con le sede e fanno gli altri essercizi di bottega, e loro vecchi sono quelli che parecchiano i panni di seda ed ordinano e fanno il tutto; e, medesimamente dell'arte della lana, li vecchi, che governano il Stato, spartono e cernono la lana e li figliuoli revedeno li panni e fanno gli altri essercizi, dalli vilissimi e sporchi adietro. Adeo che, essendo tutti li fiorentini impliciti in questi essercizi vili. . . ." Arnaldo Segarizzi, ed., *Relazioni degli ambasciatori veneti al senato* (3 vols.; Bari, 1912-16), III, Pt. I, 17.

salary from the family business (Table 20). Jacopo knew
that in his new company with Signorini he had a successful
business going; for when his father died in December 1513,
he took his share of the liquid assets of the estate (919
florins) and added cash of his own to buy complete control
of his company. Over the next fifteen years profits amounted
to two and a half times the original capital. This was the
main source of cash income for Jacopo during that period
when his household expenses covering ten children were at
their highest. At the same time, Jacopo decreased his investment in the much less flourishing family company to the merely nominal amount of 400 florins (out of a total capital of
6,300 florins).

TABLE 20. INCOME OF JACOPO GUICCIARDINI, 1505 TO 1530
(All figures are in florins *larghi d'oro in oro*)

Profits from investments, 1508-29		6,569
Earnings from real estate		3,987
Wife's property, 1520-28	1,833	
Jacopo's property, 1514-28	2,154	
Salaries in business, 1505-16		195
Salaries from political offices		636
Profits from papal offices in which he substituted for his brother		2,721
Total		14,108

Source: AG, Libri 12-15, *passim*; 22, f. 1.

Beyond the capital in his silk firm, Jacopo was not able to
increase his liquid assets appreciably. He had liquidated his
wife's dowry in 1503, and his share of his father's liquid assets had gone into his own silk company. The considerable
profits from that company went mostly for the expenses of his
large family and only slight amounts were available for other
business ventures, by far the largest being his investment
with his brother in Flanders. Originally, he put 500 florins in
that company; after his own sons went into the company,
his investment increased to 1,000 florins but it never went any

higher. Even the large inheritance of his wife in 1519 brought him no immediate cash rewards.[85] Although that estate amounted to almost 15,000 florins, most of it was in land and this was not sold. There was one debt of 1,629 florins owed to his father-in-law by the city of Florence, but through special agreements this was paid off in small sums over a twenty-five year period. He liquidated the 2,057 florins his wife inherited in Monte stock and invested it in a company with his partner, Andrea Signorini, in Pescia; but those assets were kept apart from Jacopo's estate because they were committed by an obligation in the will to the support of his wife's mother.

Although Jacopo did not increase his liquid assets, he did inherit considerable real estate. His father's death in 1513 left him with a couple of farms and several miscellaneous smaller properties, along with a share in the family palace; and in 1519 he added the property inherited by his wife, which he estimated to be worth about 7,000 florins. His total land holdings, therefore, may have amounted to about 8,500 florins.[86] During the period covered by his accounts, up to

[85] Here is an itemization of his wife's estate (AG, Libro 25, ff. 13-14):

	Florins
Real estate (four farms, a villa, town shops)	7,000
Monte credits	2,057
Dowry (already liquidated)	3,300
A credit with the commune	1,629
Furnishings, silver, jewels, etc.	1,000
Total	14,986

The original value of the dowry was 2,500 florins, but it rose to 3,300 florins as a result of an increase in the value of Monte holdings.

[86] This figure is only an estimate. The 7,000 florins was his own estimate of the market value of his wife's property. This included 2,000 florins for a farm with a "casa da signore." The *decima* value of all this was 20 florins, 1 *soldi*, 9 *denari* (AG, Filza XLV, undated *decima* report) and this would be for the income property only, which, allowing 1,000 florins for the country house, might be worth 6,000 florins. The *decima* of Jacopo's own property was 5 florins, 13 *soldi*, 11 *denari*; and if there is a ratio between *decima* and market values, Jacopo's own property would be worth about 1,500 florins.

1531, he did not sell any of this nor did he buy any additional land until 1528, when he paid 130 florins for a farm, and 1530, when he paid 457 for three pieces of land.[87] He also bought a town house in 1515 for 1,874 florins, but he was still paying on this property when he closed his books in 1531.

From Table 20, which summarizes Jacopo's income from all sources, and Table 21, which is a balance sheet for the

TABLE 21. ASSETS AND LIABILITIES OF JACOPO GUICCIARDINI, 1505 TO 1532
(All figures are in florins *larghi d'oro in oro*)

Assets		
Real estate acquisitions		3,743
Land	667	
House and furnishings .	3,076	
Investment credits in 1532		2,741
Expenditures, 1505-32		13,514
Living expenses	8,754	
Taxes	2,664	
Three dowries	1,756	
Interest, losses	340	
Cash on hand in 1532		253
	Total	20,251
Liabilities: credits received		
Wife's dowry		2,455
Father-in-law's estate		1,637
Profits, income, credits from father's estate .		15,337
Owed on house		728
Miscellaneous credits		935
	Total	21,092

Source: AG, Libro 15, ff. 236-37.

first twenty-eight years of Jacopo's career, it is apparent that Jacopo—with his large family of ten children—was not able to accumulate capital for further investment despite the large value of his estate. That, of course, consisted mostly of land which for purposes of security he did not choose to liquidate. In fact, one might conclude that Jacopo was only able

[87] AG, Libro 15, ff. 139, 201.

to make ends meet. He certainly must have welcomed the opportunity to supplement his income by temporarily replacing his brother in the Romagna, although that kept him away from his family for considerable periods of time. What is most significant in all of this is the relatively slight income value of his land. Although with his own inheritance and that of his wife his income-producing land must have been worth about 7,500 florins, the return on that investment was relatively small; and during the 1520's all of it is credited on his books against family expenses.

After 1530 those family expenses were considerably reduced—one son died in 1529, three others had left for the Lowlands and the rest were soon to follow, and one daughter was married and her dowry paid; and with his own town house by now decorated and furnished, the income from his lands must have sufficed to pay the relatively smaller costs of living. Furthermore, with the return of the Medici in 1530, he could hope for a relaxation of the heavy tax burden which had consumed a great deal of his liquid assets, especially during the years of the last Republic. Jacopo's books do not survive for the period after 1531; we have only a few books of real estate accounts and *decima* reports. But already before he closed out his book in 1531, he had liquidated all his local business investments. The family company had long been out of business; and after the last renewal of his own company in 1529, that investment also began to be liquidated and the capital itself had been paid back by 1533. The company in Flanders was still going but, as we shall see, it was never to pay any profits and the capital was completely lost. After 1531 Jacopo bought only a few more pieces of land, including a country house, although he inherited some land from his brother Francesco.[88] Despite an active and successful

[88] AG, *Decimario*, ff. 298-302; also Libro 22, ff. 260, 354. The *decima* value of his additional acquisitions, which included two farms, amounted to 5 florins, 18 *soldi*, 9 *denari*.

business career early in life, the patrimony Jacopo handed over to his sons consisted mostly of properties he had inherited from his father, his brother, and his father-in-law; and in these he had rooted his security.

Perhaps the fact that he had so many children indicates in itself his confidence that they would somehow be able to fit into the world with the dignity of their family's tradition even without the benefit of a great fortune. And it was into the business world that he directed his sons, giving them a business education[89] and setting them up in a family company. Jacopo, therefore, was undoubtedly willing to undertake an enterprise that not only offered to pay profits much larger than his silk manufactory but one that at the same time would give his sons a secure niche in the business world. Such was the new company organized in 1519 by his youngest brother, Girolamo, for commerce in the Lowlands. This partnership was to last five years and had a capital of 4,500 florins: 2,000 from Bartolomeo di Bartolomeo Nasi, and 2,500 florins from the Guicciardini—500 from Jacopo and 1,000 each from Francesco and Girolamo, who was also to assume the management in the Lowlands.[90] The Guicciardini must have had high hopes for the company's prospects. Its capital formation was probably the occasion for the eventual dissolution of the older silk manufactory of the brothers, for we hear nothing more of it after its reorganization in 1525. But those hopes were not unbalanced by an awareness of the risk involved in such a venture. The capital was very small for international operations, and the original agreement stipulated that all profits were to be plowed back into the organization.[91] Moreover, the investments had been made with a good deal of caution: Jacopo's initial investment was very modest and

[89] AG, Libro 23, f. 59.
[90] AG, Libro, 14, ff. 84, 92; Libro 25, f. 13; *Mercanzia*, 10831, f. 176r. In 1521 Jacopo increased his capital to 650 florins, entitling him to 9 percent of the profits; AG, Libro 15, f. 9.
[91] AG, Libro 15, f. 9.

conservative considering his resources at the time, and the investment by both Nasi and Francesco was made with the understanding that they were not to be responsible for any losses.

This was obviously a venture undertaken primarily by Girolamo. He was twenty-two and unmarried at the time, and it was he who went off to Flanders to assume the management of the company. The next year, in 1520, he was joined by Jacopo's oldest son, Agnolo (1506-68).[92] Girolamo, however, did not stay abroad very long. Jacopo had long been negotiating a marriage for Girolamo with his sister-in-law, another one of the three heiresses of Agnolo Bardi; and by 1524 these arrangements had been made.[93] Thereupon, Girolamo returned to Florence, settled down to the comforts of his wife's estate (presumably as large as that of Jacopo's wife), and spent the rest of his years in his native city. This occurred just at the time that the articles of the company were to be renewed, and so there was a considerable reorganization that year. The new company was now represented by Jacopo's eighteen-year-old son Agnolo, who went into partnership with Giovanni Vernacci in Flanders. It was named Agnolo Guicciardini and Giovanni Vernacci and Company, and had a capital of 7,000 florins, of which 5,600 came from three of the brothers.[94] The capital was increased to 7,500 florins in 1527, and the company headquarters in Antwerp saw the arrival of two more of Jacopo's sons, Giovanbattista (b. 1508) and Lorenzo (1513-94), who also entered into the management. By 1533 Vernacci had withdrawn from the

[92] AG, Libro 25, ff. 175, 177, 182.

[93] For an account of the negotiations, see P. Guicciardini, *Un parentado fiorentino nei primi del Cinquecento e riflessi di vita umanistica della campagna valdelsana* (Florence, 1940), pp. 18-21.

[94] AG, Libro, 15, f. 234; *Mercanzia*, 10831, f. 203r; F. Guicciardini, "Ricordanze," p. 90. The partners were Vernacci and the three brothers, Jacopo, Girolamo, and Francesco. The capital investment of Francesco was 1,500 florins and that of Jacopo, 1,000 florins; and apparently Girolamo put in 3,100 florins.

company and it became an exclusively Guicciardini enterprise.[95] Meanwhile, the company paid no profits, for all the
successive contracts continued the agreement that they were
to be plowed back into the company.[96]

At one time or another, all of Jacopo's sons made the trip
to Antwerp. Agnolo and Giovanbattista, the oldest, were the
first to go and the affairs of the company were in their hands.
Giovanbattista in 1534 became in addition a consul of the
Florentine nation in Antwerp. The younger brothers went to
Antwerp by way of Lyons, where they all took an apprenticeship in one of the great Florentine companies in that financial
capital. By 1540 all were, or had been, in the company headquarters in Antwerp. From there they began to move out, this
time to make those contacts in the great international centers
of commerce and banking so important to the success of a
Renaissance company. Agnolo and Raffaello (1516-92) had
returned to Florence by 1540, but Raffaello moved on to
Naples in 1543 and in the following year was consul for
the Florentine nation there. Lorenzo moved to Ferrara in
1540, and Vincenzo (1519-67) went to London in
1541. Giovanbattista and Lodovico (1521-89) remained in
Antwerp.[97]

With these six brothers now moving anxiously throughout
the business world of the sixteenth century, the years around
1540 must have seen the greatest activity of the Guicciardini
company. We know from a surviving book of Jacopo's

[95] *Mercanzia*, 10832, ff. 8r, 16r.
[96] Thus the agreements of 1521, 1527, and 1536. Moreover, Jacopo's
accounts indicate no income from this source.
[97] The Archivio Guicciardini contains some notes by the late Mario
Battistini on the Antwerp company and the Guicciardini associated
with it. Battistini, who taught for some years in Antwerp, was making
a study of the Flemish branch of the family when he died, and his
notes were given to the Guicciardini family. They are very disorgan-
ized and were found not to be altogether reliable when checked out
against information in the family archives. Nevertheless, he had done
some original genealogical research on those members of the family
who were in the Lowlands, and much of the information used here
comes from his notes.

that the company and its numerous outposts were part of a
network of commerce and banking. There are records of
shipments of silk to Antwerp, London, and Ferrara, and of
exchange transactions, particularly in Ferrara. When the company was renewed in 1543, the two centers were Antwerp, under Giovanbattista's direction, and Ferrara, under
Lorenzo's.[98]

The Guicciardini company, however, never was successful.
Despite the policy of taking out no profits ever since its incep-
tion in 1519 and despite the frenzied activity of six brothers strategically located in important centers where they stood
in high regard among their Florentine confreres, the company
went under in 1543. It became insolvent, as a family document dated 1567 informs us,[99] because of various accidents:
losses on land and on sea, bad debts, and especially because
of confiscation of much of the company's money and goods
at the instigation of Gaspard Ducci, an unprincipled Italian
financier who wielded much power in the government of the
Lowlands.[100] The company was declared officially bankrupt
with debts of more than 25,000 florins; and the two directors
were imprisoned—Giovanbattista for more than three years,
and Lorenzo, in Ferrara, for more than eight years. This led
to even greater losses because the company was deprived of its
directors at a most crucial moment.[101] Jacopo had to alienate
property received from his wife worth 4,000 florins in order

[98] For the company in Antwerp there is some extant material,
including a few miscellaneous incomplete account books and books
with copies of commercial correspondence: AG, Libri 26, 27, 31, 33-
36; Filza LI, LIV, LIX. Ehrenberg does not mention the Guicciardini
firm in his study. For references to activities of Giovanbattista and
Vincenzo in England, consult James Gairdner, ed., *Letters and Papers,
Foreign and Domestic, 1509-1546* (21 vols.; London, 1864-1912),
XVIII, Pt. I, Nos. 208, 282, 353, 566, 763, 774, 789, 623.

[99] AG, Filza LXVI, document dated 1567.

[100] On Ducci, see Émile Coornaert, *Les français et le commerce
international à Anvers (fin du XVe-XVIe siècle)* (Paris, 1961), I,
351-52; and Ehrenberg, pp. 222-26.

[101] AG, Filza, LXVI, document dated 1567.

to pay off debts;[102] and as late as 1568, Giovanbattista, Lorenzo, and even the other brothers still had hanging over them the debts incurred by this failure.[103]

And so it was that the great effort came to naught. The Guicciardini did not emerge as a great financial house in the sixteenth century business world, and Jacopo's six surviving sons did not find their fortune. Three never returned to Florence: Vincenzo remained in London until his death in 1567 and continued to have a good enough standing among merchants there to become consul for the Florentine nation in 1564; Giovanbattista married a Flemish girl and, as far as we know, lived out his days in Antwerp; and Lodovico also remained in the Lowlands, where he continued in business as a representative for several Italian business firms although he had no business of his own.[104] Two of these brothers, like many of their forebears, achieved some intellectual distinction in their own day. Giovanbattista was a geographer of some note;[105] and Lodovico is, of course, the most famous Guicciardini after his uncle. Truly a Renaissance man, with interests in art, philosophy, mathematics, history, and sci-

[102] AG, Filza, xxvii, No. 35.

[103] The will of Agnolo di Jacopo, dated 1568, declares that his heirs are not to be responsible for the debts of his father and his two brothers because of accounts in Ferrara and Antwerp, and the latter two are excluded from Agnolo's inheritance. His other surviving brothers, Raffaello and Lodovico, on the other hand, are specified as his eventual heirs in the event of the death of his sons. See AG, *Spogli*. Earlier, in the will of Bongianni (d. 1549), Roberto and Vincenzo were excluded from the share of his estate which went to their brothers, Agnolo, Raffaello, and Lodovico, as sons of Jacopo, although they were to receive their shares in the event they settled their debts. The same stipulation is found in the will of their mother Camilla, dated 1555, where Roberto, Vincenzo, Giovanbattista, and Lorenzo were excluded until their debts were cleared; AG, Filza xxvii, No. 35.

[104] J. A. Goris, *Étude sur les colonies marchandes méridionales (Portugais, Espagnols, Italiens) à Anvers de 1488 à 1567* (Louvain, 1925), p. 604; Coornaert, i, 351 n. 2.

[105] Negri, p. 288. A few of his letters have been published by Mario Battistini, ed., *Lettere di Giovan Battista Guicciardini a Cosimo e Francesco de' Medici (1559-77)* (Brussels-Rome, 1949).

ence, as well as skill in the merchant's profession, he is a notable example of a well-educated, refined patrician in the noble tradition of his family and of his native city.[106]

The other three sons, who lived out their lives in Florence, removed themselves from the world of business.[107] Raffaello and Agnolo, along with Lodovico, had inherited a part of the small estate of their uncle, Bongianni, in 1549; and from their father's estate in 1552, each may have received property worth about 5,000 florins, about a third of which would not have been income property.[108] With this they had the security of sufficient income but little promise of capital accumulation. What happened to the estate of Lodovico, who was in the Lowlands, cannot be determined. Neither Agnolo nor Raffaello appreciably added to their land holdings up to the time of their deaths.[109] Both held numerous political offices, especially external offices, which may have appealed to them as sources of income. Agnolo became a senator in 1557 and appears frequently on the Grand Duke's council. Lorenzo, who, having lost out on the inheritance of his father

[106] On Lodovico, see the bibliography in P. Guicciardini, *Ritratto vasariano . . .* , p. 40 n. 25.

[107] The account books of Lorenzo's heir (AG, Libro 166) and of Agnolo's estate (AG, Libro 57) reveal no business interests.

[108] Here is an estimate of Jacopo's properties:

		Florins
From his father, 1514		1,500
Wife's estate, 1519		7,000
Palace, 1518		2,500
From Francesco's estate, 1540		1,625
From Bongianni's estate, 1549		1,549
Acquisitions, 1528-52		1,500
	Total	15,674

The inventory of Agnolo's properties in 1568 (four farms, miscellaneous smaller parcels, a country house, one-fourth part of the town house, a part of the *castello*) would confirm the proximity of this value; AG, Libro 57, inventory attached to front of book. The gross income from these properties from April 1568 to December 1570 amounted to 675 florins; *ibid.*, ff. 43, 84.

[109] AG, *Decimario*, ff. 316-27. Three small account books of Raffaello survive: AG, Libri 51-53; and there is a series of accounts of Agnolo and his estate: AG, Libri 55-60.

and uncle because of his misfortunes in business, nevertheless returned to Florence, where he appears as an officeholder more frequently than either of the other two brothers. In 1570 he too became a senator. His estate, however, was not impressive; it was certainly smaller than his brothers', and he likewise had no business investments.[110] All three brothers, in short, had very modest if secure incomes. Nevertheless, they had a great deal of dignity and status in their native city, and they had leisure. For such men as these the prestige of an office in the ducal government—as well, no doubt, as the modest stipend which went along with it—befitted their dignity, and they must have entered into the courtly life of the new princes with quiet resignation if not with positive enthusiasm.[111]

Girolamo (1497-1556).[112] In this survey of Piero's six sons and what they did with their lives, one son remains—Girolamo. As we have seen, he had gone off to Antwerp in 1519 supplied with 4,500 florins of capital to establish himself in business but was soon lured back to Florence by the prospect of marriage with one of the Bardi heiresses, the sister-in-law of Jacopo, who had negotiated the marriage. He took over the family palace as his residence—which had been a stipulation of his bride—and lived the rest of his life in Florence. He seems not to have abandoned his interest in the business world. His one extant account book (1527-30) records many commercial transactions in luxury materials as well as accounts with international bankers, and there are a few surviving busi-

[110] This is the general impression one has from the book of *entrata e uscita* of his heir, Jacopo d'Agnolo di Jacopo; AG, Libro 166.

[111] Of all of Jacopo's sons, only three themselves had sons—Vincenzo, Lorenzo, and Agnolo. Only Agnolo's provided further descendants, but they did not extend this line of the family beyond the eighteenth century; Litta, *Guicciardini*, Tavola III.

[112] On Girolamo, see AG, *Spogli*. Only a part of one of his account books survives: a commercial book of *debitori e creditori*, 1527-30 (AG, Libro 10). There is also a record of property acquisitions by his line of the family: AG, Filza XXVII, No. 47.

ness letters from him in Rome and in Venice for the years
1525 to 1527. He retained his investment in his nephews'
company in the Lowlands; but what other investments he
had are unknown except for 1,500 ducats put into a silk
manufactory in Florence in 1548. His *decima* reports reveal
several additions to his land holdings, though he did not increase by very much the property inherited from his wife and
from his own family.[118] He was a frequent officeholder in the
ducal government and had several ambassadorial missions.
In 1551 he became a senator, probably replacing his brother
Luigi, who died that year. Girolamo died in 1556 leaving one
heir, his son Agnolo.

The life of Agnolo di Girolamo Guicciardini (1525-81)
goes somewhat beyond the scope of this study, but it so dif-
fers from that of his relatives of the same generation that it
is worth at least a brief sketch.[114] It was Agnolo who built
up the great family fortune which still provides the Guicciardini with their wealth, and this fortune was made in both land
and business. For the period after his father's death there is a
record of continual investment in silk, wool, and dye businesses in Florence.[115] These companies apparently made
handsome profits with which Agnolo was able considerably to
increase his patrimony by acquiring land. Within eight years
following the death of his father he had spent 7,446 florins
alone on land purchases; and thereafter until his death his
land holdings grew steadily.[116] Meanwhile, Agnolo played
an important role at court. He, too, held many offices, including a number of ambassadorial assignments of more cere-

---

[113] AG, *Decimario*, ff. 303-6.

[114] On Agnolo, see AG, *Spogli*. Three of his letters have been published: *Tre lettere di Agnolo Guicciardini mandate da Cosimo I a
Venezia nel 1519* (Florence, 1906), an extract from *Arte e storia*,
17-18 (1906). Several miscellaneous account books survive, none of
great value: AG, Libri 43-49, 54.

[115] Agnolo's investments, extracted from Mercanzia records, are
enumerated in AG, *Spogli*.

[116] AG, *Decimario*, ff. 398-429. From 1569 to 1574 his property
grew in value from 15,081 to 22,889 florins; AG, Libro 43, f. 30.

monial than diplomatic importance. He was frequently on the Duke's Council, and in 1565 became a senator.

Agnolo's three sons were also wealthy men; they continued to invest heavily in the cloth industry, and in addition they had investments in Rome. In 1593 his sons had 36,000 ducats in credits with a number of such manufactories. The two younger brothers followed other patricians into the ducal court, both becoming, however, more than just courtiers but also court functionaries at the highest level. They both ended their days abroad as resident ambassadors of the Grand Duke. The oldest brother, Girolamo (1550-1621), remained in Florence, where he made a handsome marriage that brought him a dowry of 8,000 ducats; and it is from him that the Guicciardini line descended into the present century.[117]

The journey through the economic history of seven generations of Guicciardini has had a varied course along which it has been possible to take a broad survey of the Florentine patriciate. We have encountered a number of patrician types —rentiers and entrepreneurs, politicians and administrators, lawyers and scholars. Their wealth in the course of the century and a half traversed reached at times the pinnacle, but it also descended to more modest levels, although it never fell altogether outside the economic sphere of the patriciate. Over so many generations there could be no stability in the economic fortunes of the family as long as investments were in liquid wealth and therefore subject to unpredictable fluctuation and as long as there was the prospect of periodic division of estates every generation. Up to the very end of the story we have found men turning to business to replenish their wealth and make their own fortunes. Most striking of all in this survey of the Guicciardini is the lack of a main genealogi-

---

[117] In the Archivio Guicciardini the number of account books which survive for this and subsequent generations is almost overwhelming. There are also some books of the heirs of Agnolo in ASF, *Miscellanea repubblicana*, Buste L-LIX.

cal trunk: there is only periodic branching, and in pursuing the rambling genealogical growth of the family it has been necessary at each juncture to select one branch alone and abandon its parallels in order to proceed with a degree of continuity. Otherwise, the efforts would be hopelessly diffused and the result would be utterly amorphous. The decision as to which branch to follow has necessarily been made on the basis of surviving documentation, but that criterion should not blind us to the nature of the growth itself. The economic history of a family in the Renaissance has a notable lack of cohesion and continuity. Familial relationships had economic meaning only within one man's household; and beyond those confines, where the economic ties were loosened or altogether severed, relationships are more likely than not to be of genealogical interest only.

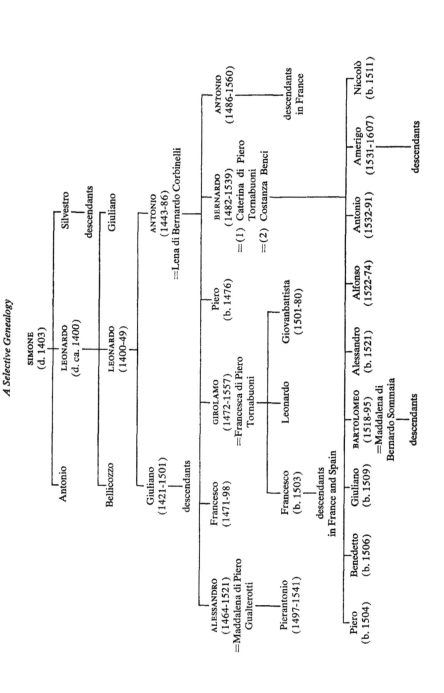

GENEALOGICAL CHART 3. THE GONDI

A Selective Genealogy

Chapter v

THE GONDI

ALTHOUGH the Strozzi and the Guicciardini did not leave for posterity an imposing collection of personal documents, their participation in public life is recorded in official documents and in the comments of contemporary writers. It is otherwise with the Gondi: there are no letters, no diaries, no family commentaries, only an occasional comment here and there in the contemporary annals. That is all we have—except for the account books. These are not the records of personalities, but of careers and businesses; and as woefully impersonal as they are, they nevertheless provide the materials to delineate at least one remarkable career, the story of an impressive business and the fluctuating fortunes of another great Florentine family.[1]

Hints of the Gondi family appear as early as the late twelfth and early thirteenth century.[2] They possessed a tower in the same parish as the Strozzi in the quarter of S. Maria Novella,

---

[1] The Gondi materials relevant to this study are found in the Archivio Gondi in the Archivio di Stato, Florence. For a description, see Cesari Paoli, "Le carte dei Gondi deonate all'Archivio di Stato di Firenze," *ASI*, XII (1883), 296-300; and "Notizie degli archivi toscani," *ibid.*, CXIV (1956), 423-24. The archival Inventario is particularly useful, for it includes a very thorough chronological *spogli* of the surviving documents. Also in the Archivio di Stato of Florence there is a Fondo Gondi in the Archivio Mannelli-Galilei-Riccardi. For other Gondi records still in private hands, see Roberto Ridolfi, *Gli archivi . . .* , pp. 55-93; and Rudolf Hirsch, "Gondi-Medici Business Records in the Lea Library of the University of Pennsylvania," *Renaissance News*, XVI (1963), 11-14. The standard genealogy of the Gondi is Monsieur de Corbinelli, *Historie généalogique de la maison de Gondi* (2 vols.; Paris, 1705), which publishes a number of documents (*preuves*).

[2] *Delizie degli eruditi toscani*, VII, 163, 247. See also the documents cited in Corbinelli, I, *preuves*, *passim*.

and their name appears among the earliest merchants of the city who held political office. The family took its name from one of these ancestors, a certain Gondo, whose name is found several times in the official records, and whose descendants identified themselves as "de Gondi." By the early fourteenth century a number of Gondi were participating in the international import-export business, where many Florentine patricians originally made their fortunes.[3] How active the Gondi were in the tumultuous politics of fourteenth century Florence is difficult to say. In 1358 one of the leaders of this house, Simone di Geri Gondi, was disqualified from public office—along with his descendants up to the third generation—for his Ghibelline sympathies;[4] but they do not appear to have played a very important role in the city's political affairs.[5]

Simone di Geri Gondi matriculated in the merchants' guild in 1352; and, despite his political misfortune, by the year of his death in 1403 he was one of the wealthiest citizens in the city.[6] How Simone had made his wealth and in what it consisted we do not know. He owned properties in the Mugello, east of Florence, and the family genealogist describes him as a lord over a sizeable fief in this area and the owner of a tower.[7] But again, as we have seen before, because of division of estates among children and then further divisions

---

[3] Davidsohn found six Gondi brothers active in commerce in 1322 (*Forschugen zur Geschichte von Florenz* [4 vols.; Berlin, 1896-1908], III, 159) and four brothers conducting business in Forlì in 1329 (*Geschichte von Florenz*, IV, Pt. 2, 468). Many of them were matriculated in the silk guild.

[4] Corbinelli, I, li.

[5] The name does not appear at all in the recent study of Brucker already cited. Before 1438, when the ban on Simone and his descendants was lifted, there had never been a Gondi on the Signoria. Corbinelli lists the offices held by the family over four centuries, and the record is not impressive; Corbinelli, I, ccccxiv-ccccxx.

[6] He paid a *prestanza* that year of 26 florins, which put him among the 126 citizens who paid more than 20 florins; Martines, *The Social World* . . . , p. 359.

[7] Corbinelli, I, xlix.

thereafter, the wealth of one man, however great, did not assure his descendants of wealth. In the *catasto* of 1427 one of Simone's grandchildren, Simone di Silvestro Gondi, declared a net worth of 6,279 florins, putting him also among the wealthiest patricians.[8] On the other hand, another grandson, Leonardo di Leonardo, declared a taxable worth of only 650 florins;[9] and the three sons of Giovanni, a brother of Simone, reporting together on one return, declared that their debts and deductions more than canceled out their assets.[10] At the same time, while the various descendants were finding their fortunes along separate paths, the bonds tying them together became more and more tenuous. For a while the ancestral home, under a fideicommissum, was held by them all, but its ownership became more fragmented as the family passed it from one generation to another. In 1428 the Gondi residence in the parish of S. Maria Ughi belonged to the sons of Simone's brother Giovanni, a son of Simone (Silvestro), and a grandson by another son of Simone (Leonardo di Leonardo); but in that year these three parties severed even that tie by selling the property outside the family.[11] Thereafter the cycle of family history must start all over again; and with the characteristic fluctuation in the fortunes of Florentine families, the descendants of Leonardo, whose extremely modest wealth was mentioned above, were again among the city's richest men. Fortunately, family records of this line survive which let us trace these fluctuations over several generations.[12]

THE FIFTEENTH CENTURY

Leonardo (1400-49). In his *catasto* of 1427 Leonardo di Leonardo di Simone Gondi declared his total worth as 1,832

---

[8] Martines, *The Social World . . .* , p. 373.

[9] *Catasto*, 76, ff. 123r-24v. The smallest value in Martines' list of the top 150 reports from the same quarter is 1,346 florins.

[10] *Catasto*, 76, ff. 2r-3r.   [11] Corbinelli, I, clxxxvi.

[12] There are no surviving personal records of the descendants of Silvestro di Simone. They appear quite frequently, however, in the *Tratte*.

florins before deductions. This included 968 florins credit in the Monte and land worth 598 florins, consisting of one farm with a residence and eight other smaller parcels of land. In addition, he owned a half of the family house in which he resided in the city—it was next door to Matteo di Simone Strozzi's house—but it, of course, had no income value. He mentions no business investment. Leonardo's financial position was very modest indeed for one whose grandfather had been one of the city's wealthiest men.

In 1428 Leonardo inherited the estates of his only two brothers and hence came into possession of the entire patrimony of his father, a son of Simone Gondi.[13] How large that was cannot be determined, but all indications are that Leonardo immediately began to raise capital by selling his properties and investing that capital in business. In 1428 he sold his share of the house in which he lived; and by 1433 he had sold whatever property he must have inherited from his brothers, for he declared in his *catasto* that year no more holdings than those on the 1427 return. By 1442 he owned no property at all except for one farm and he was even paying out rent for his residence in the city. At the same time, after 1427 he began to invest in business, although the values of his assets as entered on his tax reports are not at all reliable. In 1433 he mentions a company of his own, investments in two other companies of indeterminate nature, and an asset of 3,000 florins for a loan he had made. In 1442 he refers to his company as a shop "del mestiere dell'oro."[14] For lack of further documentation, we have to assume that Leonardo met with considerable success in his business ventures, or at least that he was able to introduce his sons to a business in which they could build their own fortunes, for in 1457, eight years after Leonardo's death in 1449, his oldest

[13] See the biography of Leonardo in Corbinelli, I, clxxxv-cxc.
[14] For the changing financial interests of Leonardo, see his tax reports for 1433 and 1442: *Catasto*, 461, ff. 48r-49r; 620, ff. 639-40.

son, Giuliano, paid an impost which indicated that he had brought his family back into the upper ranks of the city's wealthiest patricians.[15]

Giuliano di Leonardo (1421-1501). Of Giuliano's considerable wealth, there are only the vaguest hints in his tax reports of 1457 and 1480.[16] The foundation of his fortune was the workshop "del mestiere dell'oro" mentioned in both returns, but this was a much larger business than the same kind of shop operated by his father. In 1457 he declared its value to be 4,000 florins. He also included several pages enumerating his debtors and creditors, and the totals of each of these categories approaches 15,000 florins. The itemization of these alone indicates that he was operating more than just a workshop, for besides stock on hand of silk, silver, gold thread, and other shop materials, his liabilities included many amounts held in deposit.

The activity of the company, furthermore, reached far beyond the confines of Florence. Among his bad debtors in 1457 he lists Federigo, Count of Urbino, and his testament includes instructions to his heirs to be diligent in their efforts to collect a sizeable debt from Ercole, Duke of Ferrara.[17] The King of Naples was another prince with whom Giuliano had good personal relations, no doubt arising out of business dealings.[18] Giuliano was active in Naples as early as 1452,[19]

[15] *Catasto*, 816, No. 126. Giuliano paid 14 florins, 6 *denari*, and hence he was among the 227 men who paid over 10 florins in tax that year; see de Roover, *The Rise and Decline . . .* , p. 29 (Table 4).

[16] *Catasto*, 816, No. 126; 1003, f. 434.

[17] Corbinelli publishes the will: I, *preuves*, cccclxxviii-cccclxxxiv. In 1492, 12,916 florins remained to be paid, and Giuliano and the heirs of Antonio made a convention for dividing these credits; A Gondi, Inv., No. 2.

[18] In 1477 King Ferdinand intervened in Giuliano's behalf with the Florentine government. Furthermore, either Ferdinand or his successor granted Giuliano and his heirs the right to incorporate a ducal crown into their coat of arms.

[19] In that year he was given 500 florins as an *accomanda* for three years for business in Naples; *Mercanzia*, 10831, f. 28r.

and it became a center of the Gondi business interests. In 1457 he mentions material possessions there worth 5,711 florins; and in 1480 he refers to certain business operations there done under his name and that of his brother Antonio. At the same time, in 1480, one of his sons was in Naples and two others were away from Italy, one in Hungary and one in Constantinople, both very likely traveling to make business contacts.[20] The picture is very hazy, but from all this evidence emerges the vague outline of a company centering on a workshop in Florence and extending into banking and commercial activities throughout Italy. A base was established in Naples, where, it will be recalled, the Strozzi centered their business network at about the same time. If the general picture of late fifteenth century business history is a gloomy one, this is not to say that there were no successes alongside the many houses that were contracting their operations or actually closing shop. The Gondi numbered among the fortunate.[21]

How extensive Giuliano's wealth was cannot be determined. None of his accounts survive. It is interesting, however, that in his two returns he indicates almost no possession of land. In 1455 he moved out of the quarter which had long been inhabited by his family and established his residence in the quarter of S. Croce, where he purchased a house. In 1457 this was the only property he possessed other than the one farm mentioned earlier in his father's returns. In 1480 this farm had passed to Antonio, and the residence therefore was the only property henceforth owned by Giuliano. In fact, he was actually paying out rent for his workshop as well as for three houses adjacent to his which were apparent-

[20] For all this, see the tax reports cited above. The son in Hungary, Simone, died there in July 1480 at the age of twenty-three; and that event was commemorated in a dialogue by Francesco Bandini, his friend and mentor; Paul Oskar Kristeller, "Francesco Bandini and his consolatory dialogue upon the death of Simone Gondi," in *Studies* . . . , pp. 411-35.

[21] Ehrenberg does not mention this Gondi firm in his study.

ly needed as additional space for his large family of twelve. In 1488 construction was begun on the great family palace, and it continued until his death in 1501. After that, it lapsed for several generations, probably because the division of his estate that year among his five sons discouraged them from further dissipating their reduced wealth by carrying on work on their father's monument.[22]

It is not only in his business career that there are certain similarities between Giuliano Gondi and his contemporary, Filippo di Matteo Strozzi. Giuliano, like Filippo, appears to have detached himself from political involvements. He held a couple of major posts: he was prior in 1469 and served on the Monte in 1479. In 1464 he was ambassador to Ferrara, where his presence—like Filippo's in Naples—was perhaps valuable to the Medici because of his personal influence with the Duke.[23] Otherwise, however, Giuliano, like Filippo, did not burden his days with the endless rounds in state offices which occupied many of their fellows like the Guicciardini and the Capponi. Nor does Giuliano appear to have been associated with Lorenzo de' Medici either in the inner councils of state or in the literary circle of Lorenzo's court. After 1494, however, Giuliano, although by that time over seventy, was twice a Conservator of the Laws[24] and he died the creditor of the republic for a very large sum.[25]

Giuliano and his immediate descendants did little to imprint their family name on the history of their city, and the reader encounters it surprisingly seldom in the contemporary annals. Nevertheless, Giuliano left his mark on Florence with monuments constructed to honor himself and his family. The Gondi chapel in S. Maria Novella is as impressive as

[22] The palace was not completed until 1874; von Reumont, *Lorenzo de' Medici*, II, 156 n. 1.

[23] It will be recalled that Giuliano died the creditor of the Dukes.

[24] *Tratte*, 83, ff. 18v, 19v.

[25] See his testament; A Gondi, Inv., No. 57 (published in Corbinelli, I, *preuves*, cccclxxviii-cccclxxxiv).

Filippo Strozzi's on the other side of the main altar.[26] The great palace also caused much wonderment among the populace when its construction began,[27] and it stands today as majestic a monument as Filippo's to the wealth and taste of a Florentine patrician of the Renaissance.[28]

Antonio di Leonardo (1443-86). The family of Giuliano's brother Antonio elevated the Gondi to a more honored status. Not only did Antonio's sons establish a great banking house in Lyons but from that foothold in France they stepped upward into the life of the court, joined the ranks of the nobility, and won for themselves a place in the history of that kingdom. Fortunately, a few early records of this branch of the family survive which tell more than just the genealogical story of this ascent and, at the same time, disperse some of the obscurity of Florentine social and economic life of the period.

Of Antonio himself, very little can be ascertained. Although he was considerably younger than his brother and was only a child of six when his father died in 1449, he was nevertheless brought into Giuliano's businesses, both the silk and *battiloro* manufactories in Florence and the business in Naples.[29] The company's name included Antonio's, and he shared equally with his brother in the profits.[30] Like his brother, he appears to have had no political role whatsoever in Florence.[31] He died in 1486 in Ferrara, leaving behind a

[26] When Filippo di Filippo Strozzi made provision in his testament for the remodeling of his family chapel, he refers to Giuliano's chapel in the same church as the model which was to be followed: Niccolini, p. 323.

[27] Landucci, p. 48; Giovanni Cambi, *Istorie*, Vols. xx-xxiii of *Delizie* . . . , ii, 51.

[28] For a sketch of Giuliano's life, see Corbinelli, i, cxcii-cxcix.

[29] *Catasto*, 1064, f. 489r.

[30] His heirs continued to share in the profits of Giuliano and Heirs of Antonio Gondi and Company, *battiloro*, at the rate of 10 *soldi* per florin (50 percent); A Gondi, 33, f. 23.

[31] His name does not appear in the *Tratte* records.

dozen children. His large estate, like his brother's, included almost no real estate. He did not even own a residence in Florence,[32] and his only real property consisted of two farms and a small parcel of land located at Ponte di Mezzo just outside Florence toward Prato, altogether valued in 1480 at 1,054 florins.[33] The balance of his estate was his share in the company owned with his brother: but without any documents from the company itself, it is not possible to evaluate its worth. It is obvious, however, that it was a large business, for it provided Giuliano with the resources to build his great palace, and it provided Antonio's heirs with a handsome patrimony.

Antonio had six sons and six daughters who were to reach maturity; but when he died in 1486, all of these except one were still minors. His estate, therefore, was not immediately divided but remained intact until the youngest son reached his majority and a division among the six sons could be effected. Consequently, for the next twenty years, up to 1506, the patrimony Antonio left was administered as a single property; and fortunately some of the records of that administration survive, bringing us as close to the extent of Antonio's wealth as we can hope to come.[34]

Except for his farms, Antonio's estate consisted entirely of liquid assets, apparently with the company he owned with his brother Giuliano; for when the patrimony was finally divided in 1506, it consisted of the real estate, worth 1,480 florins, and the accumulated credits from "Giuliano and Heirs of Antonio Gondi and Company," worth 53,316

[32] *Catasto*, 1004, f. 489r. He was paying 60 florins a year rent for a house, part of which he subleased for 7 florins.

[33] A Gondi, 33, f. 278. The value, for purposes of division among the heirs, was 1,480 florins, which included capital expenditures on the land in the meanwhile.

[34] There are two books of *debitori e creditori* of the sons and heirs of Antonio, 1486 to 1514: A Gondi, 32 and 33. In addition, there is a book of *debitori e creditori* of three of the brothers, Alessandro, Bernardo, and Antonio, 1498 to 1506: A Gondi, 34.

florins.[35] In what form these credits were extended to the heirs and how they were used cannot be exactly determined. They were partly absorbed by the family's ordinary living expenses during these years, and partly by the acquisition of real estate, including a residence, the construction of a villa, and several farms (these expenditures are summarized on Table 22).[36] There was also the expense of three dowries,

TABLE 22. PARTIAL EXPENDITURES OF THE FAMILY OF
ANTONIO GONDI, 1486 TO 1506
(All figures are in florins *larghi di grossi*)

Real estate purchases		10,425
House in Florence	2,400	
Construction of villa	2,196	
Five farms	5,829	
Real estate improvements		1,639[a]
Household furnishings		1,322
Living expenses (clothing, food, etc.)		10,300
Taxes		3,231
Charity		94
Total		27,011

[a] Estimated by comparing purchase costs with assessment value made for purposes of division in 1506, taking into consideration "losses" recorded as a result of that assessment.

Source: A Gondi, 33, ff. 31, 83, 142, 179, 249, 269, 286 (profit-loss accounts); *ibid.*, 36, ff. 6, 34, 103, 136, 163, 189, 278 (property-accounts).

each worth 1,700 *fiorini di suggello* on maturity. Finally, a considerable amount of capital had been available to the brothers for investment; and with the oldest, Alessandro, tak-

[35] A Gondi, 33, f. 23.

[36] The palace was purchased for 2,400 florins on 3 August 1496 and, curiously enough, was located in the quarter of S. Maria Novella, where the family had resided in the early part of the century. The villa was on the family property at Ponte di Mezzo, where one of the five new farms was also located. The other four farms were scattered in other areas: two in the valley of the Greve, one at Grassina, and one at Querceta. Some of the purchase documents survive: A Gondi, Inv., Nos. 28, 35, 39.

ing the initiative, they used it to embark on joint business ventures of their own.

As noted above the estate of Antonio Gondi remained intact as the patrimony of his sons until 1506; and at that time, when his youngest son, also called Antonio, reached maturity, it was completely divided. By 1506 there were only four brothers who were eligible for shares. Piero (b. 1476 or 1477) had become a Dominican monk in 1496, receiving his habit from Savonarola, and so renounced his share of the patrimony,[37] and a sixth brother, Francesco, died in 1498 and his share was divided among the four remaining brothers.[38] Thus in 1506 the estate was divided four ways, among Alessandro, Girolamo, Bernardo, and Antonio; and the division included all property. The family residence went to Alessandro and Antonio; and on 6 June 1506, three months after division of the estate had been arranged, the brothers drew up an agreement concerning living arrangements in the house until the other two brothers could find their own accommodations. It was a very businesslike agreement: each was to pay a share of the general living expenses according to the number of his dependents (including one servant each); each was to pay the salary of his one servant, but those of two others serving the whole household were to come out of the general fund; the expenses of their mother and her servant were to be shared equally; and, finally, Girolamo and Bernardo were each to pay fifteen florins to Alessandro and Antonio for rent. In November, Girolamo moved out and Bernardo followed in December; and since Antonio had gone off to Lyons to establish a branch of the family business, the house remained the residence of Alessandro and his mother alone.[39]

This kind of family agreement even for temporary living

[37] He died in Rome in 1512; A Gondi, Inv., No. 38.
[38] A Gondi, 33, f. 151.
[39] A Gondi, Cassetta VIII, No. 44, ff. 14-15.

arrangements, which was made in the presence of two outside witnesses (Francesco da Sommaia and Giuliano Scarfi), indicates just how distinct each adult male in a "family" must be considered. Whatever kind of association a family of adult brothers may have been, the economic bonds were no tighter than any one of them desired. Even before the division of 1506, each brother could apparently appropriate some capital from the patrimony for himself. As we shall see, Alessandro had long been investing on his own; and the "family" company which he organized with the capital of the brothers' patrimony did not include Girolamo as a partner. At any rate, the division of 1506 was complete; each brother had his own estate thereafter and was free to go his own way. Nothing further is known of Girolamo; he does not appear in the records of the family company, nor is his name found in the *Tratte*.[40] He had two sons, however, and their names appear here and there in family records; he himself died in 1557. The other three brothers, Alessandro, Bernardo, and Antonio, remained investment partners in an ambitious and partly successful venture to raise their fortunes; and with the survival of some of their account books, it is possible to trace something of their efforts.

ALESSANDRO AND THE FAMILY COMPANY

As the oldest son and as the only son who was an adult when his father died, Alessandro assumed the responsibility for administering the estate, and he remained throughout his life the driving force behind the further growth of the Gondi fortune. Fortunately, the documentation of the career and fortune of Alessandro is remarkably complete.[41] He had prob-

[40] The family genealogist has nothing further to say of him; Corbinelli, I, ccxliv-ccxlv.

[41] His private ledgers exist in a series of three books, from 1486 to 1519: A Gondi, 35, 36, 37. The last is incomplete owing to his death. There are also three secondary books: A Gondi, 5, 6, 38.

ably started out his career in 1482 at the age of eighteen as an apprentice in the business of his father and uncle in Naples, where he may have been when his father died.[42] After 1486 he was in Florence, where he apparently supervised his patrimony for his family and kept a separate account of his own on the side. For the first two and a half years he was salaried in his uncles' silk and *battiloro* establishment;[43] and thereafter for three years, up through 1493, he was employed in the company of his uncle where his own patrimony was invested.[44] After that date there is no evidence of further association with his uncle, and Alessandro began to undertake his own ventures. Already before 1493, however, he was committing small amounts of his capital. In 1489 he made his first investment on his own when he put a small sum in a wool manufactory; but the profits were not large, even though he plowed them back into the company, and in 1497 he withdrew altogether from the business.[45] In the meantime, ever since 1488, he had been collecting small premiums—usually under five florins—for underwriting marine insurance up to one hundred florins at a time. Up to 1499 he had suffered only one loss of fifty florins and had netted 856 florins profits from such transactions.[46]

In 1493 Alessandro apparently withdrew altogether from the company of his uncle and organized his own investing company to handle the liquid assets of the patrimony.[47] The

[42] In an entry dated 1486 he records his salary for four years (1482-86?) in Naples as 36 florins, 1 *soldo*; A Gondi, 35, f. 6.

[43] He received 13 florins, 17 *soldi*, from the silk company, and 80 florins from the *battiloro* company; A Gondi, 35, f. 44.

[44] His salary for thirty-five and a half months was 118 florins, 6 *soldi*, 8 *denari*; A Gondi, 35, f. 102.

[45] He originally invested 333 florins, 6 *soldi*, 8 *denari*, for a share of 6 2/3 percent of the profits, which totaled 218 florins, 1 *soldo*, 8 *denari*, in eight years; A Gondi, 35, ff. 62, 101.

[46] A Gondi, 35, f. 189.

[47] The earliest company book that survives is Book E, dating from 1506. If this were the fifth *ragione* and the previous *ragioni* were all three years in duration as the subsequent ones were, then the first *ragione* would have been opened in 1493 or 1494. The year 1493 is

company was initially called Alessandro d'Antonio Gondi
and Company. The books for this new company do not survive for the early period, and the amount of its initial capital
and the range of its original investments are not clear.[48] It
was something like an investment company for the brothers,
using the capital of their patrimony. Among other things, the
capital was put in cloth manufactories in the names of Alessandro's younger brothers as they reached maturity. A company of *battiloro* was set up in 1493 with the names of two
brothers, Francesco (1471-98) and Girolamo (1472-1557),
but it did not continue for long.[49] In 1496 a wool manufactory
was established with the name of Bernardo (1482-1539),
but it too has an obscure history.[50]

Whatever the early organization of this company may have
been, it eventually became distinct from the brothers' patrimony itself and, in fact, its ownership was shared by only

also the date of the founding of the company of Francesco and Girolamo, in which Alessandro's company participated.

[48] The early investments of the brothers can be traced in A Gondi,
34, a book of *debitori e creditori* of the joint capital accounts of
Alessandro, Bernardo, and Antonio, from 1499 to 1506. There are
two extant books of the *battiloro* company, 1506 to 1513: A Gondi,
1 and 2; and two books *dello scrittoio*, 1516 to 1533: A Gondi,
3 and 4.

[49] This company was called Francesco and Girolamo d'Antonio
Gondi and Company, and had a capital of 6,000 florins: 3,000 from
the Gondi, 2,000 from Bernardo di Stefano Segni, 700 from Pagholo
di Francesco Falconieri, and 300 from Giovanni di Bernardo Vecchietti, who was the manager. The contract survives: A Gondi, Cassetta
I, No. 20. The tenure was three years, and the company probably did
not go beyond 1496, when Vecchietti became manager of the new
company organized that year by the other three brothers.

[50] According to a surviving contract, this company had a capital of
8,000 florins (6,667 from the Gondi, the rest equally from Andrea
di Zanobi Guidotti, the manager, and Michele di Leonardo Pescioni,
who had married sisters of the Gondi), which was to be used for two
shops; A Gondi, Cassetta I, No. 22. In their joint accounts, however,
there is an entry of 4,000 florins invested in Bernardo d'Antonio
Gondi and Company, a wool shop, in 1497; A Gondi, 34, f. 16. In
1500 the brothers received 1,435 florins in profits (40 percent of the
total); *ibid.*, f. 23. The shop was closed in 1506; A Gondi, 36, f. 242.

three of the brothers—Alessandro, Bernardo, and Antonio. Girolamo's name does not appear on the company records, and so presumably he did not participate in the business enterprises of the others, although he came in for his one-fourth share of the patrimony when it finally was divided in 1506. The youngest son, Antonio (1486-1560), is listed as a shareholder along with Alessandro and Bernardo, although he was still a child; but when he came of age in 1506 he became an active partner and went off to France to establish a branch. Even after the division of the patrimony in 1506, these three brothers kept their capital in the company.

In 1496 the company had 10,000 florins capital. The manager was Giovanni di Bernardo Vecchietti, who had also been the director in the earlier wool company of the two other brothers, Francesco and Girolamo. Vecchietti shared in the profits but as usual had no capital investment himself. Alessandro also was actively involved in the direction of company affairs, and his services were capitalized at 500 florins for purposes of increasing his share in the profits beyond his capital investment.[51]

The brothers' ambitions for growth is reflected in the fact that at least up to 1503 profits were kept in the company in order to increase its capital, and thereafter very little of the profits were taken out. In seven years, from 1496 to 1503, the accumulated profits of the company were 11,314 florins, which was more than the 10,000 florins originally invested, or a return of slightly over 16 percent a year. The increase in the capital of the company up to 1506, shown in Table 23, represents these accumulated profits which were not removed from the company. Profits came mostly from production of cloths, especially from the *battiloro* shop; but the company slowly entered into the marketing of these cloths as well. Alessan-

[51] Bernardo and Antonio put in 3,500 florins each, and Alessandro, 3,000 florins, but they shared equally in the profits; A Gondi, 34, f. 14.

TABLE 23. CAPITAL INVESTMENT AND PROFITS OF THE COMPANY OF
ALESSANDRO, BERNARDO, AND ANTONIO GONDI, 1496 TO 1516
(All figures up to 1506 are in florins *larghi di grossi*;
thereafter, they are in florins *larghi d'oro in oro*)

Tenure of contract	Capital[a]	Profits	Gondi's % Share	Alessandro's share		
				Capital	% share	profits
1496-1499	10,000	4,646	85	3,000[b]	25-2/3	1,185
1499-1503	13,949	6,668	80	4,185	24-1/6	1,612
1503-1506	16,205	.	80	5,796	22-11/12	.
1506-1510		5,508	80	4,871	22-11/12	1,267
1510-1513	17,800	6,134	80	4,871	24-1/6	1,482
1513-1516	23,578	13,640	89-1/12	6,354	26-11/12	3,613
1516	34,000[c]		89-2/17	9,000	26-8/17	..

a The figure for 1496 is the actual capital put in by the brothers,
and the figures for 1499 and 1503 represent the increase of that investment by the amount of their profits, which were not removed. The
figure for 1510 and thereafter include Vecchietti's investment, but it
cannot be determined whether that was a cash investment or a value
derived from a capitalization of his services to the company.

b This does not include 500 florins for the capitalized value of his
services.

c This figures includes 1,300 florins for the capitalized value of
Antonio's services, in addition to his capital investment worth 10,000
florins.

Source: A Gondi, 34, ff. 13, 14, 40; 36, ff. 74, 81, 118; 37, ff. 7,
12, 15, 23.

dro's accounts show that by 1503 he was making agreements on his own for commercial ventures abroad;[52] and presumably the company had been doing this for some time
before it finally sent its own representative to establish a
branch in France.

In 1506, when the company was renewed and the youngest

[52] On 19 May 1503 Alessandro entered into agreements with his
brother-in-law, Antonio Gualterotti, by which he gave Antonio 2,000
florins for commercial ventures in England, Flanders, and elsewhere
for three years. Alessandro was to be reimbursed the 2,000 florins plus
8 percent interest on it per year and to share half the profits; A Gondi,
36, f. 230. On 24 September 1503 he made an agreement with Bernardo Segni concerning shipments of cloths to Ancona; *ibid.*, f. 234.
Throughout his *ricordanze* there are notes recording shipments of
luxury cloths (*drappi d'oro*) and references to correspondents in
Bruges (his brother-in-law, Filippo Gualterotti), London, and the
Levant; *ibid.*, ff. 220-51 *passim*.

son, Antonio, entered into the business, it was decided to extend operations to Lyons; and Vecchietti and Antonio were sent off to reside there and to engage in marketing the luxury cloths made in Florence.[53] In 1510 a separate company, named Antonio Gondi and Giovanni Vecchietti and Company, was organized for the business in Lyons.[54] Vecchietti was the manager, and both he and Antonio lived in Lyons. By 1513 Vecchietti had returned to Florence, where he joined Bernardo in the direction of the *battiloro* company; and Antonio assumed the direction of the Lyons branch. In 1516 the company of Lyons substituted the name of Pierantonio Gondi (1497-1541), the son of Alessandro, for that of Vecchietti, Pierantonio having apparently joined his uncle in Lyons.

The company in Lyons was an impressive success.[55] Its profits were extraordinarily large; and since they were at first put back into the company, the capital grew rapidly, in 1516 reaching 20,000 florins, almost three times the original investment (Table 24). The company engaged primarily in mar-

TABLE 24. CAPITAL AND PROFITS OF THE GONDI COMPANY IN LYONS, 1510 TO 1521
(All figures are in écus)

Tenure of contract	Capital	Profits
1510-1513	7,000	3,334
1513-1516	10,000	. ..
1516-1521	20,000	22,914

Source: A Gondi, 4, f. 446; 7, f. 8; 8, ff. 7, 444; 36, ff. 248-49; 37, ff. 12, 120-29.

keting of merchandise, especially the luxury cloths from Florence; but it also made profits from exchange transactions and commissions. Its success along with that of the other great

[53] A Gondi, 36, ff. 243-49; Ehrenberg, p. 219, is mistaken in dating Antonio's move to France in 1527.

[54] A Gondi, 37, ff. 120-21.

[55] Three books of the company survive: A Gondi, 7 (1516-20), 8 (1520-21), 9 (1521-23).

Florentine houses located in Lyons in the early sixteenth century is proof enough that there was still considerable enterprising spirit among Florentine patricians, even those who had wealth, and that fortunes could still be made by selling their city's products abroad. By 1515 the prosperity of the Gondi company was sufficient enough to permit Antonio to establish himself in a sumptuous residence in the Florentine community at Lyons.[56]

In Florence the parent company, acting partially as a holding company, was identified on the title page of its books as a company "dello scrittoio" of Alessandro and Bernardo Gondi. In 1520 it listed as its investments 6,500 florins in the family *battiloro* company[57] and 3,200 florins with Zanobi Buondelmonti and Piero di Bernardo Gondi and Company "dello scrittoio."[58] Besides these companies, jointly owned with other investors, the parent company wholly owned the company in Lyons although that investment is not listed with its assets. The parent company, however, was more than just a holding company; it also engaged in commercial ventures, and its assets other than investments included large credits with the Lyons company and a large cash reserve (3,922 florins in 1520).[59] Personnel of the company included two partners: Vecchietti, who was paid 50 florins a year, and Bernardo Gondi, who received 73 1/4 florins a year. Besides these expenses, the company paid a couple of *giovani* and rent for its headquarters, which altogether amounted to

---

[56] Charpin-Feugerolles, p. 119.

[57] A Gondi, 3, f. 781. The original contract for the company is dated 1 November 1516 and shows that the Gondi invested 4,000 florins for 80 percent of the profits, with Filippo d'Agnolo Guiducci, who was the manager; A Gondi, 37, f. 124. In November 1518 the company paid 1,848 florins in profits to the brothers, but this was kept in the company and added to the capital; A Gondi, 3, f. 206. On 19 January 1519 the company was reorganized with 6,500 florins from the Gondi, for 65 percent of the profits; and a new partner was added, Pagnozzo Ridolfi; *ibid.*, f. 568.

[58] A Gondi, 3, f. 781. The company had begun 11 September 1518.

[59] A Gondi, 3, ff. 780-82.

about 100 florins annually, and small interest payments of 7 to 8 percent on capital which was probably invested in the company by outsiders.[60] The profit-loss sheet lists these fixed expenses as well as a number of losses owing to varying exchange rates in transactions with the Lyons Company. The only major loss in commercial ventures for the period covered by the extant books was 350 florins on a shipment of pepper in 1523.[61] The company was mostly involved in commercial dealings, in luxury cloths, pepper, sugar, and the like, although it also made profits on commissions. Altogether, its net profits from these transactions from November 1516 to April 1520 amounted to 1,498 florins, not including profits from its investments.[62]

After 1506, when Bernardo was named in the contract of the company as manager in Florence,[63] it is unclear what role Alessandro played. He was not salaried by the company: neither the surviving books of the company nor his own books list any payments for services; and it is not known whether his share in the capital continued to include a capitalized value for his services as in the earlier partnerships. He continued to be an active investor on his own (Table 25). It is interesting, however, that he himself did not enjoy the large profits which his company was piling up. A glance at Table 25 will show that the profits from 1496 to 1503 and from 1510 to 1516 went back into the company, and only the profit division of 1506 (which is unknown) and of 1510 were apparently received in credits. At the same time, apart from the growth of his credits with the brothers' company from 3,000 to 9,000 florins in 1516, his estate did not otherwise show the increase in value which one might expect from

---

[60] See, for example, A Gondi, 4, f. 394.

[61] A Gondi, 4, f. 394.

[62] A Gondi, 3, f. 781. The profits from the *battiloro* company (*ibid.*, f. 350) are subtracted from the total profit listed here.

[63] A Gondi, 36, ff. 248-49. Whereas Alessandro's services had been capitalized for purposes of profit division, Bernardo was apparently salaried; A Gondi, 4, f. 394.

TABLE 25. INCOME OF ALESSANDRO GONDI, 1488 TO 1519
(All figures are in florins *larghi di grossi*)

Miscellaneous sources		
Salaries, 1482-94		248
Profits as Official of the Monte, 1497-1500		1,623
Salary	250	
Interest on loan	1,373	
Interest on loan to unidentified friend, 1499-1500		830
Interest on Monte holdings, 1499-1507		224
	Total	2,925

Business profits		
Profits from varying exchange rates, 1497		114
Insurance, 1488-1506		1,732
Wool company, to 1497[a]		218
Alessandro Gondi & Co., to 1516[b]		10,367
Lorenzo di Bernardo Segni & Co., wool manufactory, 1503[c]		803
Venture with Bernardo di Stefano Segni, 1504[d]		1,103
Bernardo Gondi & Co., wool manufactory, 1507[e]		265
Capital invested with Antonio Gualterotti, 1507-14[f]		2,531
Gondi and Vecchietti & Co., Lyons, 1509-16[g]		1,277
Bernardino Perulli & Co., Venice, 1517[h]		476
Mainardo di Bartolomeo Cavalcanti & Co., silk manufactory, 1519[i]		1,047
Miscellaneous transactions involving luxury cloths, to 1516[j]		1,382
	Total	21,315

[a] See text, p. 169.

[b] The figures in the source after 1506 have been converted from *fiorini larghi d'oro in oro*.

[c] On investment of 3245 florins *larghi d'oro in oro* with Segni & Co.

[d] 50% profits on silk cloth with gold work purchased from Piero di Jacopo Guicciardini & Co. and sold in the Levant; A Gondi, 36, f. 234.

[e] See text, note 50.

[f] This was an investment in 1503 of 2,000 florins for trade in England, Flanders and elsewhere at Gualterotti's discretion. The capital was to be refunded in three years at 8% interest plus one-half of all profits; A Gondi, 36, f. 230. Apparently Alessandro later engaged in another such venture, judging from entries, from 1512 to 1514, of profits on 3,000 florins invested with Gualterotti. The figure for this Table has been converted from 2,127 florins *larghi d'oro in oro*.

[g] Apparently Alessandro had a private investment with this company; cf. Table 26. The figure in this Table has been converted from 1,073 florins *larghi d'oro in oro*.

[h] Alessandro invested 3,040 florins *larghi d'oro in oro* with this company in 1516; A Gondi, 37, f. 24. The figure in this Table has been converted from 400 florins *larghi d'oro in oro*.

TABLE 25 (notes).—*Continued*

[i] Alessandro loaned 4,000 florins to this company in 1517 for a return at a fixed rate of interest, from 7% to 8%; A Gondi, 37, ff. 26, 31, 33. The interest charges were later canceled because of the marriage of Cavalcanti's son with Alessandro's daughter in 1519; A Gondi, 37, f. 136. The figure in this Table has been converted from 880 florins *larghi d'oro in oro*.

[j] Converted from 1,161 florins *larghi d'oro in oro*.

Source: A Gondi, 35, ff. 6, 44, 102, 113, 166; 36, ff. 48, 74, 203, 218, 257, 263; 37, ff. 4, 8, 10, 14.

the size of his profits. Table 26 shows his net worth as he himself calculated it in 1517. Except for the other half of his palace, which he had bought in 1510 for 1,500 florins, all his real estate had been inherited from his father's estate, and that was not very much if it is considered as a capital investment for income purposes.[64] The Monte stock is likewise insignificant.

TABLE 26. The Estate of Alessandro Gondi in 1517
(All figures are in florins *larghi d'oro in oro*)

Real estate		5,500
Palace	3,100	
Two farms	2,400	
Investments		12,740
Alessandro and Bernardo Gondi & Co.	9,000	
Bernardino Perulli & Co.[a]	3,300	
Gondi and Vecchietti & Co.[a]	440	
Household furnishings		1,500
Wife's dowry		200
Credit with the Monte		260
Miscellaneous		800
	Total	21,000[b]

[a] See Table 25 for explanation of these investments.

[b] Alessandro, in his calculations, subtracted from this total 4,500 florins for miscellaneous obligations, including 3,666 florins for the dowries of his two daughters.

Source: A Gondi, 37, f. 130.

[64] Alessandro's records do not include income from these two farms, located in the valley of the Greve just south of Florence. The records of his father's estate before its division in 1506 include accounts of income from land holdings; and from these, some idea of the income value of Alessandro's farms can be had. The two farms had been

The Gondi

Whatever unfavorable signs on the economic scene of the early sixteenth century the modern historian has found in retrospective analysis, they were not so apparent at the time to men like Alessandro Gondi, a man who knew something of the business world and who possessed the means of securing his well-being in other ways had he wished. That he used his inherited wealth, already of comfortable proportions, in capitalistic ventures, is proof enough that not all Florentines regarded the economic horizon with the gloom of some modern historians. The mentality of men like Alessandro was not that of a man who seeks ways to conserve his wealth rather than to increase it; he was willing to gamble on greater returns by risking it in capitalistic ventures.[65]

Alessandro died in 1521, leaving a will reminiscent of that of Filippo Strozzi *il vecchio*, for in it he shows the same tortured concern for the inheritance of his property. After his son, it is to go to his three brothers and their progeny; their lines ending, it is then to pass to that of Giuliano di Antonio, and after that "to the nearest male relative of the latter who will die a Gondi, as long as the family and the house of

---

purchased in 1497 for 2,120 florins and brought income—in kind and in cash—totaling 749 florins over the next nine years; A Gondi, 33, ff. 163, 277.

[65] Alessandro was not politically active. He held the following offices (*Tratte*, 84 *passim*):

> 1497—Official of the Monte (three years)
> 1511—Otto di Custodia
> 1517—Prior
> 1518—Official of the Mercanzia

A final observation on the marriages in Alessandro's family is worth making in relation to his business interests. He married, in 1496, Maria Maddalena, the daughter of Piero di Bartolomeo Gualterotti. In 1518 his daughter Lena married Pagnozzo di Giovanfrancesco Ridolfi; and in 1519 (not 1523, as in Corbinelli; cf. A Gondi, 37, f. 33) his other daughter, Dianora, married Bartolomeo di Mainardo Cavalcanti. Alessandro had business dealings with all these families. He invested 2,000 florins with his brothers-in-law (Table 25). He had 4,000 florins invested with Mainardo Cavalcanti when his daughter married Mainardo's son (Table 25). In 1519, the year after his marriage, his other son-in-law, Pagnozzo Ridolfi, was brought into the Gondi *battiloro* company.

Gondi endures." And then he proceeds to make the necessary arrangements to prevent the continual fractioning of the estate.[66] Alessandro's concern, like that of Filippo Strozzi, arose from a feeling both of them had for a concept of the family which extended beyond the confines of one man's household. Both men, though bearing old Florentine names, represent new families in the sense that they were replanting their family's fortune in their native soil after exile and impoverishment had uprooted it for a generation. Neither could accept the brief formulas in the testaments of earlier generations which attempt to impose a fideicommissum on their descendants; both elaborate the plan and articulate its details. They both had rebuilt their family's fortunes, and each was anxious that this fortune endure beyond his generation.

One hardly knows whether Alessandro at the time he drew up his testament really felt that these elaborate provisions would ever have to be invoked, that, in short, his one son would be his only descendant. But, in fact, such was the case. Hardly anything is known of Pierantonio di Alessandro Gondi.[67] Apparently he did not continue to share partnership with his father's brothers. The book "dello scrittoio" of the family company opened in 1520 was not continued after Alessandro's death but was closed out over the next few years;[68] and when in December 1521 a new book of the Lyons company was opened, it is identified by the names of Bernardo and Antonio, no longer including, as it had in 1516, the name of Pierantonio.[69] In 1533 he was a resident of Milan;[70] and in 1538 he was involved with his mother in a dispute with his uncle Bernardo and Giovanni di Bernardo Vecchietti.[71] He

[66] The will is published in Corbinelli, I, *preuves*, ccccIxxv-ccccIxxviii.
[67] Corbinelli assigns no date to his death.
[68] A Gondi, 4.   [69] A Gondi, 9.
[70] A Gondi, Inv., No. 108 (he names his mother his procurator).
[71] *Ibid.*, No. 113 (the Mercanzia ordered them to name arbiters to settle their dispute).

died in 1541, apparently without children.[72] Meanwhile, Alessandro's widow lived on in Florence. In 1546 she finally made a settlement of credits in capital and accrued income in the company of Bernardo and Antonio.[73] Her death in 1550,[74] postdating that of her son, was the occasion for the provisions of Alessandro's will to come into play, and there are several documents surviving from the division of his estate made over the next few years.[75] Alessandro's fideicommissum was liquidated and his property, including the palace, was divided three ways, among the heirs of his three brothers.

THE GONDI IN LYONS

After the death of Alessandro, the fortunes of the Gondi company return to the obscurity which Alessandro's books had momentarily removed. It continued to be active through the better part of the century and was, in fact, a stepping-stone for the family into the high circles of court finance in France and eventually led them out of the world of business altogether and into the ranks of the aristocracy. Antonio never returned to Florence. He married a noblewoman in 1516 and bought a seigniory in 1521. He became a large property owner in Lyons and was active in political affairs. Both the church and the throne employed him as a financial agent. In 1533, when Catherine de' Medici passed through the city, she took him into her service as maître d'hôtel for her husband, a post he retained when Catherine became queen. Antonio died in 1560 in Paris, a nobleman and a courtier. His children remained in France; one son became bishop of Paris, another was the Duc de Retz, peer and marshal of the kingdom.[76]

[72] *Ibid.*, No. 152.
[73] *Ibid.*, No. 127. She had 4,337 florins in capital and 4,614 florins credit in earnings.
[74] *Ibid.*, No. 152.
[75] *Ibid.*, Nos. 143, 146, 152, 173, 174, 178, 244, 253.
[76] On Antonio and his family in France, see Michel Jullien de

Meanwhile, the family business had attracted other members of the family to Lyons and likewise boosted them into the higher ranges of the nobility away from Florence and their bourgeois origins. Of these the most prominent were the sons of Girolamo, the fourth son of Antonio di Leonardo, who had never been active himself in his brothers' business. Giovanbattista di Girolamo (1501-80) seems to have replaced his uncle Antonio in Lyons, for he had his own company there, which was active in the Grand Parti under Henry II.[77] He too married a lady of the court, in 1558, and became a naturalized French subject and the maître d'hôtel of Queen Catherine. He remained active as a banker, however, receiving many tax farms and benefices from the throne; and he was one of the most intimate councillors—as well as a creditor—of the throne. When he died in 1580, he was considered not only one of the richest men in France but also one of the most knowledgeable in financial matters.[78] A younger brother of Giovanbattista, Francesco (b. 1503), followed a similar path although his course was not marked with such spectacular achievements. In 1532 Francesco established a business in Valencia on money he received from his uncle Antonio and Raffaello di Amerigo Corsini, also of Lyons.[79] While in Spain, however, he was knighted by Philip, then governing for his father; and his one son eventually entered

---

Pommerol, *Albert de Gondi, Maréchal de Retz* (Geneva, 1953), especially pp. 7-44; and Corbinelli, II.

[77] Roger Doucet, "Le grand Parti de Lyon au XVIe siècle," *Revue historique*, CLXXI (1933), 485.

[78] See the notice of his death and impressive funeral in *Journal de L'Étoile pour le règne de Henri III (1574-1589)*, ed. L.-R. Lefèvre (Paris, 1943), p. 246; and for other brief notices of his banking activities: Maurice Carmona, "Aspects du capitalisme toscan aux XVIe et XVIIe siècles: les sociétés en commandite à Florence et à Lucques," *Revue d'histoire moderne et contemporaine*, XI (1964), pp. 92-93; and Lapeyre, pp. 51 and 54.

[79] *Mercanzia*, 10832, f. 3v. This was an *accomanda* of 5,000 *monete* of Valencia—1,000 from Antonio, the rest from Corsini. Bernardo Gondi was their agent in Florence through whom the investment was made.

the service of the French king and lived out his life in France. The third son of Girolamo, Leonardo, also left Florence to reside in France, under what conditions we do not know; and, finally, a son of Bernardo, Alfonso, made the same trip to end his days a knight in the service of the French crown.[80] By the end of the century the Lyons company of the Gondi probably went the way of all Florentine companies in that city—if, indeed, it even survived the death of Giovanbattista; but meanwhile it had opened a well-traveled path for the family leading away from Florence and their bourgeois origins and into the ranks of nobility and the life of a royal court.

THE SURVIVAL OF THE FAMILY IN FLORENCE

Of the four sons of Antonio di Leonardo Gondi, three failed to continue the lineage in Florence. Alessandro's one son was himself childless; Antonio established himself and his branch in France; and while Girolamo himself resided in Florence, his sons all eventually left their native city permanently. It is only through the fourth brother, Bernardo, who had married twice and had nine sons, that the line of the elder Antonio Gondi continued in their native city to the present, and with the subsequent extinction of collateral lines with earlier origins, it is their descendants alone who keep the name alive in Florence today.

Bernardo seems to have had an active business career. Unlike Girolamo he had been an investor in the family company and, in fact, at one time had been one of its managers. He was most likely its Florentine agent after Alessandro died. The very few personal records of his which survive indicate that he engaged in all kinds of transactions on his own although on a very small scale.[81] Furthermore, he groomed

---

[80] For all this, see the biographical sketches in Corbinelli, I, *passim*; Charpin-Feugerolles, pp. 118-28; and Picot, pp. 37-43 and 97.

[81] His books include accounts with several banks, and accounts of insurance transactions and sales of various kinds of luxury cloths.

his sons for business careers. In 1522 there is reference to a bank in the name of two of them (one still a minor),[82] and before his death he had at least two sons doing business in Spain. Despite his family connections in Lyons, however, Bernardo does not seem to have met with much success, for when he died in 1539 he did not leave a large estate;[83] and by the time it was divided among his nine sons, it was hardly a patrimony which allowed them to live at the level their family had long enjoyed.

Bernardo's sons were thus very much thrown on their own resources; and, like the sons of Jacopo Guicciardini a generation earlier, they sought their fortunes in the business world abroad. With one exception, the records of none of them survive, but reading over the collection of miscellaneous family papers one can discern something of their efforts to make their way in the world—and it is not apparent that they derived any advantage from their well-placed French relatives. Already before Bernardo's death, two brothers were in Spain—Bartolomeo in Seville, Benedetto in Valencia; and in 1540, they were together in Valencia where they were joined by a third, Alessandro.[84] That same year four of the brothers remaining in Florence—Piero, Giuliano, Niccolò, and Alfonso —organized a company for commerce and banking with a small capital of 4,500 florins (perhaps with the capital of their father's estate):[85] and Giuliano went off to Naples with 2,000 florins *in accomandita* from the other three.[86] A few

[82] A Gondi, Inv., No. 89: the Ufficio dei Ribelli permitted them to continue their bank despite the branding of the partner, Zanobi Buondelmonti, as a rebel.

[83] A Gondi, 44, f. 15. It consisted of only 6,004 florins in liquid assets.

[84] A Gondi, Inv., No. 119: they named their mother and a brother as their procurators in Florence.

[85] *Ibid.*, No. 120: they put in 4,000 florins, and Francesco Marucelli put in 500 florins.

[86] *Mercanzia*, 10832, ff. 33v-34r. The contract is dated 12 February 1541/42, but the capital was committed for five years beginning in July 1540.

years later, in 1545, Bartolomeo also went to Naples, where he established residence long enough to marry and have two sons, although by 1549 he was back in Florence.[87] Very little is known about any of these brothers, and there is nothing to indicate that their various efforts were markedly successful.

Of the nine brothers, the career of only one can be fully documented. This is Antonio, a much younger son of Bernardo, who was born in 1532. In 1554 he began keeping his own accounts, and with one short hiatus they survive to his death in 1591.[88] Like his brothers he too went into business, and his modest beginnings further substantiate the decline of the fortunes of this branch of the family. In 1552, at the age of twenty, he entered into the service of a Spanish wool merchant, Lope Gallo, with a starting salary of 30 florins a year. For the next ten years while he was with Gallo his salary never rose over 100 florins; but meanwhile he invested on his own, especially in wool transactions, and so gradually accumulated some capital. In 1562 he left Gallo's service and went into business for himself; and unlike any of his brothers he met with remarkable success. By the time of his death he had investments in three wool companies of 6,000 florins each, and it was estimated by one of his heirs that throughout his career he had made about 70,000 florins, mostly from wool and *provvisioni*. He gave generously to religious foundations and spent little on himself, living frugally in the house of his brother Bartolomeo. Being childless, he left his estate to his only two surviving brothers, Bartolomeo and Amerigo, on his death in 1591.

These two heirs were the only sons of Bernardo who themselves had sons to carry on this line of the family. To these two brothers, presumably, devolved the estates of their other

[87] A Gondi, Cassetta VIII, No. 44, f. 43.

[88] A Gondi, 45-54; these include all the master books, except Book C (1568-72), and several books of first entry. A *spogli* of his books along with additional biographical information is found in the genealogical compilation of 1609, already cited: A Gondi, Cassetta VIII, No. 44, ff. 61-66.

six brothers, including the residue of the estate of their uncle Alessandro, one-third of which had passed to Bernardo and his heirs after the death of Pierantonio. Yet, judging from what is known of Bartolomeo's estate, it was Antonio's legacy which must have formed the major part of Bartolomeo's patrimony.[89] At any rate, it is clear enough that it was Antonio who made the strongest impression on the family records of this branch of the family. In the anonymous genealogical *spogli* of 1609, most likely compiled by one of Bartolomeo's sons, Antonio receives all the attention. There is considerable information about him and especially his financial affairs, whereas of the other brothers of Bartolomeo there is no information at all. One can conclude that it was Antonio's estate which put the Gondi back on firm financial ground.

The history of the Gondi through the period of the Renaissance shows nothing more clearly than the almost regular fluctuation of the level of their wealth. At the very end of the fourteenth century, Simone di Geri had been one of the wealthiest citizens of Florence; two generations later, his grandson, Leonardo di Leonardo, had only a modest estate and did not even own his home. Leonardo's two sons, however, again raised the family to what must have been close to the uppermost stratum of the patriciate; yet, the grandsons of Antonio di Leonardo—those who were not syphoned off to the French court but remained in their native city—had to start almost from scratch by patrician standards. At least one

[89] Only two of Bartolomeo's books survive (A Gondi, 55-56), and the one that was still open at the time of his death does not reveal extensive property possessions. A few months after his death a settlement was made among his three sons, between Bernardo and Marcantonio on one hand, and Alessandro on the other. A surviving document enumerates Alessandro's one-third share of his father's estate, consisting of three *poderi* with cottages, several pieces of wooded land, and a part of a meadow; and in addition the other two brothers agreed to pay Alessandro an income judged to be equal to one-third of the rents from the property owned in Florence (a *casa*, a *casetta*, and a *bottega*); A Gondi, Cassetta VII, No. 23.

of these, Antonio di Bernardo, struck it rich on his own; and it was his fortune that reëstablished the status of this branch of the Gondi as it entered the seventeenth century. Some of this fluctuation was undoubtedly caused by the rough current of business fortunes in the Renaissance; but much of it was brought on by the natural process of succeeding generations with the periodic fragmentation of the estate, the severing of economic ties among the heirs, and the disparate fortunes of each as he took his share and went his own way. The history of the Gondi is as multiple and variable as the branches on its genealogical tree.

Chapter vi

THE CAPPONI

IN THE annals of Florentine history, from the beginning to the end, probably no family appears as frequently—almost on every page—as the Capponi. In the fiery politics of the fourteenth century, at the side of the Medici in the fifteenth century, at the helm of the last republic in the early sixteenth century, in the vanguard of the Florentine nation in its financial and commercial conquests abroad throughout the entire period, and still in the foreground on the cultural scene as late as the nineteenth century, the Capponi bring us to the very center of life and civilization in Florence. The surviving records of the family are vast, and fortunately the documentation of their fortune extends back into our period, the late fifteenth and early sixteenth century. From these records the Capponi emerge not only in their unique role as a leading family in Florentine affairs but also as a part of that economic structure which formed the solid backbone of the city's life during the Renaissance.[1]

As early as 1210 the Capponi are listed as residents of the

[1] For genealogical information, consult the manuscripts of Luigi Passerini in the Biblioteca Nazionale: MSS Passerini, 48 (Capponi). Although Passerini did the Capponi genealogical tables in Litta, this manuscript is often more detailed; cf. *Capponi di Firenze*, in Litta, XI (1869-75). The Capponi documents are located in the Archivio di Stato and the Biblioteca Nazionale. For a description of the holdings in the Archivio di Stato, see "Notizie degli archivi toscani," *ASI*, CXIV (1956), 418. There is an inventory in typescript of this collection: ASF, Inventario 342 bis. There is also an uncatalogued inventory in typescript for the collection of documents in the Biblioteca Nazionale. Some family documents are still in the family's possession, in their palace in the via de' Bardi. I have not seen these; but I have been assured by Dr. Gino Corti, a professional archivist who knows the collection, that none of them date from before the late sixteenth century.

GENEALOGICAL CHART 4. THE CAPPONI

A Selective Genealogy

GINO
(1350-1421)
=(1) Francesca di Niccolò Serragli
=(2) Margherita di Jacopo Nasi

NERI
(1388-1457)
=Selvaggia di Messer
Tommaso Sacchetti

Agostino
(1390-1470)
descendants

Lorenzo
(1391-1473)
descendants

Tommaso
(1417-44)

GINO
(1423-87)
=Maddalena di Raimondo
Mannelli

PIERO
(1446-96)
=Nicolosa di Luigi
Guicciardini

Tommaso
(1447-1528)
descendants

Neri
(1452-1519)
descendants

Cappone
(1453-1521)

Alessandro
(1458-1503)

Girolamo
(1459-1526)
descendants

NICCOLÒ
(1473-1529)
=Alessandra di Filippo Strozzi

GIULIANO
(1476-1565)
=(1) Alessandra d'Antonio Attavanti
=(2) Ginevra di Niccolò Sassetti

Piero
(1504-68)
descendants

Cappone
(d. 1527)

Filippo
(1505-63)
descendants

LUIGI
(1505-84)
=Luisa di Filippo
Strozzi

ALESSANDRO
(1512-86)
=Elisabetta di Francesco
Guicciardini

oltr 'Arno section of the city where they continue to reside;[2] and they are among the few families whose prominence in the city's political and economic life can be traced back into the thirteenth century. The family was strongly Guelf;[3] and Compagno Capponi, the direct ancestor of the line we shall be studying, lost his life in 1260 in the battle of Montaperti fighting for the Guelf cause.[4] Compagno's son Buonamico became the family's first prior in 1287; and the family continued to have a leading political role throughout the fourteenth century.[5] Compagno matriculated in the silk guild;[6] but his son matriculated in both the silk and wool guilds, and subsequently the Capponi can be found in all the major guilds—the *Lana*, the *Seta*, the *Cambio*, the *Calimala*—and frequently were consuls.[7] Already in the second half of the thirteenth century they had extended their business activities beyond their cloth workshops to build up one of the great financial and commercial houses in that heyday of Florentine ascendancy in European economic affairs.[8]

GINO (1350-1421) AND NERI (1388-1457): STATESMEN AND PUBLIC SERVANTS[9]

By the time we reach Gino di Neri di Recco and his son Neri, the family had become so prominent in the political life of the city that it begins to emerge from the obscurity of earlier

[2] *Delizie degli eruditi toscani*, VII, 159.

[3] Ottokar, p. 74.

[4] BNF, MSS Passerini, 48 (Capponi), f. 8.

[5] See the biographies of Buonamico, Recco, and Neri—Compagno's direct descendants—in BNF, MSS Passerini, 48 (Capponi), ff. 10-12, 23-24, 138-39. For the importance of the Capponi in later fourteenth century politics, consult the index in Brucker, *Florentine Politics.* . . .

[6] BNF, MSS Passerini, 48 (Capponi), f. 8.

[7] See, for example, the matriculation lists in ASF, *Carte dell'Ancisa*, AA, ff. 701r, 703r, 705r, 716r; also, the biographies in MSS Passerini cited in note 5 above.

[8] Davidsohn, *Geschichte von Florenz*, II, 412-13; III, 368; IV, Pt. II, 437, 459-60.

[9] For political biographies of both Gino and Neri, see two articles by Ida Masetti-Bencini: "Neri Capponi: note biografiche tratte da

generations. The political careers of these two men are too well known to bear retelling here. They were both at the very center of the city's political life, forever appearing in the highest councils of state, going on important embassies, taking charge of military operations in the field against the republic's enemies; and probably no two names appear more frequently on the rosters of officeholders, from modest positions on lower councils, where assignments were routine, to the highest councils of the state, the Signoria and the Ten of Liberty, where major policies were determined and decisions made.

Gino and Neri above all were political men; one might even add, they were professional politicians. Certainly, Gino had little time for anything else. He was continually holding posts in the Florentine state which tied him down to administrative responsibilities for months at a time, and his numerous commissions and embassies also took him away from the city for long periods. Gino had no time to be a merchant or a banker or to manage a cloth manufactory. He was not, however, ignorant of business matters. He had received the kind of practical education that Florentine merchants gave their sons.[10] He owned at least one wool manufactory and had

---

documenti," *Rivista delle biblioteche e degli archivi*, xvi (1905), 91-100, 136-54, 158-74; and "Note ed appunti tratti da documenti sulla vita politica di Neri Capponi," *ibid.*, xx (1909), 15-31, 33-56. Included are complete listings of the offices held by both father and son. On Gino, see Marisa Mariani, "Gino Capponi nella vita politica fiorentina dal 1393 al 1421," *ASI*, cxv (1957), 440-84. There is a brief political biography by Platina, "Vita Nerii Capponii florentini," *Rerum italicarum scriptores*, ed. Lodovico Antonio Muratori (25 vols.; Milan, 1723-51), xx, cols. 477-516. The political and historical writings of Neri and Gino are also published in Muratori, *ibid.*, xviii, cols. 1103-1220. On the problem of the authorship of these, see *Raccolta di cronichette antiche*, ed. Domenico Maria Manni (Florence, 1733), pp. 25-30. Gino's *ricordi* are translated in Renzo Sereno, "The *Ricordi* of Gino di Neri Capponi," *American Political Science Review*, lii (1958), 1118-22.

[10] Gino himself recorded the completion of his study of the abacus in 1363 when he was thirteen, the usual age for completing this funda-

some knowledge of the cloth industry.[11] We do not know how much wealth he may have inherited, or even to what extent his immediate forebears had enjoyed the earlier good fortune of the family in finance and commerce.[12] If his *prestanza* in 1403 is any indication, however, one would have to conclude that Gino was hardly a wealthy man—in fact, one of only modest means—and that a substantial part of his livelihood came from his political employment.[13] The fact that he was willing to accept administrative posts away from Florence, especially before 1405, would seem to corroborate this conclusion. On the other hand, in the *catasto* of 1427, only six years after his death, each of Gino's three sons appears in the upper ranks of taxpayers;[14] so perhaps Gino made his fortune sometime before his death.

On the Capponi genealogical tree three branches extend from Gino. Fortunately, the branch which continued to bear fruit worthy of its stock in the political history of Florence— that of his son Neri (1388-1457) and his descendants—has also been fecund for social history because of impressive collections of family documents. This archival record, however, does not begin until late in the life of Neri's son Gino (1423-87); and in the interim, from the generation of the elder Gino to that of the younger, the *catasto* records are the points of

---

mental schooling of Florentine boys; "Ricordi di Gino di Neri Capponi," *Rerum italicarum scriptores,* xviii, col. 1151.

[11] The ownership of a wool shop is known from a reference in his son's *catasto* of 1427 to credits he had in the old *ragione* of his father's business; *Catasto,* 65, ff. 97v-100r.

[12] Of this line of the Capponi—from Compagno, Buonamico, Recco, Neri to Gino—only Recco's name is mentioned among the Capponi engaged in finance and commerce; Davidsohn, *Forschungen,* iii, 270.

[13] In this *prestanza* Gino and his brother together paid six florins, which barely ranked in the highest 600 assessments; Martines, *The Social World . . . ,* p. 364.

[14] The declarations were: Neri, 4,720 florins; Agostino, 4,409 florins; Lorenzo, 2,664 florins; *ibid.,* p. 377. This put Neri and Agostino among the 247 taxpayers who declared 4,000 florins or more; all were among the upper 500.

departure for an exploration into the obscure realm of family wealth.

In the case of the Capponi we learn again how inadequate the later *catasto* records are, however useful and suggestive they may be.[15] Table 27 summarizes these returns of Neri

TABLE 27. SUMMARY OF CATASTO RETURNS OF NERI CAPPONI IN 1427
AND HIS SON GINO IN 1457
(All figures are in florins)

Assets	1427	1457
Real estate (income property only)	1,777	5,541
Monte credits (market value)	4,864	7,090
Business investments	5,366ª	1,800ᵇ
Miscellaneous (balance of all credits and debits)	—5,567	58
Cash	280	..
Total (before deductions)	6,720	14,489

ª Wool shop: 1,266 florins; *banco*: 3,000 florins; one-fourth interest in a Flemish venture with Gualterotti: 1,100 florins.
ᵇ Wool shop.
Source: *Catasto*, 65, ff. 97v-100r; 688, ff. 389r-90r; 994, ff. 377r-81v.

and his son Gino and indicates the transformation of their wealth. It is worth noting that Neri in 1427 numbered among the 247 men who declared a net value of over 4,000 florins (Table 27 shows the value before deductions) and that Gino in 1457 paid the eighth highest tax (almost 64 florins) and in 1480, when a sliding tax scale was applied, paid at the highest rate, 22 percent.[16] Obviously, the Capponi, unlike any of the other families examined in this study, maintained their personal fortune at a high level throughout the century.

Table 27 would seem to establish what most students of Florence would expect to find in the fifteenth century: a

---

[15] The *catasto* reports consulted are: *Catasto* 65, ff. 97v-100r (1427); 434, ff. 216r-17r (1433); 688, ff. 389r-90r (1451); 789, ff. 97r-102v (1457); 994, ff. 377r-81v (1480).

[16] De Roover, *The Rise and Decline* . . . , pp. 27-28 (and Table 2), 31 (Table 5).

diversified portfolio, with especially large holdings of government bonds, a steady and impressive increase throughout the period in real estate holdings, and a decline in business investments. And, for lack of any further documentation, all this would seem to apply at least to Neri.[17] Neri was, like his father, a political man; and his prestige as one whose extraordinary talents were dedicated to public service was certainly no less than that of his father. Although he was only a lukewarm supporter of the Medici, his talents as a military commissioner and as a diplomat were too valuable to be dispensed with. Even after 1434 he continued to be one of the most active men in the state, serving on every Medicean *balìa* up to the time of his death.[18] It is not surprising, therefore, that Neri appears as a conservative investor, putting his wealth in government bonds and land, and yet keeping some of it in the profitable wool industry—investments not requiring the vigilant attention demanded of the more ambitious commercial and banking activities for which he would have had no time.[19]

Nevertheless, Neri must have had a handsome income and no extraordinary expenses for he more than doubled his

[17] In considering his wealth, we can include the report of 1457 for although that was submitted by his son, this was the year of Neri's death; and Gino being an only surviving son, his report must represent his father's estate.

[18] For a more general picture of the Florentine political scene at this time and of Neri's role in it, see the numerous references in Gutkind, *Cosimo de' Medici.*

[19] It is always the business investment which is the most obscure aspect of the *catasto* return, especially after 1427. In that year Neri showed an active portfolio of business investments (Table 27) which at least indicates a willingness to invest. In subsequent reports (1451 and 1457), however, only a wool manufactory in the name of his son is declared; and although the values listed for this company might not be accurate, he most likely had no other investments or he would have at least mentioned them (cf. the report of 1480). As can be seen in Table 27, in 1427 Neri's debts exceeded his credits (including the capital invested) by about 200 florins; and considering the usual accuracy of the reports for this year, one is tempted to conclude that Neri met with no great success in these ventures. This might explain a subsequent disinclination for such investments.

worth in thirty years, and he was affluent enough to share the cost of the church of S. Spirito along with a few other wealthy patrician families of the *oltr'Arno* quarter of the city. Not much of his total earnings over these years came from public office, however, for he held only a dozen administrative posts in the Florentine state. Only these paid attractive salaries although even they were no road to wealth, as we saw in the case of the Guicciardini. Moreover, we have to assume that, with his untarnished reputation as a man of public service among his contemporaries, he was not guilty of serious peculation. His land holdings were more than sufficient to meet the needs of his household; and if his wool company paid the normal return, he had those profits available for modest but steady reinvestment. Finally, the Monte stock paid dividends which also were a portion of his income.[20] All this is very speculative, of course, but the point remains that it is not very difficult to explain the growth of Neri's estate considering its initial size and the investment opportunities available to him in fifteenth century Florence: one need not have been a banker or a merchant engaging in risky foreign ventures to enjoy at least a modest prosperity.

GINO DI NERI (1423-87):
BUILDER OF A FAMILY BUSINESS

Only one of Neri's sons survived him;[21] and although we know even less about this son than we know of his father, the evidence hints at a man of a very different stamp. Perhaps because he grew up in Medicean Florence, he lacked the ardor for republicanism and public service that had so distin-

[20] According to the 1457 return, the book value of the Monte holdings was 29,222 florins (the market value was 20 percent of this figure); and two of the three yearly payments due him that year were worth together 315 florins, 8 *soldi*—certainly a handsome income in fifteenth century Florence.

[21] Neri had at least five sons (Litta, *Capponi*, Tavola XI); but only one of them, Gino, along with three daughters, outlived him and had descendants (see his testament, AC [ASF], 67, No. 2).

guished both his father and grandfather. He never served the
state as a diplomat or as a military commissioner, the roles
for which the particular competence of his forebears had
made them indispensable to the state. As a member of a
wealthy and honorable patrician family, he held some of the
state's most important offices: he sat on the Signoria twice—
once as Gonfaloniere—and was included on all the *balìe*, including the Council of Seventy in 1480. But although he was
a frequent officeholder, his name has not otherwise been recorded in the political annals of the period.[22]

Gino, however, did not live a life of retirement, enjoying
his handsome patrimony as a rentier. On the contrary, it was
during his life that the family's fortunes reached their highest
peak, undoubtedly through his initiative, although there are
no extant documents which allow us to follow this upward
course with any precision. As far as can be ascertained from
the tax records of 1451 and 1457, the only business of the
family was a wool shop in Gino's name (Table 27). By
1460, however, we know from a contract for an *accomanda*
which survives in the records of the merchants' court that
Gino had organized at least two companies, one in Florence
and one in Pisa, with the names of his sons, Piero (1446-96)
and Neri (1452-1519), at the time still minors; and through
these companies he was investing abroad in a company in
Catalonia.[23] After 1463 a family bank appears regularly

[22] Litta lists his most important offices; besides these, he held over
a dozen minor posts (*Tratte*, 81 and 82, *passim*). Litta adds that "si
tenne il più che poté lontano dai publici affari," but his authority is
not cited; Litta, *Capponi*, Tavola XI.

[23] *Mercanzia*, 10831, f. 43r. This is a record of an *accomanda*
contract by which three parties gave 3,000 *lire di Barzalone* to Jacopo
and Bindo di Coppo di Bindo Canigiani for trade in Catalonia. The
parties were: Luca d'Agostino di Gino Capponi and Piero di Gino di
Neri di Gino Capponi and Company of Florence; Neri di Gino di
Neri Capponi and Piero di Giovanni di Jacopo Bini and Company of
Pisa; and Agostino di Sandro Biliotti, resident of Avignon. In 1471
Biliotti became the manager of the Medici bank in Naples; de Roover,
The Rise and Decline . . ., pp. 257, 304-5, 457 n. 22.

on the official company lists of the *arte del Cambio*;[24] and two decades later, in 1480, Gino's tax report declares just how much investing he had been doing in the interim. There he lists—without declaring any values for a number of specious reasons—a bank in the name of his sons, Piero and Neri; a company at Pisa with Lorenzo di Francesco Strozzi; a company in Avignon and Lyons with Bartolomeo Buondelmonti; a silk manufactory in the name of his son Tommaso; and a one-sixth interest in copper mines at Montecatini, in the val di Cecina, near Volterra.[25]

Very little has been known about these Capponi enterprises other than the mere fact that the Capponi were engaged in such activity, although business historians tend to include the name of Capponi whenever they discuss banking and commercial activities of Florentines in the late fifteenth century.[26] The Florentine archives contain none of the books of the individual companies, but there are among the family papers records that help to document the organization of Gino's businesses and the wealth of his family especially after 1485.[27]

[24] ASF, *Arte del Cambio*, 15 *passim*. In this *libro di compagni*, covering the years 1460 to 1487, the first mention of the family is the company of Piero and Tommaso di Gino in 1463, and it is identified as "giallo A" (f. 10r). Thereafter, there were eleven reorganizations up to 1487; and outside partners included Piero Bini, Leonardo Mannelli, Niccolò di Leonardo Mannelli, and Bartolomeo Buondelmonti.

[25] Here are Gino's excuses for omitting values for these investments: because of expenses and heavy taxes, everything has been withdrawn from the bank, and although the accounts are still open, there is no capital left; the company at Pisa cannot be maintained any longer and there is only hope that all its creditors can be paid; the company at Lyons is closed and there will be a personal report to the *signori* on it; as for the silk company, there is only hope that all Tommaso's debts can be paid and his disorders cleared up; and since the copper venture has just been undertaken and the expenses—which are enough to completely ruin one—cannot yet be known, no value can be set; *Catasto*, 994, f. 381r.

[26] See, for example: Ehrenberg, p. 203; and de Roover, *The Rise and Decline . . .* , p. 310.

[27] Besides the account book of Gino already mentioned, which is too incomplete to be very useful, there is a book of the investment

The Capponi

The documents tell us nothing more about the copper mines near Volterra or the silk company of Tommaso, and Gino may not just have been making excuses in his pessimistic evaluations of these ventures.[28] But the other companies, of Florence, Pisa, and Lyons, were prospering although before 1485 information regarding them is very scarce and it is difficult to draw a very clear picture of their formation and growth. The company (*banco*) of Florence mentioned in the *accomanda* of 1460 was undoubtedly the parent company through which capital was invested in other enterprises, and therefore presumably it was the first to be organized. From this base in Florence the Capponi extended their interests to Pisa and to Lyons, and by 1485 Gino and his sons had formed an international network of commercial and banking contacts and were building a sizeable fortune.

The company in Pisa was one of a number of companies established there by Florentines following the conquest of Pisa in 1406 and the systematic effort by the state after 1421 to develop the port for Florentine trade.[29] Between 1451 and 1457—judging from the tax reports of those years (Table 27)—the Capponi purchased two houses in Pisa; and by 1460 they had a company there, presumably one engaged in trade.[30] Several of Gino's sons were active in the affairs of this company over the next few decades. Piero di Gino was a captain and one of two major shareholders of a galley which

---

accounts of Gino's five sons, Piero, Neri, Cappone, Alessandro, and Girolamo, from 1485 to 1516; AC (BNF), 2. A personal account book of Cappone also survives and it contains information regarding the brothers' investments: AC (BNF), 1. Gino's testament (1485) survives: AC (ASF), 67, No. 2.

[28] It will be recalled that Piero Guicciardini had a share in these copper mines and he seems not to have made great profits from them; see p. 129 above.

[29] There is a good unpublished study of the economic importance of Pisa in the fifteenth century: M. E. Mallett, "Pisa and Florence in the Fifteenth Century. An Economic Background to the Pisan War" (unpublished D.Phil. thesis, Oxford University, 1959).

[30] This is the company of Neri Capponi mentioned above.

left for Sicily in 1476;[31] and his brother Neri was the Pisan agent for English merchants in the 1480's.[32] A third son, Alessandro, was a resident of Pisa in 1480, when his father claimed a deduction for one of his houses there being used by Alessandro as a residence and a headquarters for the family company. There were many other Capponi who were in Pisa at the time, most probably poorer relatives brought into Gino's company. They held important political offices in the government established by Florence over the port and the city, and several of them became large property owners in the area. Gino's family, however, appears not to have been active either as office holders or as landowners.[33]

From Florence and Pisa Gino extended his connections abroad; but the expansion of his business outside Italy remains almost totally shrouded in obscurity.[34] By 1480, however, a company in the name of his son Neri was so well established in Lyons that it was considered one of the chief rivals of the Medici bank there.[35] Their partner was Bartolomeo Buondelmonti, who earlier had been the manager of the Mannelli bank in Avignon. Another of Gino's sons, Alessandro, was probably in residence in Lyons most of his life as the family representative.[36]

[31] *Tratte*, 82, f. 24r.

[32] M. E. Mallett, "Anglo-Florentine Commercial Relations, 1465-1491," *Economic History Review*, xv (1962), 259.

[33] Mallett, "Pisa and Florence . . . ," pp. 256-57, 280-84; *Tratte*, 81 and 82 *passim*.

[34] For the few references to various Capponi in Lyons in the late fifteenth century, see Charpin-Feugerolles, p. 44; and Abel Desjardins, ed., *Négociations diplomatiques de la France avec la Toscane* (6 vols.; Paris, 1859-86), I, 167. Cf. Picot, pp. 106-8.

[35] De Roover, *The Rise and Decline . . .* , p. 310; Ehrenberg, p. 203.

[36] In the assignment of the credits of the Lyons company in 1485, Alessandro comes in for an extra one-tenth share, beyond what he shared equally with his brothers, of their father's credits, and this would seem to indicate a compensation for services; AC (BNF), 2, f. 13. We know that he was in charge of the bank there in 1495, for he was the agent of the republic in paying 30,000 écus toward its debt to Charles VIII; Desjardins, I, 605. Alessandro died in France in 1503.

The Capponi

On the basis of the surviving documents, it is futile to attempt to estimate the size of the Capponi business complex before 1485. Nevertheless, at least a suggestion of the prosperity of all the Capponi businesses together is found in the personal account of another son of Gino, Cappone. He recorded that the profits on his share of 2,275 florins in the capital of the companies of Pisa and Lyons amounted to 6,316 florins from 1475 to 1485, an average annual return of almost 28 percent on his original investment.[37] Rather than withdraw any of these extraordinarily handsome profits, Cappone kept them accumulating in the company, where they were added to his capital in successive reorganizations. By 1485 the value of his capital had thus grown to 8,050 florins. The family company, hence, was not only prospering but it was also undergoing a dynamic expansion during this decade.

The first precise details of the investment portfolio of the Capponi come from a copy of the contract by which the family renewed the articles of association of their jointly invested capital in 1485.[38] As usual, the basic organization resembles a holding company, of which members of the family shared ownership; and the capital was distributed in a number of subsidiary organizations. The company carried the name of Gino's oldest son and was called simply Piero di Gino Capponi and Company. Their capital of 42,000 florins was shared unequally by five of the brothers (Tommaso was not included).[39] More than one-half came from Piero and Neri, and they were to have control over the company with the authority

[37] AC (BNF), 1, ff. 3, 6. Cappone had 1,275 florins in the company of Lyons, which in ten years earned him 3,929 florins; and 1,000 florins (one-tenth interest) in the company of Pisa, which earned 2,387 florins.

[38] A *ricordo* of the contract along with an additional note made at the time of Gino's death two years later, in 1487, is found in AC (BNF), 2, ff. 126v-29r.

[39] The shares were: Piero and Neri—11,550 florins each; Cappone—8,050 florins; Alessandro—6,650 florins; Girolamo—4,200 florins.

The Capponi

TABLE 28. CAPITAL INVESTMENTS OF PIERO CAPPONI AND
COMPANY IN 1485

Company in Lyons
(All figures are in écus[a])

Capital[b]

The Capponi, in names of Piero and Neri . . .		21,375
Bartolomeo Buondelmonti .		7,125
Giovanni di Piero Gaetani and Niccolò d'Albertaccio del Bene		3,000
	Total	31,500

Disposition

Company with Giovanni Tosinghi and Albizzo del Bene at the court of the King of France		5,000
Company *di drappi* with Girolamo Niccoli .		3,500
Company in Venice . .		8,000
Balance		15,000
	Total	31,500

Company in Florence[c]
(All figures are in florins)

Capital

The Capponi . . .		22,105
Bartolomeo Buondelmonti		7,368
	Total	29,473

Disposition

Company in Rome with Antonio di Bindo Altoviti .			12,473
Company with Guido and Niccolò Mannelli			17,000
Capital: The Capponi and Buondelmonti . .		17,000	
The Mannelli . .		1,400	
	Total	18,400	

Disposition:

Company in Pisa with Lorenzo di Francesco Strozzi .		4,350	
Wool and dye company		4,500	
Battiloro company with Piero Corsini		1,500	
Balance for the *banco* .		8,050	
	Total	18,400	
		Total	29,473

Note: Figures in italics are not in the documents but are calculated on the basis of evidence therein. Capital values may include capitalized value of personal services in the case of lesser parties.

ª The écu was worth slightly less than the florin. The Capponi interest of 21,375 écus in the Lyons company had a value of 19,848 florins on their own books; AC (BNF), 2, f. 22.

ᵇ One-seventh of the profits were to go to Gaetani, del Bene, and Alessandro Capponi, apparently for personal services; after that deduction the profits were to be divided with three-fourths going to the Capponi and one-fourth to Buondelmonti.

ᶜ The figures are taken not from the *ricordo* of the contract but from an appended note concerning arrangements following the death of Gino in 1487 where there is greater clarification and more detail (although also a few very slight discrepancies). In the contract the company with the Mannelli seems to be a separate entity apart from subordinate companies, but the added note two years later outlines the structure represented here.

Source: AC (BNF), 2, ff. 126v-29r. This is a copy of the agreement drawn up on 4 November 1485 and a further *ricordo* of 26 April 1487 following the death of Gino.

to withdraw capital from any venture and to reinvest it at their discretion. They were joined by an outside partner, Bartolomeo Buondelmonti, who contributed one-third as much capital as the Capponi (14,000 florins), and together these two parties formed two major partnerships and a host of subsidiary ones. The structure had its center in Florence with a bank and several cloth manufactories and radial branches in Pisa, Rome, Venice, Lyons, and the French court (Table 28 above).

None of these companies' records survive; but the profits they paid to the Capponi, on paper at least, are known, and they are impressive. In 1489, after four years, the brothers recorded 19,324 florins in profits, an average annual return of 11 1/2 percent on their original investment.[40] A portion of these profits was left in the company to be added to the capital, which was thus increased to 48,000 florins in that year.[41] The Capponi firm, therefore, must have been one of

[40] AC (BNF), 2, ff. 30, 31; also, see the accounts of Piero, *ibid.*, ff. 8, 32. The accounts of Cappone record only his share in profits from 1487 to 1489, and nothing for the years from 1485 to 1487; AC (BNF), 1, f. 9.

[41] AC (BNF), 2, f. 32.

the largest of its day.[42] With two cloth manufactories, a bank in Florence, a company at the port of Pisa, and bases in Rome and Lyons, it was a complex of industrial, commercial, and banking interests operating through an international network. It is not surprising that the Medici brought this prominent business family into its plans to exploit the alum mines discovered near Volterra in 1470. Had those efforts been successful, the state would have needed the kind of organization and capital which the Capponi had at their disposal in order to realize the anticipated profits in the international markets.[43]

How had Gino built up this flourishing business? He had, of course, inherited a handsome patrimony, which gave him working capital.[44] But the initiative had been his; he had been able to forego the temptations to withdraw much of the large profits and instead was willing to risk the large sums necessary for such adventurous undertakings in order to build up the business into an even larger structure. Furthermore,

[42] Compare, for example, the total capital investments of the Medici banks: in 1420, 31,370 florins; in 1441, 44,000 florins; in 1451, 72,000 florins; de Roover, *The Rise and Decline* . . . , pp. 50 (Table 10, to which has to be added 3,800 florins for the wool company), 61 (Table 13), 66 (Table 14). At the same time, the older Filippo Strozzi's capital investment was 24,750 florins in 1471, and 35,195 florins in 1491; see Table 4 above, p. 60.

[43] Gino was one of the members of the original society organized to exploit the mines at Volterra in 1470. After the war with Volterra he had a continuing interest in these mines; and Piero Capponi was included in a new society organized in 1484 by Lorenzo de' Medici for the same purpose. But all these efforts apparently met with no success. See Fiumi, *L'impresa* . . . , pp. 36, 160, 165.

[44] How Gino actually formed the capital for his companies cannot be known on the basis of the records used here. He did not sell any real estate (Table 29). His 1480 tax report includes no Monte stock, yet in 1457 he had such credits worth 7,090 florins (Table 27); whether he was able to sell these bonds cannot be ascertained until some research has been done on the very difficult problem of the state debt in fifteenth century Florence. It is not at all certain that holders of these bonds, the market value of which was steadily depreciating throughout the early fifteenth century, were ever able to liquidate their credits. Gino, of course, may have received a large dowry from his wife, which would have assisted in his capital formation.

it may have been no coincidence that his wife was a Mannelli, another of the great banking families of mid-fifteenth century Florence. Her father, Raimondo (1390-1464), was a distinguished naval commander who also engaged in commercial ventures.[45] He had companies in Spain in 1446; and his son Amaretto was a treasurer for the Duke of Milan in 1459 and a partner of the Medici branch bank in Milan. Amaretto possibly had some ties with the Capponi, for his death apparently sufficiently compromised the interest of the company of Capponi and Buondelmonti that the government of Florence sought special favor for them from the king of France (1485).[46] At least three other men with the name Mannelli had been partners at one time or another in the company of Gino's sons,[47] and the Mannelli were in fact leading bankers in both Lyons and Avignon at the same time the Capponi were active in those places.[48] One can hardly speak of the Capponi-Mannelli marriage as an "alliance," but there can be little doubt that such personal relations between important business families facilitated the conduct of business among the Florentine nation abroad.

From the very beginning Gino brought his sons into his businesses. He made his investments in their names and incorporated them in the titles of the companies before they could have been old enough to assume the management of them. In fact, in the surviving documents there is no Capponi company which includes the name of Gino himself except the

[45] Her mother was a daughter of Piero di Filippo Strozzi and hence a first cousin of Matteo di Simone Strozzi.

[46] Desjardins, I, 205 (here Amaretto is referred to as "fils" of Gino, but surely this is a mistake). In fact, Amaretto's death may have occasioned the Capponi reorganization of that year.

[47] Leonardo, in 1467 and 1468, and Niccolò di Leonardo, from 1471 to 1474; *Arte del Cambio*, 15, ff. 20v, 23v, 33r, 37r, 41v, 45v. And Guido and Niccolò in 1485; see Table 28.

[48] On the Mannelli, see: de Roover, *The Rise and Decline* . . . , pp. 91, 270, 310, 315; and Charpin-Feugerolles, pp. 133-34.

wool manufactory which he had before his father's death. The company in Florence carried the name of Piero (1446-96), his oldest son; that in Pisa, and later the one in Lyons, carried the name of Neri (1452-1519), his third son. The second son Tommaso (1447-1528) operated a silk shop in 1480—which, in his tax report of that year, Gino claimed was losing money and was in much disorder—but otherwise we hear nothing more of him in the family company. Alessandro (1458-1503) in 1480 was in Pisa and, as we have already observed, later moved on to Lyons, where he died. The other two sons, Cappone (1453-1521) and Girolamo (1459-1526), do not appear as active partners.

So it was that Gino had been able to make his family's fortune: ready funds, important family business connections, a willingness to risk capital and to sacrifice profits, and, above all, sons who were capable of assuming the responsibilities of directing the entire enterprise. Gino had built up a successful business organization engaged in a complex of business and financial activities on an international scale. It was one of the largest firms of his day, and it was still growing at the time of his death in 1487.

Gino's personal fortune cannot be exactly appraised. His son Cappone recorded his one-sixth share of his father's estate as being worth 5,574 florins.[49] Hence, the appraised value for purposes of division among the six sons was in the neighborhood of 33,500 florins. Of Cappone's share, 2,275 florins represented his capital investment in the company in 1475, which therefore must have been a credit extended to him at the time by his father and now, in 1487, charged to his share of the estate. This would mean that the growth of the company after 1475 was not, for bookkeeping purposes at any rate, credited to Gino himself but to his sons, in whose names his investments had been made. In other words, Gino's estate in 1487 as reflected in Cappone's share does not repre-

[49] AC (BNF), 1, f. 4 (and the cross-references cited there).

sent the considerable expansion of the family business in the last decade before his death.

Cappone evaluated the real estate he received from his father at 2,847 florins; but it is not certain that this represents a one-sixth share of all of Gino's land holdings. Gino had continually bought land and by 1480 had added considerably to his patrimony (Table 29). How much he added after

TABLE 29. REAL ESTATE HOLDINGS OF NERI CAPPONI
AND HIS SON GINO, 1427 TO 1480

Type of holding	Quantity				
	1427	1433	1451	1457	1480
Residence in Florence (non-income)	1	1	1	1	1
Houses in Florence	1	1	2	1	1
Villa (non-income)	1	1	1	2	2
Farms	5	10	12	17	16
Parcels of land	2	3	1	5	27
Cottages	...	...	3	3	8
Houses in Pisa (one used as residence)	..	.	...	2	2
Value of income property	1776		3933a	5541	7588

a Calculated by capitalizing the *stima* at 7 percent.
Source: Catasto, 18, ff. 1177-81; 65, ff. 97v-100r; 434, ff. 216r-17r; 688, ff. 389r-90r; 789, ff. 97r-102v; 994, ff. 377r-81v.

that date cannot be determined; there are a few entries in his accounts which survive, but these are too incomplete to be conclusive.[50] Of all the families examined in this study, the Capponi alone possessed much land in the fifteenth century although their holdings were certainly not so large that they can be considered great landowners. Up to 1457 the family owned land in only one area, at Legnaia, in the valley of the Arno down-river just outside the city walls. Capponi had owned land in this area since the end of the thirteenth century;[51] and in the fifteenth century our line of the family

[50] AC (BNF), 140, ff. 18, 113, 114, 172. A number of purchase deeds of Gino and his descendants are collected in AC (ASF), 67.
[51] BNF, MSS Passerini, 48 (Capponi), ff. 10-12.

had a villa there suitable enough to be selected by Charles VIII for his residence before entering the city in 1494.[52] In addition to these properties, to which Gino from time to time added, he had bought the two houses in Pisa but no other lands in the Pisan countryside, unlike many of the other mercantile families who had a vested interest in the port of Pisa.[53] In 1468 he purchased a small holding at Marti, in the lower valley of the Arno toward Pisa, and subsequently added to his holdings there. He also built up a small holding at Vico, near San Gimignano. But in 1480 the largest collection of farms still was at Legnaia, and his sons concentrated their acquisition of land in that area as well.

THE SONS OF GINO

In the absence of personal accounts, or any other personal records, it is impossible to know just what kind of living arrangements Gino's numerous progeny had and to what extent their property was shared. In his 1480 *catasto* report Gino lists nineteen dependents—he and his wife, eight sons, and two daughters, three daughters-in-law, and four grandchildren —and so presumably the whole family, including five grown sons, three of them with their own families, lived in one household at that time. In this study this is the only instance of such a large family group remaining together, and whether it had broken up by the time of Gino's death in 1487 cannot be ascertained from the extant documents. The account book of Cappone, already cited, indicates that Gino had assigned credits to his sons long before his death although the sons were living together with their father and those credits remained in the family enterprise. With Gino's death, however, the estate was most likely broken up and the six surviving sons began to build their own estates. In that year, 1487, Cappone recorded a division of both credits and property

[52] Landucci, p. 64.
[53] Mallett, "Pisa and Florence . . . ," pp. 280-84.

among the brothers; and thereafter he listed real estate acquisitions in his own name alone, indicating that he was now building an estate separate from his brothers'. None of the personal accounts of the other brothers survive, but beginning in 1496, only a decade after Gino's death, there is a complete series of the personal accounts of the two sons of Piero di Gino, who died that year; and these records show that their estate as well as their household was completely separate from that of any of their uncles, the other sons of Gino still alive.

Further evidence that Gino's death loosened the fraternal bond can be found in the history of the brothers' investment in the family company. One of them, Tommaso, does not further appear at all as an investor after 1487; and the subsequent history of the others' investments shows markedly individualistic behavior. In 1494, after a five-year hiatus in the documents, the companies of Florence and of Lyons were legally separated; and Piero and Girolamo withdrew all their capital from the company of Lyons, while Neri withdrew his from the company of Florence.[54] Henceforth there were two companies—one under Neri and Alessandro in Lyons, and one under Piero in Florence.[55]

[54] The evidence is too flimsy even to propose a possible reason for this division. One suspects that it had something to do with internal affairs of the company since no profits were recorded after the surviving documents—which, however, are not company books—become silent in 1489, long before the reorganization was effected. Yet business relations between the two brothers, Piero and Neri, continued. Piero invested in Neri's company in Pisa, and he sent his oldest son, Niccolò, to Lyons to get a business education in Neri's company. The political uncertainties of these years undoubtedly complicated the conduct of business and may have necessitated a reorganization.

[55] See the second paragraph on the title page of the book of the brothers' joint investments, AC (BNF), 2. The subsidiary company in Rome meanwhile had apparently been dissolved. In 1489 profits of 4,739 cameral florins were recorded, but in the reorganization that year the Capponi share of the capital was reduced from 9,000 to 8,764 cameral florins. By 1492, 2,973 cameral florins were recorded as profits but the credits on the company account were assigned to "un conto di tempo" in Lyons. *Ibid.*, ff. 36, 45.

The Capponi

After the division of 1494, the history of the Lyons branch of the Capponi bank fades away into obscurity. Cappone, who kept some capital in the company, recorded a profit in 1498; but thereafter his account with the company remains blank although the book in which it appears continues to his death in 1521.[56] Alessandro, who was the family representative in Lyons, died there in 1503 without children; and there is no evidence that any other member of the family replaced him.[57] Neri, whose name was carried by the company, was active in Florentine politics up to his death in 1519 and therefore could not have been in residence in Lyons for very long periods of time.[58] In the later sixteenth century one of the most important banks in Lyons was a Capponi firm and, in fact, it was the last Florentine house on record in the city;[59] but it is not clear that there was a continuity between the bank of Gino's sons and this later company.[60]

In Florence, the new organization of 1494 came under the direction of Piero, Gino's oldest son. Its capital amounted to 22,000 florins and was contributed in unequal shares by only four of the brothers—Piero, Cappone, Alessandro, and Girolamo (Table 30). Piero was by far the largest contributor and the company carried his name until his death on the battlefield just two years later, in 1496. Thereafter it was

[56] AC (BNF), 1, ff. 24, 31.

[57] One book survives of Alessandro and Neri's joint accounts at Lyons: AC (ASF), 55. It is a book of *debitori e creditori*. It was opened in 1500, but after 1502 the entries are much less frequent although there are further entries in various other hands as late as 1544. Alessandro's death probably accounts for this incompleteness.

[58] The major offices are listed in Litta, *Capponi*, Tavola xx. In addition, see *Tratte*, 84, ff. 1r, 6r, 13v, 47r, 51v, 66r, 84r, 94v, 123v, 152r, 157r.

[59] Ehrenberg, pp. 216-18; Charpin-Feugerolles, pp. 45-46.

[60] Lorenzo and Piero Capponi, who had an important bank in Lyons in the mid-sixteenth century and who became naturalized and ennobled, were descended from a collateral line; Litta, *Capponi*, Tavola xvi. There is a brief study of this bank based on feeble documentary evidence surviving in Lyons by Roger Doucet, *La banque Capponi à Lyon en 1559* (Lyons, 1939). Cf. note 118 below.

TABLE 30. CAPITAL AND PROFITS OF PIERO CAPPONI AND COMPANY,
1494 TO 1521
(All figures are in florins *larghi d'oro in oro*)

Dates	Total Capital	Total Profits	Niccolò and Giuliano's share Capital	Profits
1494-1503[a]	22,000	8,874	10,450	4,215
1503-1513	9,000	8,666	4,275	4,116
1513-1516	11,500	5,312	6,900	3,164
1516-1521	13,200	13,048	9,680	9,569

[a] Figures for these years are in *fiorini larghi di grossi*.
Source: AC (BNF), 2, ff. 77, 82, 85, 87, 91, 92; 3, ff. 58, 61, 184,
190, 235; AC (ASF), 142, ff. 84, 86, 123, 150.

known as the Heirs of Piero Capponi and Company; but although it remained in existence until 1521, Piero's two sons,
Niccolò and Giuliano, were by far the largest investors in it.
Their uncles became less and less important in its affairs:
Alessandro died without children in 1503; Girolamo withdrew his capital after 1516; and when Cappone, also without children, died in 1521, the company was dissolved. After
1496 it is quite clear that Piero's brothers were but passive
investors and that the history of this company belongs more
properly with an account of the wealth of Piero's sons.

Despite the unusual cohesion of the Capponi while Gino
lived, the financial history of his family after his death disin-
tegrates into concurrent but separate lineages and ceases to be
an integral whole. The personal accounts of none of Gino's
six sons survive, except the one book of Cappone already
mentioned; and although there are four branches of Capponi
which extend beyond their generation, only the descendants
of Piero have left a record which can be traced through successive generations.[61] Once again we find that as the past of
these Florentine families becomes unraveled, the multiplic-

[61] There is a collection of documents belonging to later descendants
of Girolamo; it forms the *patrimonio vecchio* of the Archivio Capponi
(ASF). The rest of this collection, as well as that in the BNF, belongs
to the descendants of Piero.

ity of threads defies a comprehensive view; and the historian pursuing the story of a family's fortunes must take up one strand at a time, periodically leaving behind a number of loose ends, many of which fade away from his historical vision altogether.

PIERO DI GINO [62]

Piero was raised by his father with the intention that he should go into business. Fortunately, he had talents for this profession and he met with considerable success.[63] The business world, however, could not contain the energies and interests of Piero Capponi. His wealth, after all, only complemented the prestige which his family enjoyed in the city as a result of a time-honored tradition of political service and close association with the Medici.[64] For Piero, also, politics had its fascination; and he had an active career in diplomatic service to the state. In 1478 and 1479, with the diplomatic debacle following the Pazzi conspiracy, he was busy as ambassador and military commissioner in Tuscany; in 1482 he was ambassador to Naples; the next year he was a prior and one of the Otto di Guardia; and again, in the war over Sarzana against Genoa, from 1484 to 1486, he was active as a field commissioner of the Republic; in 1490 he was Captain of Cortona and in 1492, Podestà of Greve; and in 1493 he

[62] On Piero, see: Vincenzo Acciaioli, "Vita di Piero di Gino Capponi," *ASI*, iv, Pt. 2 (1853), 13-40; and the sympathetic sketch in Pasquale Villari, *Life and Times of Girolamo Savonarola*, trans. Linda Villari (New York, 1898), pp. 235-37. None of Piero's accounts survive, but the documents of his descendants constitute the two family archives in the Biblioteca Nazionale and the Archivio di Stato (the *patrimonio nuovo*).

[63] "Letterato, et nelle mercantie expertissimo," was the judgment of Piero di Marco Parenti, quoted in Macinghi negli Strozzi, p. 75. Passerini's opinion that he had no interest in business affairs is apparently based only on the assumption that an active political career precluded such interests.

[64] There are numerous letters from Piero to Lorenzo de' Medici; see *Archivio Mediceo avanti il principato. Inventario*, ii.

held the city's highest official post, Gonfaloniere di Giustizia.[65] When the death of Lorenzo de' Medici in 1492 created a vacuum in the political leadership of the city, he was one of the first to step in and dedicate himself wholeheartedly to the service of the state, even to the neglect of his private affairs[66] and ultimately at the cost of his life, for he was killed in the field in 1496 while directing operations for the reconquest of Pisa.

In 1494 with the French invasions, Florence found herself for the first time caught up in the great dynastic struggle of Europe and was compelled to handle the problem of a French alliance. This was to be a major issue in city politics for the next forty years, for it had obvious importance for Florentine commercial and banking interest in Lyons and was bound to have been an immediate concern of families like the Capponi who had interests in both camps. Whatever the threat of Franco-Florentine relations to business interests in Lyons in 1494, Piero may have played an important role in establishing an accord between the Florentine financial interests and the King of France in that year. Piero was on good terms with the King. In March 1494 he had gone to France as the ambassador of Piero de' Medici to the King; and subsequently he met with the King after his arrival in Italy. Before Charles moved into Florence, he stopped at the Capponi villa at Legnaia;[67] and although Piero a few days later in an incident famous in Florentine history stood up solidly against the King's harsh demands on the city and threatened to answer French cannons with Florentine bells, the King at the time

[65] He also had a number of internal offices (*Tratte*, 82-83 *passim*).

[66] His grandson, the historian Bernardo Segni, asserts that when Piero died in 1496 his affairs were in much disorder because his political involvements distracted him from his private matters and necessitated extraordinary expenses; Segni, "Vita di Niccolò Capponi," p. 220.

[67] Landucci, p. 64, recorded that the King "was stopping at Legnaia, in the house of Piero Capponi" on 12 November, and yet it was not until 17 November that he entered the city.

was much more amused than offended by this bold bourgeois and was even patronizingly affectionate toward him.[68] And when Charles made his exit from Florence, Piero's brother Neri accompanied the King to Naples and then followed the royal court back to France as the city's ambassador.[69] Piero was on the commission dealing with the King and the provisions agreed upon included privileges for Florentine merchants in France.[70] The Capponi business came off particularly well from the events of that year, for their bank in Lyons subsequently became the agent for indemnity payments and other business between the two governments.[71]

In turning from business to politics, Piero was remaining true to an old Capponi tradition of civic duty, and it is ironic that he should die fighting to reconquer the prized possession his great grandfather had originally subjected to Florentine rule. Although his father had withdrawn from active political

[68] Jacopo Nardi, *Istorie della città di Firenze* (Florence, 1888), Bk. I, sec. 17. Ehrenberg misunderstood the King's attitude and therefore doubts the authenticity of this story, thinking that Piero, with his financial interests, would never have dared so to risk offending the King; Ehrenberg, p. 205. Piero may have been impulsive in his patriotism at this point, but he surely knew Charles well by this time and was aware how far he could go with the King.

[69] Gino Capponi, *Storia della repubblica di Firenze* (Florence, 1876), III, 19 n. 2, 34 n. 2.

[70] See provisions 12 and 13 of the original document, published in Pagnini della Ventura, II, 308-9.

[71] Ehrenberg, p. 205. Whether all of this has anything to do with the company reorganization in 1494 remains an unanswered question. Commines asserted that Piero, when he was in France to see the King in March, wanted to make a pact with him by which he would assist Piero's political efforts—according to Commines—to rally support in Florence against Piero de' Medici by the ruse of temporarily expelling Florentine merchants from France; see Villari, p. 202 n. 1, who doubts the story. The story finds some substance, however, in a dispatch of 17 April 1494 from Francesco della Casa in Lyons, who warns Piero de' Medici of the secret hostility of the Capponi toward him; Desjardins, I, 291. This may have just been a rumor, however, for in two ciphered notes from Piero Capponi to Piero de' Medici he is frank about having heard such talk but professes his innocence; *ibid.*, I, 393-94. If the story is true, it might explain why there was a legal separation of the two Capponi companies before such a precarious venture.

involvement during the Medicean ascendance, the republican spirit of former times lingered on in Piero; and when that ideal once again inflamed the politics of his own day, men like him proved that the Medici had not yet mastered the hearts of a proud patriciate.

NICCOLÒ (1473-1529) AND GIULIANO (1476-1565) [72]

Both of Piero's sons received a sound business education. Niccolò, the older, spent two years in his uncles' company in Lyons, but he had little disposition for business and was willing to entrust his finances entirely to his younger brother. Niccolò was attracted to politics, and, in the grand tradition of his family, he distinguished himeslf as the city's most prominent leader in its final effort to reinvigorate its constitutional tradition in opposition to a Medicean principate. He was active in the first period of the revived republic, after 1494, as an ambassador and a military commissioner and was particularly instrumental in the final defeat of Pisa in 1509 when he took charge of the city. After the Medici restoration in 1512 he was less active although he was an official of the Studio in 1515, a Monte official in 1520, and held a number of other posts. Niccolò had his finest moment as Gonfaloniere in 1527 when the Medici were again expelled from the city and he took up the reins of power in the early stages of the revived republic. He died in 1529, before the final demise of the Florentine republican tradition and the return of the Medici.[73]

[72] The personal joint accounts of the two brothers are complete from 1496, when their father died, to 1529, when Niccolò died; thereafter, there are accounts for the jointly held property of Giuliano and the sons of Niccolò, but these are not complete: see App. IV. Litta, *Capponi*, Tavola XII, includes a third son, Gino, but none of these Capponi documents record his existence.

[73] On Niccolò there is the life by his contemporary, Bernardo Segni, "Vita di Niccolò Capponi," already cited; cf. Michele Lupo Gentile, "Sulla paternità della vita di Niccolò Capponi," *Giornale storico della*

Niccolò left financial matters to his younger brother, Giuliano, who directed the family company established by his father and uncles. This company was something like a holding company, consolidating the capital of its members and investing it in various enterprises. Its portfolio varied throughout its history, and Table 31 summarizes several of the investments which can be identified from the documents. The only subsidiary company which continued throughout the duration of the parent company was the *battiloro* company in Niccolò's name although the surplus capital of the parent company was continually employed in banking activities. It will be observed that up to 1503, profits were not impressive and the capital was considerably reduced. Political conditions, Piero's neglect of business matters, and the relative inexperience of Piero's sons following his death in 1496 may all account for difficulties initially encountered by the brothers in managing their finances; but after 1503 profits improved, reaching an annual average return of 20 percent in the years 1516 to 1521.

By 1521 the uncles of Niccolò and Giuliano, Alessandro and Girolamo, were no longer included in the organization; and the death of Cappone in that year was the occasion for the company's final dissolution.[74] Thereafter, in the absence of company records, the only details of the investment history of the Capponi brothers are widely scattered throughout their personal accounts. These are frequently imprecise, and after fitting them together the picture of that history is less complete than it had been for the earlier years. There is no indication, however, that there was any appreciable reorganization of their finances until after the death of Niccolò in 1529. Up until the settlement of his estate a few years later

---

letteratura italiana, XLIV (1904), 126-36. See also BNF, MSS Passerini, 48 (Capponi), pp. 194-99. His political ideas are discussed in von Albertini, pp. 108-22; and his role in the republic is best summarized in Roth, *The Last Florentine Republic*.
[74] AC (ASF), 142, f. 84.

TABLE 31. INVESTMENTS OF PIERO CAPPONI AND COMPANY (CALLED
AFTER PIERO'S DEATH, HEIRS OF PIERO CAPPONI AND COMPANY),
1494 TO 1521
(All figures are in florins)

Dates	Investments	Share of profits	Profits	Partners
Niccolò di Piero Capponi & Co., silk manufactory,[a] *1491-99*				
1491-1494	5,600	60%	1,007	Giovanni Bini, Girolamo Niccoli, and Amerigo Antinori
1494-1497	6,607	60%	215	Bini, Niccoli and Antinori
1496-1499	7,500	85%	2,125	Amerigo Antinori
Niccolò and Giuliano Capponi & Co. of Pisa,[b] *1509-16*				
1509-1511	3,000	60%	1,800	Simone di Matteo Botti
1512-1516	4,000	66-2/3%	1,667	Botti, Lodovico Dossi, and Gino di Neri Capponi
Niccolò di Piero Capponi & Co., battiloro,[c] *c. 1492-1516*				
1492-1496	2,950	45%	1,050	Giovanni Bini, and Simone (?)
1496-1499	3,900	50%	1,380	Giovanni Bini
1500-1502	6,200	90%	2,470	Giovanbattista (dei Galilei?)
1502-1506	3,808	. .	..	... .
1506-1510	. .	. .....	2,067	....
1510-1512	4,182	. .	1,182	... .
1512-1516	4,500	67-1/2%	1,985	Lodovico and Giovanni Dossi
Neri di Gino Capponi & Co. of Pisa,[d] *1492-99*				
1492-1494	4,461	51-2/3%	1,118	Simone Botti, and Francesco da Empoli
1494-1497	.. .	....	−464	....
1497-1499	3,552	60%	1,332	. ...

Source:
   [a] AC (BNF), 2, ff. 48, 54, 63, 68. Figures are in *fiorini larghi di grossi.*
   [b] *Ibid.,* 2, ff. 83, 89, and unnumbered folios at end of book. Figures are in *fiorini larghi d'oro in oro.*
   [c] *Ibid.,* 2, ff. 63, 67, 70, 71, 82, 83, 90 and unnumbered folio at end of book. Figures after 1502 are in *fiorini larghi d'oro in oro.*
   [d] *Ibid.,* 2, ff. 64, 69. The loss in 1497 was a consequence of the rebellion of Pisa. Figures are in *fiorini larghi d'oro in oro.*

the capital of the brothers was employed through a company which assumed both of their names, and the *battiloro* and Pisan companies remained their chief investments.[75] They continued to prosper impressively and considerably increased their capital investment.[76] Furthermore, sometime before 1532 an entirely new company was organized in the names of the two oldest sons of the brothers, Piero di Niccolò and Luigi di Giuliano. It is known only through references in Giuliano's personal accounts to his earnings from it. Its capital and activity cannot be determined, but it appears to have been a sizeable organization.[77]

Although the wealth of the Capponi did not approach the extraordinary resources at the disposal of Filippo Strozzi, they were nevertheless very rich men, certainly ranking far above the middle ground of the patriciate represented by a family such as the Giucciardini. The brothers, of course, had had a handsome inheritance;[78] but despite that security and

[75] For the company of Pisa, see the records of its periodic reorganization from 1519 to 1552; AC (BNF), 117, No. 77, ff. 1-8. For the *battiloro* company there are records of reorganization from 1516 to 1543; *ibid.* Nos. 66-73; and, in addition, its accounts survive in an incomplete series: see App. IV.

[76] After 1521 there were only three entries of profits, totaling 1,035 florins, made in the brothers' joint accounts, Niccolò dying before any major assignment was made. In Giuliano's separate accounts, however, which open in 1532, a profit was assigned in 1534 from "Giuliano e rede di Niccolò Capponi"—undoubtedly their jointly held capital account; and this amounted to 7,622 florins for Giuliano alone; AC (BNF), 9, f. 12. This presumably was the first profit assigned since 1521. Giuliano's credit with the sons of Niccolò in 1532 was 9,500 florins (*ibid.*, f. 1), whereas in 1516 the total capital of both the brothers together amounted to 9,680 florins (Table 30).

[77] In opening his accounts in 1532 Giuliano listed credits of 4,441 florins with this company apart from his investment in the older company with his brother: AC (BNF), 9, f. 1. In this entry the reference is to book "E" of this company, so presumably it had gone through five reorganizations and had existed for a number of years.

[78] There is no inventory of the estate of Piero, but it must have been worth about 15,000 florins. The value of the real estate inherited by his sons was 5,822 florins (AC [BNF], 3, ff. 16, 236); and two years before his death he had 10,450 florins in the family business (Table 30).

despite the uncertainties on the economic and political scenes of their day, there was no retrenchment in the capitalistic employment of their wealth. In the early years, for reasons already suggested, their capital investment fell off considerably from what it had been in 1494, two years before their father's death; but after the turn of the century, in the capable hands of Giuliano, their wealth was steadily and impressively augmented over the next few decades. In 1511 the brothers were worth 14,826 florins (Table 32); two dec-

TABLE 32. ESTATE OF NICCOLÒ AND GIULIANO CAPPONI IN 1511
(All figures are in florins *larghi d'oro in oro*)

Real estate	7,476
Heirs of Piero Capponi and Company	6,900
Other credits	450
Total	14,826

Source: AC (BNF), 3, f. 231.

ades later, after the death of his brother when the estate was divided, the value of Giuliano's wealth alone amounted to over 25,000 florins.[79] Another way of regarding their affluence is to relate their income and their expenditures; Table 33 contains a summary tabulation of the most important of these items, and it reveals quite clearly the splendid prosperity which the Capponi were enjoying in the early sixteenth century.

This prosperity was primarily rooted in business investments within Florence. The Capponi at this time were not engaged in business on an international scale. They had no branch organizations, although of course they undoubtedly had numerous contacts abroad through whom they marketed the products of their cloth manufactories and transacted the

[79] Besides 11,364 florins in nonbusiness investments (Table 35), Giuliano, on opening his own separate accounts in 1532, declared credits of 9,500 florins in investments with the sons of Niccolò and 4,441 florins with the company of Piero and Luigi Capponi (AC [BNF], 9, f. 1).

TABLE 33. INCOME AND EXPENDITURES OF NICCOLÒ AND GIULIANO
CAPPONI, 1496 TO 1530
(All figures are in florins)[a]

Expenditures		
Living expenses, 1496-1530		8,232
Dowries of two sisters		1,717
Taxes		3,046
Estimated value of lands purchased and of improvements		7,970
	Total	20,965
Income (incomplete)		
Heirs of Piero Capponi and Co., 1494-1521[b]		21,064
Earnings from real estate, 1496-1530		9,574
Interest on government bonds, 1524-1530		80
Profits on insurance accounts, to 1512		203
Inheritances		7,393
Estate of Alessandro	551	
Estate of Cappone	2,459	
Joint estate of Alessandro and Cappone	2,825	
Estate of mother	1,558	
	Total	38,314

[a] In the course of the first book of the brothers' accounts (AC [BNF], 3), the florin was re-evaluated, but the accounts were continued and adjustments made in the profit-loss account.

[b] Cf. Table 30. After 1521, only small amounts from this source are entered on their joint accounts; see note 76.

Source: AC (BNF), 3, ff. 60, 61, 82, 141, 184; 8, f. 87; AC (ASF), 142, f. 162.

foreign business of their bank in Florence. Their profits came primarily from the production of luxury cloths in their *battiloro* company in Florence and in their company in Pisa, which was most probably a silk manufactory. The Capponi, in short, were participating directly in the rise of the luxury cloth industry which revitalized the Florentine economy in the early sixteenth century and brought the city into another era of prosperity after a lapse following the decline of the wool trade a century earlier.

The brothers were also continually investing in land. From their father they had inherited real estate worth 5,822 florins,[80]

[80] See note 78 above.

and later they inherited from their uncles land worth 2,825 florins;[81] but at the time of the division of their estate in 1532, after Niccolò's death, their land holdings of all kinds amounted to 16,617 florins,[82] representing a capital outlay of 7,970 florins beyond their inheritances.[83]

Real estate was a secure investment, but the return was far below the business earnings (Table 33). It is perhaps worth repeating, therefore, that at the same time the Capponi were augmenting their land holdings, they were by no means divesting themselves of their business interests. On the contrary, the capital in their business enterprises grew steadily throughout the period when the wealth of the two brothers was jointly administered.

It has already been mentioned that the accounts of the Capponi brothers were kept jointly. Not only were their land holdings as well as their investments jointly administered, but their personal and household expenses were shared also, and their families lived together under one roof. In this study of four Florentine families over a century and a half, this is the only example of a patrimony so completely shared by brothers, and there is no doubt that it was unusual. The only explanation is an entirely personal consideration—the extraordinary fraternal bond between Niccolò and Giuliano.[84] Once that was dissolved by the death of Niccolò in 1529, the individual families went their separate ways; and by 1532 settlements had been made between Giuliano and the sons of Niccolò. The real estate, including their town houses, was divided,[85] and Giuliano opened his own personal account

[81] AC (ASF), 142, f. 167.

[82] AC (BNF), 8, ff. 70-71. This inventory excluded only a couple of very small holdings which were not assigned at this time.

[83] Of the total value of their real estate (16,617 florins), 5,300 florins represented the value of their residential property in the city. Their land holdings were located in the same areas where their grandfather had held property, the heaviest concentration being at Vico, in the valley of the Elsa, and at the family villa at Legnaia.

[84] Segni, "Vita di Niccolò Capponi," pp. 220-21.

[85] AC (BNF), 8, ff. 70-71; AC (ASF), 68, Nos. 6-7.

book and thereafter until his death kept his accounts separately. Meanwhile, in the book which records those joint accounts of Giuliano and the estate of his brother, entries begin
to fall off sharply after 1535, leaving many accounts unbalanced; and the book remains very incomplete.[86] Finally,
as we shall see, even the capital invested by Giuliano originally with Niccolò, and then for a while with Niccolò's heirs,
was soon withdrawn from their joint accounts; and thereafter he invested exclusively in his own private ventures and
in companies with his sons alone.

GIULIANO AFTER 1529

After the division of the patrimony following Niccolò's death,
it is only the line of Giuliano which can be further traced in
the extant archival material. Giuliano's personal records as
well as a number of his business papers survive, and the financial records of his descendants become extraordinarily abundant and more complete the further we pursue the line into
the sixteenth century. They tell the story of the remarkable
growth of a business which boosted the Capponi back into
the realm of international finance and provided them with
considerable personal wealth. The climax is reached beyond
the period with which we are here concerned; but the tale
has its beginnings during the lifetime of Giuliano, and it
clearly carries the moral that great fortunes could still be
made in Renaissance Florence.

The surviving personal records of Giuliano are two private
ledgers. They include his living and other ordinary personal
expenses of all kinds and his income from various sources,
such as salaries of public office, farm rents, and, above all,
profits from individual business deals. They do not, however,
contain accounts of capital investments in his own companies
or his returns from these sources—in other words, the core
of his fortune remains hidden. Nevertheless, such accounts,

[86] AC (BNF), 8.

through his expenditures and the variety of secondary sources of income they record, can afford at least a vague reflection of his general financial position. Unfortunately, there is a gap of a decade between the two books, which was covered by a missing volume; but each of the surviving books spans about a dozen years, and between them even with the gap they provide a fairly good record over the last thirty years of Giuliano's life, from the time of Niccolò's death to his own.[87] It is quite clear that during these years he was enjoying an ever-increasing prosperity (Table 34).

TABLE 34. PERSONAL INCOME AND EXPENDITURES OF
GIULIANO CAPPONI
(All figures are in florins)

	1532-44	1553-68
Selected expenditures		
Living expenses	5,267	15,594
Clothing	910	395
Taxes	1,058	6,093
Dowry	2,209	67
Charity	85	2,629
Total	9,529	24,778
Partial Income		
Income from real estate	5,518	25,741
Monte interest payments	90	1,071
Salaries of public office	886	253
Separate silk accounts	245	4,883
Interest on loans to the state		1,190
Income from investments	24,425	8,532
Total	31,164	41,670

Source: AC (BNF), 9, ff. 12, 98, 129, 187, 231; 21, ff. 34, 97, 129, 163, 184, 212, 235, 268, 287.

Giuliano's affluence is especially apparent in the record of his accumulation of land. Although his books do not include accounts of capital investment in business, they do contain summary accounts of real estate acquisitions which reveal

[87] AC (BNF), 9 (1532-44) and 21 (1553-68).

an impressive several-fold increase in value, especially marked
in the very last years of his life (Table 35). Here, in fact, is

TABLE 35. WEALTH OF GIULIANO CAPPONI
(EXCLUDING BUSINESS INVESTMENTS), 1532 TO 1568[a]
(All figures are in florins)

Property	1532—before inheritance	1532—after inheritance	1544	1553	1568
Government bonds	506	506	506	517	1,061
Real estate	2,000	10,206	15,225	22,867	70,616
Household goods	200	652	1,000	1,200	1,727
Total	2,706	11,364	16,731	24,584	73,404

[a] Giuliano died in 1565, but his books were not closed until 1568.
Source: AC (BNF), 8, f. 71; 9, ff. 1, 230; 21, ff. 1, 8, 17, 288-89.

one clear case in this study of a great fortune invested in
large quantities of land. It would be interesting to know
something about the administration of this property, but unfortunately the real estate accounts themselves do not survive, and our only knowledge is derived from periodic entries
of income and acquisitions in the master accounts. Everything suggests, however, that at least in accounting procedures
land was being brought under a more rational administration.
That the income entries were made only once annually in the
main ledger suggests that, contrary to earlier accounting
procedures, annual balances were being made in the real estate accounts. Furthermore, this income is entered in a
rendite account completely apart from the *avanzi* account,
where all other kinds of income are listed. One has the impression, in short, that Giuliano considered his land a capital investment distinct from his general personal and household accounts.

The income from real estate became increasingly a major
item in Giuliano's accounts. Toward the end of his life it
varied between as much as one and two thousand florins an-

nually, although it is only in the later years that his annual income from this source was sufficient even to meet all of his ordinary expenditures. His income from other sources, entered on his profit-loss account, was far below that from his real estate. In the last dozen years of his life—the span of his last book—these included profits from a great number of business ventures, most of which were not very large. The chief recurring items are profits averaging several hundred florins a year from individual shipments of silk cloths arranged by Giuliano on his own apart from any of his companies. All of this income together—from these miscellaneous business sources, from interest charges and salaries of public office, and from his real estate—does not, however, account for the enormous capital accumulation revealed in the increased value of his land holdings. Obviously, his personal accounts do not tell the whole story of his rapidly growing wealth.

The missing link is, of course, the ultimate source of that wealth, and this was his business activity. However much he increased his land holdings, Giuliano was by no means withdrawing capital from much more lucrative business investments. Unfortunately, his personal accounts divulge very little information about these investments, there being no accounts of earnings from these sources. The final page of his last account book is a concluding summary sheet drawn up to transfer old accounts to a new book; but undoubtedly owing to his death, it is incomplete: the debit entries, which include all his real estate holdings, are far from being balanced by the credit entries, which include his income and miscellaneous profits.[88] This account was obviously to be balanced by assignments of additional credits from other books no longer extant. We do not have to assume, however, the existence of extensive business investments, for there are other documents which partially relieve the obscu-

[88] AC (BNF), 21, ff. 288-89.

rity, at least to the point that we can discern some of his major business activities.[89] Giuliano's portfolio, in fact, was quite diverse and varied from time to time, and this alone indicates his active interest in the employment of his capital.

When he opened his book in 1532, Giuliano recorded business investments worth 13,941 florins—9,500 florins invested with the sons of Niccolò and 4,441 florins in the bank of Piero di Niccolò and Luigi di Giuliano Capponi and Company.[90] The former investment was his share in the as yet undivided capital administered jointly with his brother. This was re-invested mostly in the cloth industry: the *battiloro* company and the company of Pisa which had long been in operation,[91] and a silk company organized by Giuliano in 1530.[92] Giuliano retained his capital in these companies even after the division of the property between himself and his nephews.[93] The *battiloro* company was discontinued after 1543,[94] but the other two companies were renewed up to his death and over the years Giuliano increased his capital investment in both. In 1530 his investment in the silk com-

---

[89] These include, above all, the personal account book of Giuliano's oldest son, Luigi; AC (BNF), 19. The entries in this book refer to Luigi's shares in family enterprises, but there are indications in the entries which make it possible to calculate the total investments and profits of Giuliano, in his name and in the names of his two sons. There is also the collection of balances already cited: AC (BNF), 117. These balances vary in the usefulness of the information they contain, but frequently they complement information found elsewhere.

[90] AC (BNF), 9, f. 1. The credits in the bank of his son and nephew probably included undivided profits as well as the original capital investment.

[91] For surviving documents of these two companies, see App. IV.

[92] Balances of this company from 1530 to 1578 survive: AC (BNF), 117, Nos. 55-65. There are also some account books extant; see App. IV.

[93] That the earlier figure of 9,500 florins represents the approximate value of his investments in these companies is confirmed by evidence found in his personal accounts. In 1533 he had 3,000 florins in the *battiloro* company (AC [BNF], 9, f. 47) and in 1535, 3,000 florins in the company of Pisa (*ibid.*, f. 83) and 5,221 florins credit—probably including profits as well as capital—in the silk company (*ibid.*, f. 84).

[94] AC (BNF), 147, No. 73.

pany represented one-half of the capital shared with the heirs of Niccolò and 23 1/3 percent of the total capital of the company.[95] By 1540 he had bought out his nephews' share;[96] and when he died in 1565, he had 18,000 florins in this company or 75 percent of the total capital.[97] Over the same period his share in the Pisan company increased from 3,000 florins to 8,667 florins.[98] Both companies paid handsome returns on the investments. From 1553 to 1565 the profits from the Pisan company amounted to 15,367 florins;[99] and in the last seventeen years of his life the silk company averaged 1,508 florins annually (Table 36).

TABLE 36. GIULIANO CAPPONI'S SHARE OF CAPITAL AND PROFITS
IN SILK COMPANIES, 1530 TO 1565
(All figures are in florins)

Date	Capital	% share	Date	Profits
1530	. .. .	23-1/3	. . .	... .
1535	....	40	1538	1,800
1540	....	83-1/3	1546	2,750
1546	9,800	80	..... .	. . ..
1548	12,500	75	1553	7,500
1553	14,800	66-2/3	1556	6,667
1556	14,800	67-1/2	1561	11,475
1561	23,400	65	1565	711,251
1565	18,000	75	....	....

Source: AC (BNF), 12, f. 44; 14, f. 144; 16, f. 179; 24, f. 229; 30, f. 187; 117, Nos. 55-63.

By the time of his death the total capital of each of these Capponi companies had grown to a sizeable investment. The silk company represented a total outlay of 24,000 florins and the Pisan company had 19,500 florins[100]—capital investments

[95] *Ibid.*, No. 55.
[96] *Ibid.*, No. 57.
[97] *Ibid.*, No. 63.
[98] AC (BNF), 19, f. 87.
[99] These were the profits of Giuliano and his two sons, calculated from Luigi's records of his one-fourth share of three divisions made in 1553, 1558, and 1565: AC (BNF), 19, ff. 13, 31, 87.
[100] These figures are calculated from amounts and percentages of the Capponi's shares. Giuliano's 18,000 florins in the silk company was 75 percent of the total capital; AC (BNF), 117, No. 63. In his

considerably higher than that of the ordinary cloth manufactory, which had long been the basic industrial establishment of the Florentine economy. This capital growth probably did not represent any enlargement of their industrial organization but more likely is explained by the fact that materials for the production of luxury cloth, such as silk and gold thread, necessitated a far greater capital expenditure than that for the production of the more ordinary cloths of an earlier era. It is also very likely that these companies as they appear in the Capponi accounts were not shops but actually something like holding companies which placed their capital in a number of subsidiary businesses connected with the production of luxury silk cloths.[101]

In addition to his interest in the silk industry Giuliano also invested in the wool industry. His investments included relatively small amounts of capital in companies organized by others,[102] but he also had a wool company of his own. In 1548 he provided two-thirds of the capital of 8,000 florins for Vincenzo Violi and Company. This was something like a holding company with interest in several wool companies, including wool manufactories along with a *fondaco* and a dye shop.[103] Violi was apparently the over-all supervisor. Giuliano's sons shared in his investment, and in 1558 the parent company assumed the name of Luigi's son Niccolò.

---

accounts, Luigi refers to 8,667 florins capital in the Pisan company owned with his father and brother, and this, judging from division of the total capital in earlier companies, was four-ninths of the total; AC (BNF), 19, f. 87; 117, No. 77, ff. 7r, 8v. These figures probably include the capitalized value of the personal services of managers.

[101] In this respect, they would be similar to the wool company discussed below.

[102] When his last book was closed, Giuliano had credits with Bernardo Bartolomei and Company (4,000 florins) and Giovanbattista d'Antonio Miniati and Company (1,500 florins), both wool manufactories; AC (BNF), 21, f. 289.

[103] In 1561 the profits and capital of the company amounted to 20,000 florins, of which 4,000 was in a dye company, 4,000 in a *fondaco*, 2,000 in a wool manufactory and 10,000 remained in the parent company; AC (BNF), 117, No. 2.

The Capponi

The company was still operating at the time of Giuliano's death and its profits were as impressive as those from his silk companies (Table 37).

TABLE 37. GIULIANO CAPPONI'S SHARE OF CAPITAL AND PROFITS
IN WOOL COMPANIES, 1548 TO 1566
(All figures are in florins)

Date	Capital	% share	Date	Profits
1548	8,000	66-2/3	1554-55	5,333
1554	8,000	66-2/3	1560-62	5,788
1559	. ...	... .	1567	12,773

Source: AC (BNF), 19, ff. 10, 39, 124; 117, Nos. 2, 3, 4, 7, 8, 13.

Besides his investments in the cloth industry, Giuliano also operated a bank. At the center of any growing fortune in Renaissance Florence was always a *banco* to facilitate a variety of commercial and exchange transactions abroad, for great fortunes were made not in local business but in the realm of international commerce and finance. Along with their cloth manufactories, the Capponi family company had always had at its nucleus such a banking organization, and through it they undoubtedly marketed their own cloth products as well as engaged in a number of other commercial ventures. Sometime after the dissolution of their father's company in 1521, Giuliano and Niccolò organized a new bank in the names of the oldest son of each—Piero di Niccolò and Luigi di Giuliano. The records of the earliest stages of the growth of this company do not survive, but some documentation of it can be found in Giuliano's personal accounts. For the later period, however, the company's books are extant; and along with the surviving personal accounts of Giuliano's son Luigi, they supply considerable information regarding the history of this company up to the time of Giuliano's death in 1565.[104]

[104] Balances for this company from 1553 to 1578 survive: AC (BNF), 117, Nos. 85-93. In addition, its commercial accounts survive

The initial size of this company is unknown, but from Giuliano's personal accounts it appears that in the 1530's the total capital grew from about 10,000 to about 20,000 florins.[105] From 1534 to 1539 Giuliano recorded 5,267 florins in profits from this source.[106] After 1553 Niccolò's heirs withdrew their capital altogether, and the company's only investors thereafter were Giuliano and his two sons,[107] although the managers, whose personal services were capitalized, also shared in the profits.[108] Not only did Giuliano increase his capital investment but the total capital of the company likewise grew; and up to Giuliano's death in 1565, he and his sons reaped returns from this investment averaging 4,524 florins annually (Table 38). Its profits derived

TABLE 38. GIULIANO CAPPONI'S SHARE OF CAPITAL AND PROFITS
IN THE BANCO, 1534 TO 1567
(All figures are in florins)

Date	Capital	Date	Profits
1534	. ...	1537	8,000
1535	. ...	1539	6,120
. . .	....	.. ..	....
1550	13,266	1553	16,842
1553	24,000	1559	22,500
1557	28,000	1564	24,000
1563	28,000	1567	12,600

Source: AC (BNF), 9, f. 98; 11, f. 365; 19, ff. 13, 30, 92, 144.

in a fairly complete series up to the death of Luigi in 1584: see App. IV.

[105] In 1534 Giuliano recorded his capital investment of 3,083 florins for 30-5/6 percent of the profits; AC (BNF), 9, f. 98. In 1539 his capital was 6,600 florins and he was to have 30 percent of the profits; *ibid.*, f. 129.

[106] AC (BNF), 9, ff. 98, 129.

[107] In 1553 the company changed its name to Luigi and Alessandro di Giuliano Capponi and Company.

[108] In the organization of 1557, for example, there were two other parties, Tommaso Biffoli and Pagholo Carnesecchi, whose *persone* were valued at 3,500 florins, entitling them to 20 percent of the profits; AC (BNF), 19, f. 92.

from a great variety of commercial transactions: Neapolitan silk and Spanish wool sold in Florence, finished cloth sold in Lyons and Antwerp, commissions on accounts, shipments of a variety of other products, especially sugar—to mention only the major items on some of the profit sheets of the extant company books.[109] Although it is not apparent from these surviving books, the Capponi also invested in commercial companies abroad through their bank. These subsidiary investments were *accomande* given to Florentine merchants established abroad in the major centers of trade, and it was undoubtedly through them that the Capponi company in Florence laid its own network of business contacts extending throughout Europe. From the meager documentation we know that the Capponi had at one time or another such investments in Antwerp, Seville, London, and Lyons.[110]

Besides these limited liability investments *in accomandita*, Giuliano also established an independent company of his own in Naples in 1538 with Agnolo di Niccolò Biffoli, his former partner in the silk company. The company assumed the names of Alessandro, Giuliano's younger son, and Biffoli. Although their capital increased considerably over the next decades, the share of the Capponi remained only about 40 percent of the total up to Giuliano's death. In the renewal of 1559 the Capponi capital was invested in the names of Luigi and Alessandro only, and there were two new partners added, Agostino del Nero and Raffaello Vecchietti. Thereafter the company is referred to as the company of Biffoli and Vec-

[109] See, for example, AC (BNF), 11, f. 269 (1535-40); 28, f. 466 (1560-64).
[110] The *Mercanzia* records of these *accomande* are very incomplete until later in the sixteenth century. Nevertheless, the surviving records contain several Capponi investments: *Mercanzia*, 10832, ff. 6r-6v (5,500 écus invested by the Capponi as procurator of Filippo Strozzi in Antwerp, 1533), 6v (participated with others in 11,960 florins invested in Francesco di Giovanni Lapi & Co. of Seville, 1533), 26r (£640 invested with Mariotto di Bernardo Neretti in London, 1539), 77r (2,500 écus invested with Filippo di Neri di Baldo della Tosa in Lyons).

chietti, no longer including the name of the Capponi. Like all of Giuliano's companies, it too returned impressive profits right up to the time of his death (Table 39).[111]

TABLE 39. GIULIANO CAPPONI'S SHARE OF CAPITAL AND PROFITS
IN THE COMPANY OF NAPLES, 1538 TO 1567
(All figures are in florins)

Date	Capital	% share	Date	Profits
1538	4,637	40	1540	1,824
1540	6,465	43-1/3	1544	3,727
1545	9,524	....	..	....
1548	10,000	...	1553	6,667
......	....	40	1559	17,143
1559	11,571	45	1564	9,417
1563	16,071	37-1/2	1567	11,000

Source: AC (BNF), 9, ff. 119, 213; 19, ff. 11, 100; 27, ff. 1, 22, 35.

Giuliano's business empire was founded on the Florentine cloth industry. His complex of companies included manufactories of luxury cloths, both wool and silk, dye shops, *battiloro* shops, and warehouses (*fondachi*); but besides the production of cloths, he and his sons also engaged in the marketing of them abroad through their *banco*, although apart from their interest in the company in Naples they established no branches of their own in foreign lands. The Capponi fortune, in short, was made chiefly in manufacturing and marketing rather than in high finance. It is unfortunate that nothing can be known about the internal operation of Giuliano's various companies so that more light might be shed on the conduct of business in the increasingly complex economic world of the sixteenth century. Yet, the evidence is nonetheless clear that his business ventures met with spectacular success. At the time of his death in 1565 the total value of his business investments must have been somewhat higher than 75,000 florins, a sixfold increase over his share of the family

[111] No records of this company survive. Sources for it from the earlier book of Giuliano and the book of Luigi are cited in Table 39.

business when it was divided in 1532.[112] In the last years of his life his profit from these investments averaged about 10,000 florins annually (Table 40). With these profits, he had

TABLE 40. PROFITS FROM INVESTMENTS BELONGING
TO GIULIANO CAPPONI, CA. 1548 TO CA. 1565
(All figures are in florins)

Source	Dates	Profits
Silk companies	1548-1565	25,642
Company of Pisa	1548?-1565	15,367
Wool companies	1548-1567	23,894
Banco	1550-1564	63,342
Company of Naples	1548-1564	33,227
Total	ca. 1548-ca. 1565	161,472

also increased the value of his land holdings from about 10,000 florins in 1532 to over 70,000 florins at the time his books were closed in 1568, three years after his death (Table 35, p. 222). Although his capital investment in land was therefore approximately equal to that in business, his earnings from this source were much lower, averaging between one and two thousand florins a year.[113] Even allowing

[112] A precise value of Giuliano's portfolio at the time of his death cannot be determined. Here are his known investments in various years close to the end of his life:

	Florins
Silk company (1565)	18,000
Company of Pisa (1565)	8,668
Wool company (1554)	8,000
Banco (1563)	28,000
Company of Naples (1563)	16,071
	78,739

His investments in 1532 were worth 13,941 florins.

[113] Here is the income from his landed possessions (AC [BNF], 21 *passim*):

	Florins
1554	900
1555	1,463
1556	1,892
1557	1,700
1558	2,032
1559-60	1,606
1561	2,500
1562-68	13,647

a generous value for his non-income property, such as his town house and villas, the rate of return on this investment was very small. Giuliano's accumulation of real estate no doubt represented an attempt to secure a portion of his wealth, but he by no means pursued a policy of general financial retrenchment. There were more handsome profits to be made elsewhere, and up to the end Giuliano continued his pursuit of them.

No personal papers of Giuliano have survived which give us any insight into his personality, but his financial success reveals the still flickering spark of the capitalistic spirit which had fired Florentines from the very beginning. Giuliano had inherited a sizeable fortune, and with only two sons to provide for he could not have felt a compulsive need for greater wealth. Furthermore, the Capponi had all the requisites of Florentine nobility, and their prestige in the city could hardly have been matched. Giuliano himself had an honored position in the state under the Medici dukes. He was a senator and one of the duke's regular councillors; and, in addition he frequently served in a great number of lesser offices in the state as well.[114] Yet, wealth, nobility, and status did not induce in Giuliano the mentality of a rentier. He owned land and he served at court, but he was also making money; and his fortune, which must have been one of the largest in Florence, was still growing dynamically at the time of his death.

Giuliano's two sons, Luigi (1505-84) and Alessandro (1512-86), were brought into their father's businesses as soon as they had reached maturity and both continued to be active investors after their father's death.[115] Their documents

[114] Giuliano was a councillor in 1534, 1536, 1538, 1541, 1543, 1544, 1545, 1548, 1550 and 1552; and he was chosen almost annually as one of the *accoppiatori; Tratte*, 85, ff. 145r-49v, 193r-95v, 202r-207v, 238r-40v, and *passim*.

[115] This company was one of the leading Florentine firms which had ties with the important Ruiz bank in Spain; see F. Ruiz Martín, *Lettres marchandes échangées entre Florence et Medina del Campo* (Paris, 1965).

survive in great abundance, and it is with their generation that the Capponi archives yield a continuous record of the family's fortune up to the nineteenth century.[116] The brothers enjoyed the traditional social prestige of their family,[117] and both became senators shortly after their father's death and were prominent in the court of the grand dukes. Luigi, in addition, gained considerable renown as a dilettante intellectual and was active in learned circles in Florence. Alessandro dedicated himself zealously to the family businesses and these continued to prosper.[118] Like their father, the brothers enjoyed wealth, prestige, and status, and yet they did not withdraw from the world of business. Both Luigi and Alessandro themselves had sons; but beyond this generation there was no male progeny; and so the line of Giuliano Capponi, which had shown so much vitality in an age usually characterized by its return to economic dormancy, came to a sudden end at the close of the sixteenth century.

[116] Their documents compose the *patrimonio nuovo* of AC (ASF) as well as the bulk of AC (BNF).

[117] Luigi married a daughter of Filippo Strozzi and Alessandro married a daughter of Francesco Guicciardini.

[118] Litta, *Capponi*, Tavola XIII. In AC (BNF) there are numerous ledgers of the various companies of Giuliano's two sons, most of them continuations of those established by Giuliano (the silk company, the company in Pisa, the *banco* of Florence, the company in Naples); but there are also ledgers for a company in Venice and one in Lyons (with another Capponi, Luigi di Gino).

Chapter vii

PRIVATE WEALTH AND

THE FAMILY

ALTHOUGH one can hardly hope to arrive at any final generalizations about Florentine society on the basis of these
studies of only four families over six or seven generations,
there have been recurring themes in their histories which
are very suggestive of features of the patriciate as a whole;
and it seems worthwhile in summing up to attempt to regard
these families not as separate strands but as constituent parts
of the fabric of that society. Because the primary materials
consist almost wholly of financial records, our attention has
been focused on the families' economic existence, but this
fortunately is not the least important aspect of social history.
The changing financial status and activities of successive generations of these families indicate a good deal about the
sources and uses of wealth throughout the Renaissance and
serve as a kind of commentary on the economic history of
the age, while habits of investment and spending no doubt
reflect something of the basic economic attitudes of the patrician mind. Furthermore, since economic interdependence is
one of the strongest ties binding the family together, an examination of the financial relations among members of these
families can bring us closer to a definition of the family itself
as a social institution. It is precisely these realms of social
and economic history which have been least explored by Florentine scholars, and it is therefore appropriate to conclude
this initial foray into family history with a few tentative generalizations about the nature of private wealth and the organization of the family in Renaissance Florence.

Private Wealth and the Family

PRIVATE WEALTH

Economic history is one area in which Florentine Renaissance historiography is sadly deficient. Studies of the Florentine economy concentrate on either the thirteenth and fourteenth centuries or the ducal period, leaving a hiatus for precisely our period.[1] There is, in fact, hardly a scholarly consensus even on general trends.[2] It is therefore still difficult to deter-

[1] The survey, "Della mercatura de' Fiorentini," in Vol. II of Pagnini della Ventura, is still frequently cited. The recent study by Fiumi terminates in the fifteenth century: "Fioritura e decadenza dell'economia fiorentina," *ASI*, cxv (1957), 443-510; cxvi (1958), 385-439; cxvii (1959), 427-502. There are studies on the port of Pisa and the galley trade in the fifteenth century: W. B. Watson, "The Structure of the Florentine Galley Trade with Flanders and England in the Fifteenth Century," *Revue Belge de philologie et d'histoire*, xxxix (1961), 1073-91; xl (1962), 317-47; and of course the excellent studies by Mallett already cited. Finally, there are studies of aspects of the Florentine economy which begin at the end of this period, in the mid-sixteenth century: Carmona, "Aspects du capitalisme toscan . . ."; idem, "Sull'-economia toscana del Cinquecento e del Seicento," *ASI*, cxx (1962), 32-46; José-Gentile da Silva, "Aux XVIIe siècle: la stratégie du capital florentin," *Annales: économies—sociétés—civilisations*, xix (1964), 480-91; idem and Gino Corti, "Note sur la production de la soie à Florence au XVe siècle," *ibid.*, xx (1965), 309-11; F. Braudel and R. Romano, *Navires et marchandise à l'entrée du port de Livorne (1547-1611)* (Paris, 1951). See also Amintore Fanfani, "Effimera la ripresa economica di Firenze sul finire del secolo XVI?" *Economia e storia*, xii (1965), 344-51 (a consideration of the evidence in Ruiz Martín, *Lettres marchandes* . . .).

[2] For examples of opinion regarding the Florentine economy at the end of the fifteenth century as stagnated, if not clearly regressive, see: de Roover, *The Rise and Decline* . . . , p. 5; Fiumi, "Fioritura e decadenza . . . ," *ASI*, cxvii (1959), 501-2; Sapori, "Luci ed ombre sui mercanti fiorentini del Rinascimento," *Nuova antologia*, xciii (1958), 30-31. For a more optimistic view, see Eugen S. Kominsky, "Peut-on considérer le XIVe et le XVe siècles comme l'époque de la décadence de l'économie européenne?" *Studi in onore di Armando Sapori* (Milan, 1957), i, 561-62; Gino Luzzatto, *An Economic History of Italy from the Fall of the Roman Empire to the Beginning of the Sixteenth Century*, trans. P. Jones (New York, 1961), p. 159; Carlo M. Cipolla, "Il declino economico dell'Italia," *Storia dell'economia italiana*, ed. Carlo M. Cipolla (Turin, 1959), i, 605, 609. The most positive statement comes from Federigo Melis, "Il mercante," in *Vita privata a Firenze nei secoli XIV e XV* (Florence, 1966), p. 92; "quei due secoli sono senz'altro da definirsi i secoli d'oro dell'economia fiorentina e il secondo è il più luminoso, con prolungamento almeno sino a mezzo il Cinquecento."

mine precisely what kinds of economic pressures were being exerted on the patriciate and in what ways their behavior was thereby determined by economic considerations. An alternative approach, however, to the problem of understanding the economic forces at work in their lives can be taken from the standpoint of the history of the composition and uses of their private wealth. In this respect these studies of four fortunes are very suggestive. To the extent that they can be considered a kind of index to the investment history of the patriciate they can reveal a good deal about the economic behavior and attitudes of Florentines during the Renaissance.

In the fourteenth century the financial stability of a Florentine family was secured by a portfolio of diverse investments, including usually a family business, government securities, town properties, and real estate in the countryside, as well as the usual variety of independent commercial and loan transactions which characterized Italian business operations at the time.[3] The 1427 *catasto* indicates that these investment habits had not changed appreciably by the beginning of the fifteenth century; and government securities, business, and real estate were still the three general categories into which private wealth was distributed. Of these three areas, it is obvious that new fortunes and rapid growth were traditionally found in business; and to judge from the behavior of many of the men encountered on these pages, business continued to offer happy prospects for the investor for some time to come. In fact, once their fortunes were made, some of these men showed no hurry to transfer their capital to those other kinds of investment which generally are considered more secure. Confidence in the business sector of the Florentine economy remained strong throughout the Renaissance.

As an economic man the Florentine patrician was, after all, primarily a businessman; and the prosperity of Florence had

[3] Sapori, *Studi* . . . , I, 332; Brucker, *Florentine Politics .   . ,* pp. 26-27.

always been rooted in business. It initially arose from the city's international position as a producer of wool cloth; but Florence was soon much more than a manufacturing center. To market their products, Florentines themselves ventured abroad and eventually they developed financial institutions to facilitate their international transactions and to exploit the advantages of their capital accumulation in other ways. With their refined techniques of international banking and an exclusive network of business contacts through their countrymen scattered all over Europe, Florentines long enjoyed an effective monopoly in international commerce and banking. It was in this arena that the largest fortunes were to be found, and the wealthiest Florentine families had always been those who had built up the great international commercial banks of their day.

Historians have long been hard at work on the great companies of the early Trecento, the heroic era of Florentine banking, when Florentines first climbed to the highest levels of international finance; but for the subsequent period, despite more abundant documentation and the unflagging fascination which other aspects of the Renaissance continue to have for historians, there is a remarkable dearth of studies of individual businesses.[4] It is thus difficult to form a clear impression

[4] The only studies of specific businesses active in this period are those already cited by Melis, on Datini of Prato; by R. de Roover, on the Medici bank, and on the sixteenth century Medici wool firm; and Florence Edler de Roover, "Andrea Banchi, Florentine Silk Manufacturer and Merchant in the Fifteenth Century," *Studies in Medieval and Renaissance History*, III (1966), 223-85. R. de Roover has suggested that the considerable success of Florentine commerce and banking throughout Europe in the fifteenth century eventually led to a strangulation of trade as the Florentines accumulated credits abroad, especially in London and Bruges which could not be transferred to Florence because of the one-way pattern of trade; and this inherent weakness in Florentine commercial capitalism led to the crises in Florentine banking at the end of the century: *The Rise and Decline . . .* , pp. 150, 195-96, 317, 326-27, 373-74; "La balance commerciale entre les Pays-Bas et l'Italie au quinzième siècle," *Revue Belge de philologie et d'histoire*, XXXVII (1959), 374-86. Cf. Mallett, "Anglo-Florentine Commercial Relations . . . ," pp. 258-59.

of the general course of Florentine international banking during the Renaissance, although its eventual collapse by the mid-sixteenth century is an established fact. Yet, however bleak the economic horizons appear in the retrospective view of some modern historians, there is enough evidence to suggest that in the fifteenth and sixteenth centuries a number of men—including members of each of the four families studied here—still had considerable confidence in their ability to amass a fortune in enterprising activity abroad of various kinds. Many of them kept the bulk of their estates in liquid assets and were willing to risk heavy investments in foreign ventures, and new opportunities were still appearing on the international scene which they were prepared to exploit. From their vantage point the hazards which eventually frustrated their capitalistic zeal altogether were not so apparent; and in some ways the attitude of the Renaissance businessman himself toward his own economic prospects at the time is more interesting for understanding the period than the unforeseen destiny of his efforts.

Prospects for making one's fortune in the world abroad must have been fairly promising to men like Filippo Strozzi and the Gondi brothers, Giuliano and Antonio. Starting from modest beginnings, they built up impressive fortunes in the middle of the fifteenth century. Each laid his base in Naples, where Florentines had long been established and where the king, Ferdinand, appreciated the importance of commerce and banking for the prosperity of his kingdom and encouraged its development.[5] During the lifetimes of these men, up to the last decade of the century, there is no indication that there was any loss of confidence in the economic possibilities of the Neapolitan kingdom. The records of Filippo Strozzi make it quite clear that he continued to earn profits in Naples up to his death in 1491; and he established his oldest son there

[5] Ernesto Pontieri, "La giovinezza di Ferrante I d'Aragona," *Studi in onore di Riccardo Filangieri* (Naples, 1959), I, 590-91.

in a business of his own. Although Filippo Strozzi and Giuliano Gondi were prepared to spend vast sums in building their magnificent palaces in Florence, they were not curtailing their business activities. Neither was transferring capital from Naples to investments in Florence, and certainly neither was pursuing a policy of financial retrenchment by buying land.

Naples had long been a wide open field for enterprising Florentine businessmen like Filippo Strozzi and the Gondi brothers; but with the following generation, several new financial centers of European importance appeared on the scene which excited the ambitions of many a Florentine in opening up new investment opportunities for his capital. It was at this time, at the end of the fifteenth century, that Lyons began to move into place as one of the great financial and commercial centers of Europe. Its development, like that of Naples, was sponsored by a monarch; in this case, Louis XI. In the late fifteenth and early sixteenth centuries it reached its apogee as a center especially for the international spice trade;[6] but it also became the chief European market for Lucchese and Florentine silk cloths, and so Florentine merchants and bankers came to play a prominent role in the city's economic life.[7] Furthermore, in 1494 the Florentines in Lyons gained special privileges from Charles VIII for conducting business throughout the kingdom of France. Lyons thus became a chief investment outlet for Florentine capital; and men like the Capponi, who were among the first families to appear in Lyons, and like Antonio Gondi later, built up their great financial houses and helped make Lyons one of the great international banking centers of sixteenth century Europe.

[6] René Gandilhon, *Politique économique de Louis XI* (Rennes, 1940), p. 356; Marc Brésard, *Les foires de Lyon aux XVᵉ et XVIᵉ siècles* (Paris, 1914), pp. 70-75.

[7] *Ibid.*, pp. 282-84; on Florentines in France, see the works already cited of Charpin-Feuguerolles and Picot.

Private Wealth

Rome and Antwerp were two other centers where new investment opportunities opened up to Florentine capital in the early sixteenth century. Antwerp began its impressive rise as the marketplace for the growing Portuguese spice trade, and by 1521 it too was emerging as one of the great financial and commercial centers of Renaissance Europe.[8] A number of Florentine banks, including the abortive Guicciardini venture, were established there. Rome, of course, had long been important as the banking center of the international financial structure of the church, but its importance to Florentine interests received a boost with the establishment of the Medicean pontificates, which extended over a score of years from 1513 to 1534. Through their association with the Medici a few Florentines, such as Filippo Strozzi the younger, as we have seen, and others, like Jacopo Salviati,[9] were able to build up important banking houses in Rome and Lyons and to amass extraordinarily large fortunes founded on papal finance. There were, however, a number of smaller organizations involving Florentines, many of them without a previous history in Rome, who also tied their fortunes to the fate of the Medici.

Thus in the early sixteenth century there were a number of new and promising investment outlets for Florentine capital; and from these studies of four families, it is clear that even men of already substantial means were eager to exploit these opportunities by risking their capital in new ventures. Their capital and expertise, in fact, contributed substantially to the economic growth of these new centers. Nevertheless, however bright the prospects, the city's traditionally dynamic role in the European economy was coming to an end. After 1530 political problems began to intrude in business affairs to the detriment of her financial interests. During the course of the

[8] Herman van der Wee, *The Growth of the Antwerp Market and the European Economy (Fourteenth-Sixteenth Centuries)* (The Hague, 1963), II, 199-207.
[9] Ehrenberg, pp. 206-7.

Hapsburg-Valois rivalry, Florence found herself slowly gravi-
tating toward an alliance with France. Her financial interests
in Lyons may have been a decisive influence, but the alliance
exposed Florentine commerce and banking in Europe to the
vagaries of the international power struggle. In Antwerp, for
instance, the companies of the south German towns appeared
on the scene now as the first formidable rivals to Florentine
banking interests; and with imperial patronage they and the
Genoese were destined to gain the clear ascendancy not only
in Antwerp but eventually elsewhere in Europe, wherever the
imperial power under Charles V made its influence felt.[10]
Meanwhile in Rome once the Medici were gone, the influence
of Florentines in papal finance was considerably reduced.
Florentine banking interest declined rapidly, so that by 1551
there were only twelve Florentine firms left, and few of these
carried names belonging to the old and familiar Florentine
families.[11] As the sixteenth century advanced, Florentine financial interests were more and more confined to Lyons; but
whereas earlier those interests derived their vitality from a
free and open market, after 1530 they became inextricably
wrapped up with the finances of the French crown.[12] Thus
even here there was a contraction of their banking operations.
Many loaned heavily to Henry II and, by accepting tax farms,
became bound to the financial structure of the kingdom, some
even transferring their residences to Paris. At the same time,
a number of Florentine patrician families in Lyons naturally
were attracted to the court of Catherine de' Medici. Hence,
one way or another, many Lyonais Florentines abandoned
their bourgeois origins and their native city altogether and
were absorbed into the French nobility. By the end of the
century, there were no more Florentine firms left in Lyons.[13]

[10] Van der Wee, II, 131.   [11] Delumeau, II, 277-80.
[12] Ehrenberg, pp. 205-6.
[13] *Ibid.*, pp. 211-18; Roger Doucet, "La banque en France au XVIe
siècle," *Revue d'histoire économique et sociale*, XXIX (1951), 115-23.
According to Doucet, there are no surviving private papers of Floren-

Private Wealth

The eventual fate of Florentine international banking is, however, in the long run irrelevant in many respects to a consideration of the Florentine scene in the first few decades of the sixteenth century, for however ominous the economic prospects at the time may appear to the historian, contemporaries regarded it from a different perspective. There was still Florentine capital looking for outlets; and with their long tradition of banking experience and an international network of contacts, Florentines enjoyed an initial advantage in the development of the new centers of European commerce and finance—in Lyons, Antwerp, Rome, and in England and Spain as well. Men who already had sizeable fortunes, like Alessandro Gondi and Giuliano Capponi, were ready and willing to invest; and men like Antonio Gondi and Girolamo Guicciardini even ventured abroad themselves to lay the foundations for their businesses. In an effort to build up their businesses, some of these men were prepared to sacrifice immediate profits in order to increase their capital. At the height of the Renaissance, in short, the capitalistic spirit was yet alive in Florence, and there was still considerable confidence in the possibilities for turning a quick profit in the new financial centers throughout Europe. For a while in the early sixteenth century, at any rate, the enterprising zeal of Florentines was not yet dampened by the realization that the European economy was entering a new phase which was to exclude Florence.

Even when by the second half of the sixteenth century Florentine financiers found themselves edged out of the international markets, they did not retreat altogether from the world of business; for despite the contraction of foreign outlets for their capital, they were not without attractive investment possibilities at home. Although there is yet much to be learned about the Florentine economy in the sixteenth cen-

tine residents in Lyons. Our knowledge of these families is hence very sketchy; see Charpin-Feuguerolles for the documentary evidence.

tury, all indications are that it still had a good deal of vitality. The city's industrial position remained strong: the rapid rise of the silk industry after 1450 more than compensated for the decline of wool production, and by the sixteenth century the luxury cloth industry was predominant over all other Florentine industry and commerce.[14] Furthermore, with the shrinking of her commercial horizons in Europe Florentine commerce intensified its energies on strictly Italian markets with considerable success.[15] Florentine capital remained strong into the seventeenth century even though it was channeled more into production and marketing and less into banking than in former times.[16] Handsome profits could still be made by men who, like Giuliano Capponi and Agnolo di Girolamo Guicciardini, built up a complex of cloth companies, both wool and silk, and marketed their products abroad without establishing any foreign branches. Judging from the investment history of men like these, one has to conclude that business was still good in sixteenth century Florence—or, perhaps more importantly, men at the time thought so.

Business, of course, was not the only form of wealth in Renaissance Florence; and even though the great fortunes were no doubt generally made in business, once made they would likely be secured by other kinds of investments. We have already observed that in the Trecento one of the most popular investments was, in fact, the state debt. The city's in-

[14] Carmona, "Sull'economia toscana . . . ," pp. 36-37; Piero Pieri, *Intorno alla storia dell'arte della seta in Firenze* (Bologna, 1927), pp. 34-35; Pietro Battara, "Botteghe e pigioni nella Firenze del '500: un censimento industriale e commerciale all'epoca del granducato mediceo," *ASI*, xcv (1937), II, 28; da Silva and Corti, "Note sur la production de la soie . . . ," pp. 309-11.

[15] Carmona, "Aspects du capitalisme toscan . . . ," pp. 107-8.

[16] This is the conclusion of two scholars who are working on the records of *accomande*: see the two articles already cited by Carmona, and da Silva, "Aux XVIIe siècle . . . ," pp. 480-91. See also R. Romano, "A Florence au XVIIe siècle, industries textiles et conjoncture," *Annales: économies—sociétés—civilisations*, VII (1952), 508-12.

debtedness had begun to mount after 1320, and by the 1340's it had reached such a high level that a systematic organization of it was necessary. This resulted in the consolidation and funding of the debt with the establishment of the Monte, which borrowed money from private sources and in return issued interest-bearing and negotiable stock. These government securities paid well; and since the financial needs of the state continued to mount steadily during the rest of the century and into the early fifteenth century, the Monte soon became a popular investment with a great many Florentines at all economic levels. It, in fact, absorbed so much of the private wealth of the city that the Florentine state of the Renaissance has been described as a "gigantic corporation," and the Monte, the heart of the body politic.[17]

Unfortunately, very little is known about the importance of Monte as an investment for private individuals in the fifteenth century. From the 1427 *catasto* it is apparent that many of the city's richest patricians had the bulk of their wealth tied up in the state debt;[18] yet by the end of the century not one of the men we have studied had any investment in the Monte worth mentioning. The present state of our

[17] Unfortunately, the rapidly mounting indebtedness of the government, its importance as an investment for private individuals, and the political consequences thereof are all problems in Florentine history that have never been studied despite their obvious importance. The only study of the Florentine Monte is Louis F. Marks, "The Development of the Institutions of Public Finance at Florence during the Last Sixty Years of the Republic, c. 1470-1530" (unpublished D. Phil. thesis, Oxford University, 1954), from which two articles have been published: "La crisi finanziaria a Firenze dal 1494 al 1502," *ASI*, cxii (1954), 40-72; and "The Financial Oligarchy in Florence under Lorenzo," *Italian Renaissance Studies*, ed. E. F. Jacob (New York, 1960), pp. 123-47. The importance of the Monte as an investment at the time of its organization in the 1340's has been suggested by Marvin B. Becker, "Problemi della finanza pubblica fiorentina della seconda metà del Trecento e dei primi del Quattrocento," *ASI*, cxxiii (1965), 433-66.

[18] Heinrich Sieveking, "Aus genueser Rechnungs- und Steuerbüchern," *Sitzungsberichte der Kais. Akademie der Wissenschaften in Vien. Philosophisch-historische Klasse*, 162 (Vienna, 1908-1909), 93-94; Jones, p. 197.

knowledge of the Monte hardly permits an explanation as to why in the course of the fifteenth century investment in it should have become less and less attractive with the upper classes. There is some evidence, however, that the market value of holdings declined and that interest payments were not always made.[19] After 1470 in a series of Monte reforms the stock became categorized at three different interest rates —3 percent, 4 percent, and 7 percent—depending on the length of time the stock had been held, and this was far below the rate of return one might expect from a business investment. Considering in addition the political problems of the Medicean regime, it is not altogether surprising that the rich did not continue to invest in the state debt. This kind of investment probably appealed more to men with only modest sums to invest, too little to put into a business, for it is apparent from the surviving records that the number of stockholders at the end of the century was quite large and the value of individual holdings very small.[20] By the end of the fifteenth century, in short, it is likely that the public debt was no longer

[19] In the *catasto* declarations, the declared value, which represents the market value, is always less than the value on the Monte books. Furthermore, along with Monte credits, the declarer often listed interest credits which apparently accumulated on the books and were not received in payments. Nevertheless, Monte stock was still being bought and sold on an open market in the fifteenth century; see Macinghi negli Strozzi, pp. 573-74. Cf. ASF, *Monte delle Graticole*, 954, f. 1r, where a stipulation of the provision of 17 November 1478 permits transfer and sale of credits on the Monte books without charge.

[20] My survey of the books of the 7 percent Monte from 1480 to 1487 reveals the following information. The total number of payments over 20 florins each (there were three payments annually) varied between five and twenty-one, and none of the Monte officials were among these recipients. The highest payment was 190 florins, paid in Jan.-Feb. 1483/84 to Piero di Francesco Mellini; and the payments he received from 1481 to 1487 were the only ones over 50 florins each. Hardly anyone appears to have earned more than 100 florins annually from the 7 percent Monte. Furthermore, only two Monte officials who served from 1490 to 1494 even appear in the indices of holders of Monte stock during those years, and the larger of these holdings, that of Alamanno Salviati, was 667 florins. ASF, *Monte delle Graticole*, 954, 955, 956, 957, 958.

considered a lucrative investment, and that no one was investing heavily in it.[21]

A third category of investments for Florentine capital was real estate. This was a popular form of investment in Florence and one with a more durable importance in the investment history of the patriciate. The investment portfolio of most patricians at any time in the city's history would probably include some land. Yet, it is difficult to make gen-

[21] In the articles already cited, Louis Marks has mistakenly suggested that the state debt, after the reforms of 1480, came to be regarded as a source of profits by a "financial oligarchy" and that their control of the financial machinery contributed to a rentier mentality. Marks' observation ("The Financial Oligarchy . . . ," pp. 140-41) that from 1482 to 1494 there were "only" twenty-six families represented on the board of Monte officials is deceptive in failing to point out that there were only four officials, who served from one to three years, and that only one, Giovanni di Raffaello Bonsi, served more than three years and more than one tenure (*Tratte*, 82, f. 105r; 83, f. 3r). Furthermore, his comment that the roster of officials after 1494 indicates a notable continuity of the same names and families ("La crisi finanziaria . . . ," p. 43) is likewise completely deceptive (*Tratte*, 83, ff. 3r-3v, 32r). The officials of the Monte did not constitute a financial oligarchy: they held their office for a given tenure, and very few of them ever appear again on the rosters.

The office carried with it the obligation to make a large loan of several thousand florins to the state; and this provision was obviously designed in order that the government could obtain large sums easily and quickly. The officials received a very modest salary and were to be paid back the capital with a just interest, and they held their office, administering the finances of the city to assure them on this point. See the specific provisions of 1478 and 1479: ASF, *Provvisioni*, 169, ff. 53r, 87r-87v; 170, ff. 47r-47v.

From the personal accounts consulted in this study, we have two clear examples of the financial importance of this office to its holder. When Alessandro Gondi was an official from 1497 to 1500, he and his two brothers loaned the government 5,000 florins, for which they received altogether 2,468 florins in interest up to 1506; A Gondi, 34, ff. 1, 28, 43, 50. This being his only involvement with the Monte, Alessandro hardly qualifies as a "financial oligarch" and he certainly did not have a rentier mentality. Lorenzo Strozzi, as an official of the Monte, loaned 5,000 florins to the city in July 1513. This was paid back by March 1515 with 897 florins in interest; CS-v, 94, ff. 50, 65. Other men in this study who were officials include Filippo Strozzi (1478-79), Jacopo Guicciardini (1472) and Piero Guicciardini (1503), none of whom appear to have steadily reaped extraordinary profits from this office.

eralizations about the land-buying habits of Florentines. A great many of them owned at least a few parcels of land in the immediate vicinity of the city, and there had always been a class of men who were large landowners and who lived from their rents alone. Furthermore, there were men who, having made their fortunes, wanted to sit back and enjoy it and who therefore bought land for security and leisure. But examples of men who turned away from business and secured their wealth in land can be found in the fourteenth as well as the sixteenth century; and although it is often assumed that with the decline of the Florentine economy in the Renaissance there was a marked transfer of capital from business to real estate, it seems much more likely that the "return to the land" was a very slow process lasting many generations.[22]

However popular land was as an investment for the bourgeoisie, there is little indication that their ownership of it led to a more rational and efficient agriculture. Although the percentage of land owned by townsmen was very high, most of their possessions were only large enough to provide them with their own needs; and in the fifteenth century there was no marked tendency toward formation of larger agricultural units. Significant improvements on the land in Tuscany had come in the late twelfth and early thirteenth centuries, and thereafter further capital expenditures fell mostly in the luxury category with the establishment of country residences by townsmen. Improvements were, therefore, found only on those estates in the immediate vicinity of the city; and elsewhere, in the outlying regions, the land generally remained in its pristine condition. Likewise, the administra-

---

[22] For a general statement of this thesis, see Niccolò Rodolico, "Il ritorno alla terra nella storia degli italiani," *Atti della R. Accademia dei Georgofili di Firenze*, Ser. v: xxx (1933), 326-29. Cf. Jones, p. 198; Sapori, *Studi . . .* , I, 212. For examples of men who in the fourteenth century were buying land in large quantities, there is Luigi Guicciardini in this study and the subject of the study by A. Fanfani, *Un mercante del Trecento* (Milan, 1935), pp. 101-4.

tion of farms remained almost entirely the traditional *mezzadria* system.[23]

In fifteenth century Florence, therefore, investment in land was hardly the best way to put capital to work. The rents from farms hardly compared with the profits from a cloth manufactory or a commercial bank, which normally ran somewhat higher than 10 percent. For example, the handsome income of Giuliano Capponi from extensive holdings which he accumulated in the mid-sixteenth century represented a very low rate of return on his capital investment compared to his impressive profits from an almost equal sum invested in business. Once a fortune was committed to land, therefore, it was diminished in income value. It also became stagnate, for the possibility of further capital accumulation was considerably reduced. A man who, like Jacopo Guicciardini, had a comfortable fortune in land was hardly able further to increase his estate after he had divested himself of his business interests. Even the large income of Giuliano Capponi from his real estate holdings barely met his living expenses. Men invested in land to diversify their portfolio and to secure a part of their wealth; but as long as they wanted to make money, they did not confine their investments to land alone.[24]

[23] The monumental work of Elio Conti on rural Tuscany is now being published: *La formazione della struttura agraria moderna nel contado fiorentino*, I and III (Rome, 1965). See the review article by Giovanni Cherubini, "Qualche considerazione sulle campagne dell'Italia centro-settentrionale tra l'XI e il XV secolo (in margine alle ricerche di Elio Conti)," *Rivista storica italiana*, LXXIX (1967), 111-57. Of very limited use is Enrico Poggi, *Cenni storici delle leggi sull'agricoltura dai tempi romani fino ai nostri* (2 vols.; Florence, 1845-48).

[24] See, for example, Rinuccini's complaints of taxes on real estate, which, unlike business and professional employment, did not assure one of a cash income; Martines, "Nuovi documenti . . . ," p. 84. Cf. Giovanni Rucellai's serious reservations about the advisability of investing in land: *Zibaldone*, p. 8. Likewise in Venice land was not considered an important income investment, and little was spent on improvements; Gino Luzzatto, "Les activités économiques du Patriciat

There is no doubt that in the fifteenth century some wealthy Florentines possessed large tracts of land,[25] but it is just as certain that some of them—like the elder Filippo Strozzi, the elder Antonio Gondi, and Alessandro Gondi—had no inclination to invest in real estate, either in the countryside or in the city itself. In fact, some men did not even own the premises in the city on which they conducted their very prosperous businesses. Their land holdings, such as they were, were fairly confined to the immediate vicinity of Florence, generally in an area long associated with the family. One has the impression that they regarded land not so much as an investment as a convenience for a country residence as well as for the produce it supplied for the family's own household.

In Renaissance Florence men bought land for a variety of personal reasons or because eventually economic circumstances left them no alternative; but there is no indication that the possession of land became associated with new concepts of social aristocracy or, conversely, that social forces led men to detach themselves from the world of business.[26] A "return to the land," by one man did not commit his descendants to a rural life or induce in them the mentality of a rentier or the psychology of the villa owner. Palla di Lorenzo Strozzi and Agnolo di Girolamo Guicciardini were sons of men who lived primarily off their farm income, and yet they themselves both returned to the world of business.

---

vénitien (Xe-XIVe siècle)," *Studi di storia economica veneziana* (Padua, 1954), pp. 137-41.

[25] The Medici, for example, possessed extensive land holdings, worth 59,742 florins in 1457; de Roover, *The Rise and Decline* . . . , p. 26 (Table 1). Francesco Sassetti in 1462 had 11.6 percent of his wealth, totaling altogether 26,721 florins, in real estate; Florence de Roover, "Francesco Sassetti and the Downfall of the Medici Banking House," *Bulletin of the Business Historical Society*, xvii (1943), 65-80.

[26] Jones, pp. 199-200, talks of the prestige value of land and the psychology of villa residents, but there is no indication that such ideas were widespread in Florentine society.

Giuliano Capponi and his sons, who possessed a very large fortune in land, nevertheless retained much of their wealth in mobile capital and actively engaged in business. The elder Filippo Strozzi for all his vast wealth and his sense of grandeur showed no inclination to divest himself of his business interests in order to buy land; and his son Filippo, who was not given a business education and who moved at the highest level of Italian society of his time, refused titles and fiefs and deigned to enter the business world. In whatever ways the Florentine patriciate became an aristocratic elite, it did not follow the European pattern and become a landed aristocracy with an exclusively rentier mentality.

Elsewhere in Italy the sixteenth century saw the diffusion of new social ideals among the upper classes of bourgeois origins. This was partly a result of economic circumstances which considerably contracted the horizons of Italian commerce and finance; but it is just as much a result of the heightened presence on the Italian scene of feudal Europe so that the ambitions of the bourgeoisie came more and more to be focused on the aristocratic ideal of the northern tradition. This is true in the Venetian state, for instance, where in the city itself there was a growing distaste for business among a nobility that more than any other in Europe had distinguished itself for its economic vitality;[27] while out in the Veneto there was a marked trend in the thinking of the upper classes toward the idea that nobility and commerce were mutually exclusive terms.[28] It is not surprising, therefore, that Venetian visitors in Florence were always impressed by the Florentine patrician's active engagement in trade even to the extent of performing manual labor. In 1527 the Venetian ambassador expressed considerable surprise on finding the governors of the city working in their cloth shops dirtying

[27] James C. Davis, *The Decline of the Venetian Nobility as a Ruling Class* (Baltimore, 1962), pp. 40f.

[28] Angelo Ventura, *Nobiltà e popolo nella società veneta del '400 e '500* (Bari, 1964), pp. 300-30.

their hands in the most menial of tasks;[29] and his successors throughout the sixteenth century hardly ever fail to comment with some amazement on the involvement of the Florentine nobility in the cloth business.[30] Although there are hints that the younger generations were being diverted from this traditional occupation by the attractions of the granducal court and a different style of life,[31] there was in Florence still no social ignominy attached to the man who kept his wealth in the more fluid forms of capitalistic enterprise and who himself conducted his own business. Concepts of nobility in Florence of the Renaissance and later had little to do with the kind of wealth a man might have.[32] The original foundation of the Florentine patriciate had been, after all, its business activity; in the early fifteenth century humanists like Alberti and Palmieri had given them the moral and intellectual buttressing they needed; and in the later Renaissance Florentines never betrayed their deepest tradition.

THE FAMILY IN RENAISSANCE FLORENCE

The question at the fore throughout these studies has been the family as a specific kind of social group, with its own

[29] "Relazion fatta per Marco Foscari . . . ," in *Relazioni* . . . , III, Pt. I, 17. See the quote, p. 141 n. 84 above.

[30] *Ibid.*, Pt. I, 185-86 (Lorenzo Priuli in 1566) and 210 (Andrea Gussoni in 1576); Pt. II, 42 (Tomasso Contarini in 1588). As an anonymous observer wrote in the late seventeenth century, "anche la nobiltà attende alla mercantia, non essendo punto vergogna il maneggiare la seta e la lana, et il vendere alle Botteghe," from "Arcani svelati overo la relatione del stato e governo politico di tutti i principi d'Italia l'anno 1665," *Folger Strozzi Transcript*, 141, f. 161r.

[31] *Relazioni* . . . , III, Pt. I, 186 (Lorenzo Priuli in 1566); Pt. II, 176 (Francesco Badoer in 1609).

[32] Definitions of nobility in the ducal period do not include the nature of a man's wealth: Piero di Giovanni Monaldi, "Historia delle Famiglie della città di Firenze e della nobilità de Fiorentini," ASF, MSS 421; Paolo Mini, *Discorso della nobiltà di Firenze, e de Fiorentini* (Florence, 1593); Scipione Ammirato, *Delle famiglie nobili fiorentine* (Florence, 1615), first two unnumbered pages of introduction; Giuseppe Maria Mecatti, *Storia genealogica della nobilità, e cittadinanza di Firenze* (Naples, 1754), pp. 5-7.

political, social, emotional, as well as economic life; and the ultimate goal must now be brought into focus—however vague and fuzzy it may yet appear—with an attempt to relate the changing composition and ethos of the family between the fourteenth and the sixteenth centuries to the general development of Renaissance civilization.

In Italian society, medieval and modern, the family has always enjoyed a central importance.[33] As a social institution, however, it was subject to continual redefinition following its protean adjustment to changing conditions within society as a whole; and those varying definitions themselves become touchstones to the history of that society. In the early Middle Ages the emergence of the extended family, or clan, among the upper classes corresponded to the breakdown of public authority; and the family became the preëminent fact of medieval Italian society, not only in the feudal society of the countryside but in the commune as well. Members of a clan were regarded as a totality; they lived under one roof, shared living expenses, and held their property in common. Moreover, they were subject to the legal jurisdiction of the group; and their collective association, called a *consorteria* or tower society, had its own internal organization, with councils, officials, and even statutes. It looked after the public interests of its members and played a leading role in the political life of the commune. These organizations were not limited to the nobility and, in fact, they cut across other social and economic lines. Among the upper classes the communal family was thus a well-developed social, political, and economic entity in which the individual was subordinate.[34]

[33] On the history of the Italian family, see: Enrico Besta, *La famiglia nella storia del diritto italiano* (Padua, 1933); and Nino Tamassia, *La famiglia italiana nei secoli decimoquinto e decimosesto* (Milan, 1910).

[34] On the *consorteria*, see: Gino Masi, "La struttura sociale delle fazioni politiche fiorentine ai tempi di Dante," *Il giornale dantesco*, XXXI, New Ser: 1 (1930), 3-28; Franco Niccolai, "I consorzi nobiliari ed il Comune nell'alta e media Italia," *Rivista di storia del diritto*

and the Family

By the fourteenth century the family was losing much of its cohesion and was slowly disintegrating into smaller units.[85] This development corresponded in part with the slow ascendancy of the integrated, sovereign state over the older corporate structure of political society. The *consorteria* gradually became more submissive toward the emerging authority of the state; and as it did so, it could no longer command the intense loyalties of its members as it had in the more violent days of the commune. Already by mid century the family's lateral extension was reduced to brothers and their families, and a regrouping probably occurred every other generation or so.[86] Thus, in the course of the fourteenth century the individual found his political and legal bonds of loyalty to the family, as those to the guild and other communal corporations, slowly loosened and finally dissolved.[87]

Nor did the economic bonds remain, for the disintegration of the family partly corresponded to new financial circumstances arising from the transformation of Florence from an industrial city to a worldwide financial center. In the early fourteenth century the family's common ownership of prop-

---

italiano, XIII (1940), 116-47, 292-342, 397-477; P. Santini, "Società delle torri in Firenze," *ASI*, Ser. IV: XX (1887), 25-58, 178-204; Marco Tabarrini, "Le consorterie nella storia fiorentina del medio evo," *La vita italiana nel Trecento* (Milan, 1904), pp. 98-127. The lack of documentation for this early period obviously makes it impossible to study a specific *consorteria* from within. Donato Velluti's chronicle, however, gives us evidence for the unity of a mercantile family in a matter of a vendetta in the late thirteenth century embracing three generations of three collateral lines. For other evidence of an extended family, see: S. L. Peruzzi, *Storia del commercio e dei banchieri di Firenze in tutto il mondo conosciuto dal 1200 al 1345* (Florence, 1868), p. 366; and Sapori, "La famiglia . . . degli Alberti," pp. 1005-7.

[85] Tamassia, pp. 136-45.

[86] This regrouping can be traced in the case of the Alberti: Sapori, "La famiglia . . . degli Alberti."

[87] On the state's displacement of the older corporate structure, see the analysis of Marvin B. Becker, "Florentine Popular Government (1343-1348)," *Proceedings of the American Philosophical Society*, CVI (1962), 360-82; and idem, *Florence in Transition*, I (Baltimore, 1967).

erty extended also to business organization, for the capital of a family company was not separate from the patrimony. The company was not a distinct entity, and family solidarity and honor made it entirely a family venture, with unlimited liability.[38] With the expansion of Florentine business throughout Europe, however, there was a need for additional capital for banking operations, and businesses which formerly had been exclusively family enterprises had to accept outside capital. Furthermore, with patrimonies consisting largely of liquid capital there was the possibility of division among heirs, and this assured more independent activity by individual members of the family. In the course of the fourteenth century, as a result, the private initiative of individual investors replaced the concerted efforts of families as the dynamic of Florentine banking and commerce abroad, and the structure of the Florentine company underwent a corresponding transformation. Legislation had to be formulated by the guilds to regulate the new kind of non-familial relations between partners, and by the early fifteenth century this development culminated in the apparent recognition of a company's own legal personality. In this way company organization was freed from the family and its capital became distinct from a patrimony. Private individual investment now had greater possibilities and the investor became more independent in making his own way in the business world.[39]

[38] Sapori, "Le compagnie mercantili toscane del dugento e dei primi del trecento," *Studi . . .* , II, 803; "La famiglia . . . degli Alberti," pp. 992, 996-97. In his doctoral dissertation, Max Weber examined the "analogue" of the family and early business organization in Florence: *Zur Geschichte der Handelsgesellschaften im Mittelalter* (Stuttgart, 1889), pp. 128-48.

[39] Sapori has emphasized and illustrated this development in Florence in several studies: "I mutui dei mercanti fiorentini del trecento e l'incremento della proprietà fondiaria," *Studi . . .* , I, 211; "Storia interna della compagnia mercantile dei Peruzzi," *ibid.*, II, 657-58; "Le compagnie mercantili . . . ," p. 803; "La famiglia . . . degli Alberti," pp. 981-83, 1011. Sapori regards this individualism as the decisive factor in the rapid capital accumulation at this time. The *accomanda* contract was a significant innovation (1408) in extending investment

and the Family

Furthermore, in contrast to the companies of the Bardi, the Peruzzi, the Acciaiuoli, and the other great entrepreneural families of the fourteenth century, the companies of the Renaissance were likely to have many fewer partners—perhaps no more than two or three major investors, who were not necessarily related; and partly for this reason the capital even of the largest hardly approached the size of some of the earlier giants. And finally, whereas the far-flung international structure of the Trecento company was welded into a single legal entity, the Renaissance company, like those encountered in these studies, spread its tenacles much more cautiously through a network of interlocking partnerships resembling the structure of the modern holding company. In terms of structure, in short, business became much more an individual enterprise; and the transformation of business organization from the fourteenth to the fifteenth century is analogous to what was happening to the family at the same time.

As the family began to lose its common economic interests so it also lost the property which its members had held in common.[40] Already in 1324 laws were being formulated to establish procedures for the division of property among members of a *consorteria* and for arrangements for selling shares and thus alienating the patrimony.[41] Thus the economic bonds were further loosened and property came to be held by private individuals. Some families continued to hold prop-

---

possibilities to "outsiders"; see Carmona, "Aspects du capitalisme toscan. . . ." On the ticklish legal question of the personality of the company, see Enrico Bensa, *Francesco di Marco Datini* (Milan, 1928), pp. 143-51.

[40] The gradual disintegration of the Alberti patrimony, and the consequent breakup of the common ownership of the family business, has been traced by Sapori, "La famiglia . . . degli Alberti," pp. 1005-8. The three sons of Jacopo degli Alberti, who died in 1319, kept their patrimony together until 1334 when all but the family palace and other real estate, worth 13,644 florins, was divided; then, in 1342, even that was divided, including the family palace. In 1347 when Jacopo's son Caroccio died, his sons immediately divided their patrimony.

[41] Santini, pp. 43-46.

erty in common, although with the proliferation of branches through successive generations and with the greater freedom of the individual it is not likely that common ownership extended through more than a couple of generations.[42] Even in the case of ancestral rural properties which a family might have held on to after coming to the city it was not likely that common ownership could endure. Our line of the Guicciardini, for example, took possession of its ancestral lands at Poppiano only after assembling them through various purchases. Frequently when brothers were closely bound by the ties of affection, they held their patrimony together under an unwritten contractual understanding called a *fraterna*,[43] but such an arrangement hardly outlived the lives of the parties involved. In this study, for example, we have seen that the sons of Piero di Messer Luigi Guicciardini remained in one household for about a decade following their father's death; and likewise, Giuliano and Niccolò Capponi lived together and kept joint accounts until Niccolò's death. Nevertheless, such arrangements, though perhaps not unusual, depended on entirely personal considerations and were only temporary in the over-all history of the family. Throughout this entire period there was no attempt among these four families to form a patrimony which belonged inalienably to a family and survived undivided from generation to generation. There was no fear of alienation and no practice of primogeniture: a man's property was divided equally among his "universal heirs"—normally, his sons without any special recognition of the oldest. The estates of the elder Filippo Strozzi and the elder Antonio Gondi remained undivided only because the heirs were minors; and in each

[42] The Peruzzi kept some jointly owned property, including funds for works of beneficence, for at least three generations; Sapori, "Storia interna . . . ," pp. 657-58.

[43] On the fraterna, see Camillo Fumagalli, *Il diritto di fraterna nella giurisprudenza da Accursio alla codificazione* (Turin, 1912).

case, the property was divided as soon as the sons reached their majority.

As a consequence of this complete partition of estates, there was not even an ancestral residence for some men. Simone Strozzi, the older as well as the younger Jacopo Guicciardini, Giuliano Gondi, and the heirs of Antonio Gondi, all had to buy their own residences; and until they did so, some of them rented houses. The Gondi palace was divided between two of the four brothers when the patrimony was dissolved in 1506, and eventually it was bought out entirely by Alessandro. Likewise, the Guicciardini palace was signed over to Girolamo when he married, leaving his four older brothers without a town house. The Capponi are the only family studied here which had a palace throughout the entire period; but it eventually passed to the brothers, Niccolò and Giuliano, so that presumably other lines stemming from the same branch of the family had to find their own quarters within the city.

In fifteenth century Florence the fragmentation of the family frequently reached the point at which each man established his own independent household and possessed his own property privately; and in this respect the Florentine patriciate differed from the mercantile aristocracy of Venice, where the *fraterna* was a common arrangement, and even more from that of Genoa with its remarkable *alberghi*.[44] In Florence related families, even brothers, did not necessarily live under one roof or share living expenses unless through financial necessity, as in the case of the sons of Piero di Messer Luigi Guicciardini, or because of unusually strong personal bonds, like those that kept Niccolò and Giuliano Capponi together

[44] On Venice, see Davis, p. 26, and Lane, "Family Partnerships . . . ," pp. 178-79; and on Genoa, see Heers, *Gênes au XVe siècle* . . . , pp. 564-76. In his study on Lucca, Berengo also emphasizes the importance of the wider family structure, but he presents no evidence from studies of specific families; *Nobili e mercanti* . . . , pp. 31-53.

in one household. The patrician family in Renaissance Florence was thus the smallest possible group, a fact that was recognized in the legal definition of the family as being essentially a man's immediate family.[45]

It is not difficult to see this new concept of the family symbolized in the stylistic developments in Renaissance palace architecture. In earlier times a man's actual residence was not well defined architecturally: he might share a building or even live with other members of his family, and the entire clan occupied a number of indistinguishable buildings forming a conglomerate whole around the family tower. By the fifteenth century, however, men lived apart, renting houses or building their own. The great Renaissance palace of Florence stood not only as a proud monument to a man's good taste and economic status but also as the aesthetic articulation of the physical isolation of a man's household from all others, even those with the same name.[46]

As a consequence of the fragmentation of the family and the independence of each member in the pursuit of his fortune, it was not at all unusual in Renaissance Florence to find marked differences in the financial status of members of a family even within the same generation; and with the continual redivision of wealth as it passed from one generation to another and the vicissitudes to which wealth was naturally subject as long as it was in liquid form, it was not likely that a family's financial fortune over several generations could be maintained at a constant level. Division of an estate itself reduced the wealth of the subsequent generation, depending on the number of heirs, and each one of them in turn met with varying success, depending on his abilities. Thus Gino Capponi in his *ricordi* felt compelled to advise his son Neri to keep the family united as long as possible so that he

[45] Besta, p. 32.

[46] See the provocative article by P. Francastel, "Imagination et réalité, dans l'architecture civile de '400," *Homage à Lucien Febvre—Éventail de l'histoire vivante* (Paris, 1953), II, 195-206.

would have the advantage of the entire estate for awhile at least;[47] and the histories of many family fortunes justified Gino's concern. The wealth of successive generations of all the families examined here shows considerable fluctuation; but whereas some of these fortunes approached the very pinnacle, none plunged as rapidly and disastrously as the fortunes of some other Florentine families in the same period.[48]

Without common property and with varying economic interests, the Renaissance family lost much of its inner cohesive force, for the weakening of economic bonds most likely loosened other ties as well. The cognate group never became as fragmented as it has in modern society—Florentine society after all was relatively so small and so confined that frequency of personal contact no doubt kept alive some sense of relationship. Men with the same name often lived side by side in the same parish of their common ancestor however remote, and cognate groups had a certain ritualistic unity through historical affiliations with parish churches and common chapels. Nevertheless, as the economic ties within a family were severed, individualistic behavior became more marked in other respects, especially in politics. Although in the fifteenth century there was still legislation determining the composition of various political bodies partly on the basis

[47] "Da soffrire è lo stare insieme un pezzo, tanto che abbiate il modo a dividervi con unità, e che abbiate megliorato condizione"; *Rerum italicarum scriptores*, XVIII, col. 1150.

[48] For example, the Rinuccini. Messer Francesco Rinuccini (d. 1381) was one of the richest men in the city; but his estate was divided four ways and in the 1397 *prestanze* one son, Cino, paid 260 florins whereas another, Simone, paid only eight florins. In the 1413 *prestanze*, only five of Simone's thirteen sons were inscribed, all at the level of notaries and minor guildsmen. See Martines, "Nuovi documenti . . . ," pp. 80-83. It was likewise with the Medici: Brucker, "The Medici . . . ," p. 10; Raymond de Roover, "Gli antecedenti del Banco Mediceo e l'azienda bancaria di messer Vieri de Cambio de' Medici," *ASI*, CXXIII (1965), 3-13. Sapori's study of the Alberti in the fourteenth century illustrates the fluctuations in that family's fortune and the disparity in the status of various of its members; and in his *Ricordi* Giovanni Morelli records the same phenomena in the history of his family over just two generations.

of familial traditions, the family was certainly not the active political force that it had been in the days of the *consorteria*. In the annals of Florentine politics during the Renaissance, there are many cases of "families" being found on both sides in political disputes, and even brothers could be bitterly divided in political struggles.[49] Political security was not at all assured by family relationship with men who enjoyed political influence; and conversely political condemnations of a man did not necessarily involve even his brother.[50] Gone were the violent days of the commune when a family *en masse* suffered for the political sins of one of its members, and it is likely that further researches in the political histories of families will necessitate a new political definition of the family which corresponds to its economic transformation.

The history of a family in the Renaissance shows nothing more clearly than the way in which the interests of its members follow the genealogical growth of its branches in spreading far and wide even in the course of one generation—and often the only point in common among a number of lines is that of their genealogical origin. Yet Florentine history continues to be written as if the actors were not individuals but families in the older sense, and historians too often use only surnames in discussing marriage "alliances" and political parties without any regard for the diverse interests of specific individuals who just happen to have the same name. Too much has been written about Florentine society without considering the essential difference between an entire cognate group and the family as a meaningful unit within society.[51]

[49] Examples encountered in this study include: Alfonso and the younger Filippo Strozzi, and Piero and Giovanni di Luigi Guicciardini.

[50] For example, Giuliano Capponi hardly suffered the stigma of his brother's association with the anti-Medicean party of the last republic. Lorenzo Strozzi lived on in Florence even while his brother was an active rebel against the state; and in fact, one of the very closest personal associates of both the dukes, Alessandro and Cosimo, during Filippo Strozzi's opposition to them was his first cousin, Matteo di Lorenzo; see Litta, *Strozzi*, Tavola XIX.

[51] See especially the works of Anzilotti and von Albertini already

and the Family

By the fifteenth century the encrustations of a corporate society had fallen away and man was left exposed and isolated, unencumbered with the old social obligations and loyalties. The old sociability was gone, and man had to reorient himself to a new kind of society. Whereas earlier a man was involved in a complex association which had its own social, economic and political existence, he was now detached and autonomous. He well might have ties to more remote relatives beyond his palace door, but these ties were entirely personal and therefore illusory and unstable; and whatever concrete bonds he may have had in common political and economic interests with them, they were no longer subject to a higher familial authority. Not only was he more isolated as an individual but also, with the disintegration of the larger family, he found his financial position much less secure. He could not rely on the larger association for his basic well-being; nor could he, with the division of a patrimony among all sons equally, depend on the wealth of his father to assure him a status in his society. Under these circumstances wealth was much more likely to be kept in mobile form where it had potential for growth; but for this very reason it was also subject to considerable fluctuation. One of the consequences, therefore, of this fragmentation of the family as a social organization was to throw on each man the burden of responsibility for his own well-being. He was compelled to be more aggressive in asserting his own interests, and many men had to seek their own fortunes. The resulting high premium on individual initiative in economic activity undoubtedly accounts for the continued vigor of Florentine efforts in the eco-

---

cited. The idea of the extended family is also important in the works of both Brucker and Martines and dominates their understanding of Florentine society. See, for example, Gene A. Brucker, "The Medici . . . ," p. 26. And for Martines: *The Social World* . . . , pp. 50-57; and "Nuovi documenti . . . ," p. 40. Likewise, throughout the important study by Rubinstein, *The Government of Florence* . . . , the family is taken for granted as a political unit.

nomic sphere even though the prospects for their success were growing dimmer as a result of the rapidly changing European situation.

Whatever was lost in the extensive sociability of the older family association, there was something gained in the more intensive social cohesion within the immediate family. Men came to enjoy family life in ways not formerly possible. They became more sensitive to the pleasures of domestic life and put greater stock on the value of family affections. Although it would be difficult to say that the intimacy of family life was not enjoyed previously, it is apparent that in the Renaissance these sensitivities were elevated to a level of cultural expression not formerly reached. In personal letters, diaries and *ricordanze*, sermons, moral tracts, humanist literature and poetry, much thoughtful attention is given to the sentiments of conjugal and maternal love and to the bliss and moral value of family life.[52] The humanist pedagogues recognized the unique and fundamental importance of the family in the education of children.[53] Even domestic organization received considerable attention not only in this literature but also, as we have already observed, in the mundane matters of family and household accounts. The whole body of literature is capped by Alberti's famous treatise—a systematic treatment of the subject of a man's immediate family—which embodies the spirit of the time in its emphatic statement that family life is central to man's moral existence. Burckhardt, pursuing his main theme, felt that this "thoughtful study of all questions relating to social intercourse, to education, to domestic service

[52] The Florentine literature on this subject is surveyed in Vittorio Lugli, *I trattatisti della famiglia nel Quattrocento* (Bologna-Modena, 1909), who concludes, quoting Monnier, that "il quattrocento è un secolo 'bonario, domestico, familiare'" (p. 9).

[53] Matteo Palmieri especially recognized the importance of the family in the education of children; and one can see his influence on patrician thinking in the *Zibaldone* of Giovanni Rucellai. Cf. William Harrison Woodward, *Vittorino da Feltre and Other Humanist Educators* (New York, 1963), pp. 192-95.

and organization . . . first brought order into domestic life, treating it as a work of deliberate contrivance."[54] This idea of the family as a work of art and its embodiment in the sensitivities of Renaissance man has been considered one of the most attractive features of Renaissance society.[55] The modern conception of family as a private association of a man, his wife, and their children, held together by the bonds of affection, has one of its first manifestations here and certainly it was a distinctive feature of Florentine society at the time.[56]

One aspect of this new sentiment was the liberation of women both from the obscurity of medieval life and from the idealism of medieval poetry. Salutati, for instance, rejected Petrarch's condemnation of women and marriage, and humanist invective against women becomes rarer in the Quattrocento. They took their places as partners in the direction of the household and the education of their children as well as companions of their husbands and full-fledged members of polite society. Marriage became a much more personal affair and less a matter of a family "alliance"—not that the broader interests of the family were not considered during marriage negotiations, but now there was just as much concern about the happiness of the individual parties involved. Perhaps the finest document testifying to the new status of women and the developed sentiments of familial af-

[54] *Civilization of the Renaissance in Italy*, p. 243.

[55] See, for example, C. M. Ady, "Morals and Manners of the Quattrocento," *Proceedings of the British Academy* (London, 1942), pp. 182-86. Probably the two finest expressions of familial sentiments are the letters of Alessandra Strozzi and the *Ricordi* of Giovanni Morelli.

[56] On the central importance of the family in modern European culture, see Ariès. In contrast to the Florentine family in the Renaissance, the French family was hardly endowed with those sentiments which are associated with the modern ideal of the family; Robert Mandrou, *Introduction à la France moderne (1500-1640): Essai de psychologie historique* (Paris, 1961), pp. 112-20; cf. Eileen Power, "The Menagier's Wife: a Paris Housewife in the Fourteenth Century," in *Medieval People* (London, 1946), pp. 85-110. The English family does not become "child-oriented" until the seventeenth century: Stone, pp. 591 and 670.

fection is the collection of letters of Alessandra Strozzi to and from her sons, which is one of the most appealing social documents of the era.

As the family became more confined and private, it is not surprising that children became a much more central part of family life. Even the utter delight with children in what Ariès calls their "coddling stage" seems to have quickened in the Renaissance, or at least it found more significant cultural expressions. What else can explain the happy, even sensuous fascination with infants in representations of the Christ Child and the playful *putti* which abound in Florentine art of the Quattrocento? In a society in which a greater portion of life was centered in the home, is it surprising that domestic scenes and interior settings play such a prominent part in that art? And is it going too far to suggest that the numerous representations of the Holy Family, one of the most popular themes of the time, arose from a conscious effort to apotheosize the child-oriented family?

One might suspect that the fragmentation of the extended family and the quickening of familial sentiments within the privacy of the household would weaken the very concept of the family as a more extended social organization, as a cognate group including all descendants of a common ancestor. It is not unusual in the history of a social institution, however, that precisely at a time when it is undergoing a decline and can no longer be taken for granted, a concern for it becomes more conscious and explicit, especially on the part of those who feel they have been left stranded behind by its demise. There are remarks by Alberti, for instance, in which he reveals a good deal of nostalgia for a kind of extensive familial sociability which he never really knew himself, and it was probably a similar sentiment which explains the keen consciousness of the family in some of the diaries and *ricordi* of the same period.[57] One would expect such an

[57] Alberti's ideas have been related to his own family circumstances

attitude especially from men whose families had known better times.

On the other hand, to anyone who approaches the study of Florentine family records with the usual assumption that Florentine society was based on a well-developed familial structure, it comes as a surprise that the sense of the family apart from its domestic aspect cannot, in fact, be taken for granted. In this respect the so-called "family" *ricordi* of the late fourteenth and fifteenth centuries are quite different from an earlier family chronicle like that of Donato Velluti. The expansive sociability of the communal family is revealed in Velluti's masterful genealogical methodology. He writes in the most impressive detail of all three brothers of his great-grand-father and of their descendants to his own day (three genera-tions beyond); and the wealth of factual material is handled systematically in a logical genealogical order. In contrast, the numerous *ricordi* of the later fourteenth and fifteenth cen-turies are much less articulate of the family's sense of itself. They are for the most part collections of whatever miscel-laneous information was available concerning individual members of the family, and they lack genealogical precision. Very few of them, in fact, show their authors to be interested in relations beyond their most immediate families. Further-more, to the extent that these *ricordi* are exhortations to the strengthening of familial sentiments, their tone is more didactic in general moral terms than adulatory of a specific family tradition. They certainly do not impress one with con-

---

by Sapori, "La famiglia . . . degli Alberti," pp. 1010-11. When Alberti talks of his family forming a republic in which "ogni cosa era fra loro comune e quasi propria, sì ad uso, sì a governo e mantenimento" he is engaging in wishful thinking. Likewise, when Foligno di Conte de' Medici opened his *ricordanze* in 1373 with a concern for conserving his family's status and property, he is looking back over a consider-able decline in his personal fortune; Brucker, "The Medici . . . ," p. 1. The same can be said of Giovanni Morelli, who had suffered not only from financial misfortunes but also from some unhappy family experiences.

cern for the family in a larger sense, either as an extended social group or as an historical tradition.

If with the transformation from the extended to the nuclear family the family lost its social dimension, it also lost something of its historical dimension. The family's memory image of itself became exceedingly vague if, indeed, it was not in some cases shattered altogether. Hence in the Renaissance a family's knowledge of even its most immediate history is often not impressive. After Velluti probably the most remarkable genealogical compilation of the mid-fourteenth century was that of Lapo da Castiglionchio, but by his own admission the task was not an easy one.[58] Giovanni Morelli a generation later did not do badly in pursuing his genealogy back to the twelfth century, but his information, derived mostly from a few old notarial documents, was very sketchy; he shows little interest in collateral lines and indeed confesses that he did not even know very much about the families of his own first cousins. Alberti, for all his nostalgic longing for the old sociability, seems not to know very much about his forebears, despite their preëminence in the financial life of the city just two generations earlier. In the early sixteenth century when Francesco Guicciardini and Lorenzo Strozzi wrote about their families, neither could push his historical record much before the end of the fourteenth century, although both houses had produced distinguished citizens throughout that century. Guicciardini frankly acknowledged that despite considerable research he had no information about his family until it had gained wealth and political status in the very late fourteenth century with Messer Luigi. When Paolo Velluti between 1555 and 1560 wrote an addition to his great-great-great-grandfather's chronicle, he was hard put to fill in the gap of three generations between Donato and his own father,

[58] "E se io padre a te figliuolo anzi la mia morte non avessi dato a te questa informazione la quale ho per spazio di tempo ricerca, forse non lo avresti mai saputo"; *Epistola* (Bologna, 1753), p. 52.

and the source of most of his information was an oral rather than a written tradition. The historical record of family documents appears to be no more impressive for the other Florentine families who in the course of the sixteenth century began to compile genealogical *spogli*. Indeed, as today, the most important genealogical source in the sixteenth century was the public rather than the private record.

It was precisely the desire to sharpen the historical image of the family which marks an important development in the idea of the family during the Renaissance. In other societies, including our own, the fragmentation of the family as a social institution has led to the loss of a sense of lineage.[59] In Renaissance Florence, on the contrary, the concept of the family as a cognate group, now that it was disembodied from any kind of social reality, was not abandoned altogether but was recast in a different and more nebulous form by which it came to represent an ideal rather than a fact of social life. The concept acquired a broad historical dimension and came more and more to mean a lineage, or a dynasty, which informed members of the group with a keen sense of a very particular and personal tradition of values. As an idea in the minds of men this is an all-too familiar theme in Florentine civilization of the Renaissance, and it figures prominently in much of the historical and moral literature of the period. Along with the state, the family represented a focus of men's ideological commitment and service. Guicciardini is quite explicit on its importance:

I desire two things in the world more than anything else: one, the perpetual exaltation of this city and of its liberty; the other, the glory of our house not only as long as I live but in perpetuity. May it please God to conserve and enhance both.[60]

[59] This is Ariès' explanation of the decline of the practice of primogeniture in northern Europe beginning in the later eighteenth century, when the family was becoming more cohesive and domestic as an organization; pp. 371-73.

[60] "Desidero due cose al mondo piú che alcuna altra: l'una la

Private Wealth

The interest in lineage was one aspect of the awakened historical consciousness which characterizes the Florentine mentality in the Renaissance. Just as the state has an historical continuity, so also the family; and its historical traditions, like history of any kind, can form a permanent record, one in which it is possible for the individual's role to be written. By enhancing the historical consciouness of the family and at the same time injecting himself into its history, a man could hope to achieve a kind of immortality for himself. Alberti, who like Guicciardini saw no higher duty than public service and dedication to one's family, stresses how a man thereby achieves for himself the highest glory, the greatest fame, and above all, immortality:

No one will enjoy higher and firmer glory than he who will have dedicated himself to increase the fame and memory of his fatherland, its citizens, and his family. He alone will merit having his name considered by his descendants to be worthy of praise, famous and immortal.[61]

Although he could not find glory on the battlefield and in heroic exploits as could the feudal nobleman, the Florentine merchant-patrician who had ventured alone into the world and wrested from it his fortune was not without his ambitions for the perpetuation of his name. This explains not only a good deal of art patronage by these men, especially of architectural and sculptural monuments, but also the almost obsessive concern for the family which is one of the characteristics of the Renaissance personality, true no less of the

esaltazione perpetua di questa citta e della libertá sua; l'altra la gloria di casa nostra, non solo vivendo io, ma in perpetuo. A Dio piaccia conservare e accrescere l'una e l'altra." (F. Guicciardini, "Memorie . . . ," p. 3.)

[61] "Niuno sarà più in alta et più ferma et salda gloria, che costui el quale arà sé stesso dedicato ad augmentare con fama et memoria la patria sua, e cittadini, et la famiglia sua. Costui solo meriterà avere il nome suo appresso de' nipoti suoi pien di lode, famoso et immortale. . . ." (Della famiglia, p. 39. Cf. Besta, pp. 30-31.)

patrician of Florence than of the princes of the north Italian courts.[62] It is clear in the case of Filippo Strozzi *il vecchio* that his sense of the family was dynastic: the family he had in mind was not the communal clan; it was the family which issued from him, which enjoyed his wealth and his monuments, and which was to perpetuate and enhance his fame.

In the early sixteenth century Guicciardini and Strozzi wrote a very different kind of family memoir from the *ricordi* of earlier generations, and that difference points up the more self-conscious awareness of lineage men had at a time when relationship had ceased to be a principle of social organization beyond the household. Guicciardini's *Memorie di famiglia* is a systematic historical account of his own direct line of descent,[63] and Strozzi's *Vite* is a collection of literary portraits of illustrious members of his family; but the difference from earlier works is more than one of literary form. For these men the family was not primarily a social institution representing an associative way of life but something much less tangible. It was an ideal which had emerged from a tradition of prestige established by illustrious men of the family. It found its expression in monuments to the fame of its members, in a greater awareness of its history, and in the sense of honor and pride which nourished succeeding generations with a standard of personal comportment. The family no longer rep-

---

[62] The excessive concern for the family has been commented on by Ady, "Morals and Manners . . . ," pp. 182-86. Whereas both Palmieri and Alberti favor moderation in expenditures for operation of the household, they approve of liberality and magnificence in those private expenditures which at the same time serve a public function. Contrast the advice of an anonymous fourteenth century Florentine to avoid above all "tener grande stato" ("Consigli sulla mercatura di un anonimo trecentista," p. 118) or that of Giovanni Morelli "non ti iscoprire nelle ispese . . . né con parente né con amico né col compagno" (p. 251).

[63] For the historical method of Guicciardini, see Nicolai Rubinstein, "The 'storie fiorentine' and the 'memorie di famiglia' by Francesco Guicciardini," *Rinascimento*, IV (1953), 171-225. Guicciardini's genealogical method is significantly deficient, for he is interested only in his own direct line from Messer Luigi and not in collateral lines from the same source.

resented a real association of relatives—not necessarily even an informal one, held together by bonds of affection. It was elevated to a much more idealistic realm as men began to intellectualize their sense of lineage into a concept of nobility, dignity, wealth, status or any other such nebulous ideal which they wished to attribute to their particular family tradition.

The beginning of interest in genealogy in the sixteenth century is itself a significant aspect of this awakened interest in lineage and the appreciation of family tradition. With the generation of Lorenzo Strozzi and Francesco Guicciardini, a lively interest developed in genealogical compilations which, unlike theirs, never took narrative form. Unlike the earlier *ricordi*, however, these are not just running records of the vital statistics of one man's family, but compilations of all kinds of genealogical information, and underlying them is a definite sense of the family as an historical rather than a social entity. A Buondelmonti, for instance, assembled a vast collection of notes on his family consisting of descriptive inventories of family documents then extant, descriptions of family tombs, chapels and other monuments, and extracts from various sources concerning the family; and the whole is supplied with a summary of contents and an organized index of names.[64] One of the Pitti did research in the communal archives, making a list (with references) of members of his family found in various collections of official documents.[65] This attitude toward family history, inspiring extensive and thorough research in public as well as private records and insisting on systematic organization of the vast quantity of material collected, is characteristic of amateur genealogy in the sixteenth century in contrast to the *ricordi* of an earlier era; and in compilations like those of Buondelmonti and Pitti one can sense the appreciation of a genuine genealogical

[64] "Quaderni di Memorie del Buondelmonti," ASF, *Aquisti e doni*, 186, 2.
[65] "Notizie della Famiglia de Pitti," *ibid.*, 320 A, No. 2.

methodology.[66] It is in fact with what we might call the dynastic stage of family history that the history of Florentine genealogy really begins (and it is worth emphasizing again that men at this time were not much better off than we are today in trying to uncover the record of their own historical past).[67]

This dynastic sense of the family took more concrete form than the mere expression of interest in family history and traditions. It led to a new attitude toward property, for one means of buttressing a family tradition against the ravages of time and hence of assuring a dynast of his position in history was to endow the family with grand and noble possessions. This meant not only monuments strictly speaking, but also permanent living monuments associated with the successive generations of the family—specifically, a family palace and certain other prestige properties, especially those somehow associated with the family. In the sixteenth century property slowly came to be regarded as an inalienable possession of the family; and although property may not have been held in common, there is an increasing concern that certain real estate remain in the family's possession. This is particularly true of great family palaces, which symbolized the status of the family. Wills, like the will of the elder Filippo Strozzi, show considerable concern with the inheritance of property and elaborate the precise line of descent, taking into consideration all possibilities; whereas earlier, property is left simply to "universal heirs." From prestige properties men came to

[66] This new approach inspired the *Discorso di Monsignore D. Vincenzio Borghini intorno al modo di far gli alberi delle famiglie nobili fiorentine* (Florence, 1821; originally written in the late sixteenth century), which opens with the recognition that "la via del trovare l'origine con le descendenze continuate, e come corre l'uso del dire, far albero delle famiglie nostre, come e' sia da ricercare troppo indietro, ci riesce a questi tempi tanto difficile, e impedita, che per poco si può dire chiusa affatto."

[67] Cf. Martines, *The Social World . . .* , pp. 56-57, who sees this keen interest in genealogy developing a century earlier.

apply fideicommissa to all real estate. The fideicommissum, which in Italy goes back to at least the twelfth century, was in its original form a restriction making property inalienable within the family, but it did not prevent division of property among heirs nor did it determine a particular order of succession.[68] It was only later, in the sixteenth century, precisely when the Florentine patriciate was becoming infused with dynastic ambitions, that the fideicommissum became a system of entail designed to keep all property indivisible as well as making it inalienable by fixing an order of succession.[69] Within the next two centuries the practice became so widespread that in the eighteenth century, when perhaps three-fourths of the land in Tuscany was inalienable,[70] enlightened legislation was formulated to restrict the use of fideicommissa and rectify the injustices inherent in the practice.[71]

The sense of the family not as an association of relations but as a tradition of prestige and property carried on by successive generations is a dynastic concept with obvious aristocratic overtones. In a society with no feudal tradition of hierarchical organization, one in which there was no clearly defined elitist code of behavior, and one in which the political traditions were more republican than aristocratic, the usual elements of a concept of aristocracy were lacking. Family, however—or more properly speaking, dynasty or lineage (since we are not concerned with a social institution but a social ideal)—was a possible term of social distinction for a patriciate now seeking to define itself as an elite. Family, in fact, became the principal criterion for social nobility in Florence, and the society's conscious effort to establish this

[68] On fideicommissa, see: Enrico Besta, *Le successioni nella storia del diritto italiano* (Milan, 1935), pp. 159-64; and Antonio Pertile, *Storia del diritto italiano* (6 vols.; Turin, 1896-1903), IV, 151-63.

[69] Pertile suggests that this practice came from Spanish influences; IV, 152-53.

[70] Poggi, II, 223-24.

[71] Antonio Panella, *Storia di Firenze* (Florence, 1949), p. 273.

is manifest not only in the production of genealogical works for specific families but also in those works which take a collective view of the city's leading families. Such are the well-known *prioristi*, for example, which become particularly numerous beginning with the sixteenth century. These are vast rosters of the more prominent officeholders throughout the city's history, interspersed with all kinds of historical information. Many are elaborately decorated with family coats of arms and contain a wealth of genealogical information; and it is clear that their purpose was primarily to establish a historical claim for the prominence of the city's leading families. And it is at the very end of the century that the first general treatments of the Florentine aristocracy appear, explicitly defining it in terms of familial traditions and designed to establish the right of the great patrician families to rank with the aristocracy of feudal Europe.[72]

The transformation of the upper classes in Florence into a more clearly defined and cohesive elite which increasingly identified itself with the aristocracy of northern Europe is one of the most intriguing social phenomena of the later Renaissance. During the Renaissance the Florentine patrician had lived in a relatively individualistic society; once uprooted from his old corporate loyalties he had been flung into an atomistic society and thrown very much on his own resources. In an economy based on capitalistic enterprise, wealth remained fluid; and in a state which was nominally a republic, political power was often very tenuous. Consequently, the Florentine patriciate was an amorphous elite without the certainty of status and continuity enjoyed by other patriciates of the era. The Medici regime in the fifteenth century had temporarily buttressed their political and social sta-

[72] For these works, see note 32 above. Michelangelo's obsession with the family, his insistence on its antiquity and nobility, his preoccupation with its status and wealth, has to be regarded in this context; see Giorgio Spini, "Politicità di Michelangelo," *Rivista storica italiana*, LXXVI (1964), 557-600.

tus, but the republican threat in the aftermath of Lorenzo's death confronted them with the frightening realization that their status was vaguely defined, however firm its foundations. Men at the time must have felt a pressing psychological need to distinguish themselves conspicuously from the masses and legitimize their status. This crisis of identity reveals itself clearly enough in their lively interest in political ideas at a time when the state was undergoing severe constitutional agonies in the interim between the death of Lorenzo and the final establishment of the Medicean duchy. Florentines had before them, after all, what must have been the enviable examples of the other leading mercantile oligarchies, Venice and Genoa, where the ruling classes were clearly defined. In Venice the aristocracy had long had legal status; and in Genoa, where there had always been a feudal aristocracy along with the urban patriciate, it was precisely at this time, in 1528, that there was a constitutional formulation of the definition and identification of a more comprehensive nobility.[73] Furthermore, the Florentine world view must have responded to the sudden and dramatic intrusion of northern Europe and its ideological baggage into Renaissance Italy, so that the focus of their social ambitions shifted to a clearly defined aristocracy on the feudal model. Thus one of the most fundamental laws of social behavior of the northern bourgeoisie came into play in Florentine society; and this may partly explain why for the first time in the city's history men who lived abroad, like the Gondi, the Strozzi, and the Capponi, finally found feudal aristocracy attractive enough to desert their native land for it. To be sure, the tendency toward aristocracy within Florence was accelerated by the establishment of the ducal government and the creation of a court nobility; moreover, with the contraction of the Florentine economy and the closing of investment outlets later in the century, land

[73] See Mario Nicora, "La nobilità genovese dal 1528 al 1700," *Miscellanea storica ligure*, II (Milan, 1961), 219-310.

became increasingly more important in constituting wealth, and landed possessions naturally bred economic conservatism and strengthened family cohesion. Nevertheless, the psychological orientation of the Florentine patriciate toward aristocratic modes of behavior preceded these political and economic changes in the Florentine world. More than any socioeconomic or political factor, it was the dynastic sense of the family which established the first equation between bourgeois patriciate and aristocracy. They sought the terms of their definition as an elite in notions of the family, and by establishing the prestige of their family traditions and cultivating a sense of dynastic pride they were able to reconfirm their elite status.[74] It was in their attitudes about the family, not in their economic behavior and not in their political ideas, that the Florentine patriciate first revealed an aristocratic mentality.

[74] Cf. Ariès, pp. 414-15.

Appendices

APPENDIX I

ACCOUNT BOOKS OF THE

DESCENDANTS OF

SIMONE DI FILIPPO STROZZI

A. Simone di Filippo

    1. *Debitori e creditori*
       a. 1395-1409: CS-v, 2
       b. 1410-1413: CS-v, 5
       c. 1420-1424: CS-v, 8

    2. Miscellaneous personal accounts
       a. *Quaderno* of farm accounts, 1416-1421: CS-v, 7
       b. Book of accounts kept by Simone for Andrea di Messer Antonio di Niccolò Ferrantini, 1410-1418: CS-v, 6

    3. Two books of his administration as treasurer (*camarlingo*) at Arezzo, 1409-1410: CS-v, 3 and 4

B. Matteo di Simone

    1. *Debitori e creditori*, 1424-1434: CS-v, 10 and 11
    2. *Ricordanze*, 1424-1434: CS-v, 12

C. Alessandra, widow of Matteo di Simone: *debitori e creditori*, 1453-1473: CS-v, 15

D. Lorenzo di Matteo and his descendants

    1. Lorenzo
       a. *Giornale e ricordi*, 1471-1485: CS-v, 23
       b. Book of his estate, 1479-1480: CS-iv, 357

    2. Matteo di Lorenzo: *ricordi*, 1491-1547: CS-iii, 215

3. Alessandro di Matteo: *debitori e creditori*, 1520-
   1540: CS-IV, 359 and 360

E. Filippo di Matteo

   1. Company books
      a. Naples
         (1) *Ricordanze* (records of exchange transac-
             tions, bills of exchange, commissions, notes,
             merchandise)
             (a) 1466-1467: CS-V, 18
             (b) 1470-1482: CS-V, 19, 20, 24, 25, 28,
                 29, 31, 33, 34, 37, 38
             (c) 1484-1489: CS-V, 43, 46, 47, 48
         (2) *Giornali*
             (a) 1472-1473: CS-V, 27
             (b) 1475-1476: CS-V, 32
         (3) *Libro segreto*, 1479-1484: CS-V, 35
      b. Florence
         (1) *Ricordanze*
             (a) 1472-1477: CS-V, 26, 30
             (b) 1483-1489: CS-V, 40, 45
         (2) *Debitori e creditori*
             (a) 1480-1483: CS-V, 36 (after 1483 this
                 book becomes the main ledger for the
                 businesses up to 1491)
             (b) 1486-1491: CS-V, 44, 51
      c. Balances from the companies in Naples (both the
         fondaco and the *banco*) and Florence, 1484-1486:
         CS-V, 42
   2. Personal accounts
      a. *Debitori e creditori*, 1471-1490: CS-V, 22, 41
      b. Accounts of building expenses
         (1) Villa at Santuccio, 1482-1485: CS-V, 39
         (2) Villa at Maglio, 1486-1487: CS-IV, 358

(3) Hermitage at Lecceto, 1481-1482: CS-v, 1768

(4) Palace in Florence, 1489-1548: CS-v, 49, 57, 62-64, 104

   c. Miscellaneous

     (1) *Dare e avere*, 1466-1471: CS-v, 17

     (2) *Giornale*, 1489-1490: CS-v, 50

     (3) *Quaderno* of estate at Santuccio, 1470-1477: CS-v, 21

F. Selvaggia, widow of Filippo, and his estate

  1. Personal estate

    a. *Debitori e creditori*, 1491-1524: CS-v, 55, 60, 61

    b. *Memoriale* regarding real estate, 1491-1498: CS-v, 56

  2. Accounts of the heirs of Filippo, including Alfonso

    a. *Debitori e creditori*, 1491-1505: CS-v, 65, 67 (accounts are incomplete in both books; partial copies exist in CS-v, 58, 66)

    b. *Ricordanze*, 1492-1516: CS-v, 59

  3. Book of Lorenzo and Filippo, with inventories, *ricordi* and accounts, 1491-1500: CS-v, 54

G. Filippo and Lorenzo di Filippo

  1. Accounts of expenses of Filippo's mission to the French king, 1515: CS-v, 91

  2. Business records

    a. Wool company: *giornale e ricordanze*, 1502-1508: CS-v, 89

    b. *Battiloro* company: *giornale e ricordanze*, 1519-1524: CS-v, 100

    c. Company in Rome

     (1) *Giornale e ricordanze*, 1521-1523: CS-v, 101

     (2) *Quaderno* of exchanges, 1518-1519: CS-v, 98

d. Company in Florence
  (1) *Debitori e creditori,* 1510-1518: CS-v, 92
  (2) *Ricordanze,* 1510-1521: CS-v, 93, 99
  (3) *Entrata e uscita,* 1521-1522: CS-v, 102
3. Joint accounts of the brothers
  a. *Giornale,* 1506-1511: CS-v, 90
  b. *Debitori e creditori, ricordi,* 1515-1527: CS-v, 96
  c. *Giornali* regarding real estate
    (1) 1515-1521: CS-v, 97
    (2) 1515-1526: CS-v, 103

H. Lorenzo di Filippo di Matteo and his heirs
  1. *Debitori e creditori,* 1501-1549: CS-v, 88, 94, 106, 108
  2. *Giornali, ricordanze,* 1501-1549: CS-v, 87, 95, 105, 109
  3. Real estate accounts
    a. General accounts, 1543-1552: CS-v, 111, 113, 115
    b. *Giornali, ricordanze,* 1539-1552: CS-v, 110, 112, 114, 116
    c. *Entrata e uscita,* 1533: CS-v, 107
    d. *Decimario* of Lorenzo and his heirs, 1498-1698: CS-v, 742
  4. Lorenzo's sons
    a. Palla: real estate accounts: CS-v, 133-37
    b. Giambattista: real estate accounts: CS-v, 126-32

APPENDIX II

ACCOUNT BOOKS OF

THE GUICCIARDINI

A. Piero di Ghino: general administration, 1344-1366: AG, Libro 1

B. Luigi di Piero di Ghino: general administration, 1369-1404: AG, Libro 2

C. Piero di Jacopo di Piero di Luigi di Piero di Ghino

    1. Business accounts
        a. *Debitori e creditori*, 1497: AG, Libro 6
        b. Cash book 1497-1502: AG, Libro 5
        c. Shop books, 1512-1516: AG, Libri 7 and 8
        d. Two *quadernucci*: AG, Libri 4 and 9
    2. Book of possessions, 1495-1504: AG, Libro 3

D. Sons of Piero di Jacopo

    1. Jacopo
        a. *Debitori e creditori*, 1503-1530: AG, Libri 12-15
        b. Business accounts
            (1) Silk companies, *debitori e creditori*, 1512-1542: AG, Libri 16-19
           (2) Miscellaneous commercial accounts: AG, Libri 20, 24-27, 31, 32, 35
           (3) Letter books: AG, Libri 33 (1521-1527), 34 (1534-1541), 36 (1542-1543); see also AG, Filze LI and LIV for additional commercial correspondence
        c. Miscellaneous
           (1) *Entrata e uscita*: AG, Libri 28-30

(2) Farm books: AG, Libri 21-23

(3) Accounts of widow and her estate: AG, Libri 37-42

  d. Sons of Jacopo

    (1) Raffaello

      (a) *Debitori e creditori*, 1553-1591: AG, 51-53

      (b) Letters from Antwerp and Ferrara: AG, Filza LIV

    (2) Agnolo

      (a) *Debitori e creditori*, 1540-1567: AG, Libri 55 and 56

      (b) *Debitori e creditori*, of widow, 1567-1579: AG, Libri 57 and 58

      (c) Books of children, 1571-1579: AG, Libri 59 and 60

    (3) Property acquisitions of Jacopo and his heirs in the sixteenth century: AG, Filza XXVII, No. 35

2. Francesco: *debitori e creditori, ricordanze,* 1527-1529: AG, Libro 11

3. Bongianni

  a. *Libro di conti,* 1531-1549: AG, Filza XXVII, No. 22

  b. *Debitori e creditori,* of his heirs, 1549-1551: AG, Libro 50

4. Girolamo

  a. Commercial book of *debitori e creditori,* 1527-1530: AG, Libro 10

  b. Agnolo di Girolamo

    (1) *Debitori e creditori*: AG, Libri 54 (1558-1564) and 43 (1568-1574)

    (2) Miscellaneous books; AG, Libri 44, 45, 47-49

(3) "Ristretto di memorie di beni stabili . . . ,"
1576: AG, Filza xxvii, No. 47

c. Heirs of Agnolo di Girolamo: see AG, Libri 46
and 79-151, and ASF, *Miscellanea repubblicana*,
Buste L-LIX

5. Family real estate holdings: AG, "Decimario degli ill.
Signori conti Guicciardini"

APPENDIX III

ACCOUNT BOOKS OF THE GONDI

A. Antonio di Leonardo di Leonardo: book of *debitori e creditori* of his sons and heirs, 1486-1514: A Gondi, 32 and 33

B. Sons of Antonio di Leonardo di Leonardo: capital accounts
   1. *Debitori e creditori*, 1498-1506: A Gondi, 34
   2. *Battiloro* company, *debitori e creditori*, 1506-1513: A Gondi, 1 and 2
   3. Books "dello scrittoio," *debitori e creditori*, 1516-1533: A Gondi, 3 and 4
   4. Lyons company, *debitori e creditori*, 1516-1523: A Gondi, 7-9

C. Alessandro d'Antonio di Leonardo
   1. *Debitori e creditori*, 1486-1519: A Gondi, 35-37
   2. Secondary books: A Gondi, 5, 6 and 38

D. Bernardo d'Antonio di Leonardo
   1. *Debitori e creditori*: A Gondi, 41 (1503-1511) and 10 (1538-1539)
   2. Miscellaneous books
      a. Book of possessions, 1506-1511: A Gondi, 42
      b. Cash book, 1538-1539: A Gondi, 43
   3. Book of his estate, 1539-1540: A Gondi, 44

E. Antonio d'Antonio di Leonardo: books of possessions, 1523-1545: A Gondi, 39 and 40

APPENDIX IV

ACCOUNT BOOKS OF THE CAPPONI

A. Gino di Neri; *debitori e creditori*, 1476-1487: AC (BNF), 140

B. Sons of Gino di Neri

    1. Joint investments of the five brothers, 1485-1516: AC (BNF), 2

    2. Cappone: *debitori e creditori*, 1475-1521: AC (BNF), 1

    3. Neri and Alessandro: *debitori e creditori* of Lyons, 1500-1544: AC (ASF), 55

    4. Piero: ledger of personal accounts, 1466-75: BNF, Carte Ginori-Conti, 18. This book, in a collection which has only recently been made public, was seen too late to be discussed in the text; but although it is of considerable interest for its detailed record of Piero's personal affairs, it adds nothing to our knowledge of the Capponi fortune.

C. Niccolò and Giuliano di Piero di Gino di Neri: *debitori e creditori*

    1. 1496-1511: AC (BNF), 3

    2. 1511-1531: AC (ASF), 142

    3. 1530-1563: AC (BNF), 8 (incomplete accounts of Giuliano and heirs of Niccolò)

D. Giuliano di Piero di Gino di Neri

    1. Personal accounts

        a. *Debitori e creditori*

            (1) 1532-1544: AC (BNF), 9

            (2) 1553-1568: AC (BNF), 21

b. File of balances, 1548-1631: AC (BNF), 117

c. *Decimarii* of Giuliano and heirs: AC (ASF), 60-62, 64

d. *Cassette* of miscellaneous papers: AC (ASF), 68

2. *Battiloro* company: AC (BNF), 4 (1516), 5 (1520), 6 (1527), 10 (1533), 13 (1539)

3. Silk company: AC (BNF), 7 (1530), 12 (1535), 14 (1540), 16 (1548), 24 (1556), 30 (1561), 33 (1565)

4. Bank in name of son, Luigi, 1535-84 (incomplete series); AC (BNF), 11, 15, 18, 20, 23, 25, 28, 34, 39, 40, 42, 43, 44, 47, 48, 59, 60, 67, 75, 79 (and the series continues after Luigi's death in 1584)

APPENDIX V

FLUCTUATIONS OF PRICES AND MONETARY

VALUES IN THE RENAISSANCE

In surveying private fortunes over a century and a half and assessing their vicissitudes with some precision, it is necessary to consider fluctuations of prices and money values during the same period. Price studies for Italy are not very numerous, and only two have direct relevance to Florence. Both are studies of the "price revolution" in the mid- and later sixteenth century, one for Florence, by Giuseppe Parenti, and the other for Borgo San Sepolcro and Arezzo in Florentine territory, by Amintore Fanfani.[1] Both concur that the revolution did not affect the Florentine price of grain until after 1550 and that during the entire first half of the century annual averages of grain prices in Florence remained quite stable, despite, of course, considerable temporary fluctuations owing to seasonal adjustments within the year and to political complications such as the siege in 1529. Parenti shows that the price of grain from 1520 to 1550 averaged between two and two-and-a-half *lire* per *staio*; and Fanfani, pushing his researches back into the fifteenth century, concluded that from 1477 to 1499 the prices in southeast Tuscany were on the whole about the same, between two and three *lire*. Furthermore, the value of silver in the *lira* remained almost constant throughout the period studied.

On the basis of these preliminary researches, it would seem

[1] Giuseppe Parenti, *Prime recherche sulla rivoluzione dei prezzi in Firenze* (Florence, 1939); Amintore Fanfani, *Indagini sulla "rivoluzione dei prezzi"* (Milan, 1940). Cf. Torben Damsholt, "Some Observations on Four Series of Tuscan Corn Prices, 1520-1630," *Scandinavian Economic History Review* (1964), pp. 145-64.

safe to assume that the stability of prices from 1475 to 1550 assures a common denominator in assessing changing values of a family's wealth. Before 1475, there are no price studies, and the number of account books is too small to provide the data for a tentative study. The books of Simone and Matteo Strozzi contain a number of entries which record fluctuations between one and two *lire* in the price of grain bought and sold in the early *Quattrocento*. This suggests that there was only a modest price rise in the course of the century, not enough to invalidate a comparison of face values of fortunes throughout the period.

Whereas grain prices remained relatively stable throughout the period to be studied, providing at least one constant index in comparing values, the value of the gold florin increased steadily in relation to the silver *lira* of local use. In the early *Quattrocento* the florin was worth about four *lire*, but its value rose throughout the century; and between 1500 and 1515 it was stabilized at seven *lire*.[2] In other words, considering also the relative stability of local prices over the same period, the real value of the florin increased by about 75 percent over the period which we shall be studying. This must be kept in mind while plotting the fluctuation of family fortunes, which are always expressed in florins.[3]

[2] See the chart in R. de Roover, *The Medici Bank: Its Organization, Management, Operation, and Decline* (New York, 1948), p. 61. De Roover suggests reasons for this rise on pp. 59-60.

[3] There is no need to go into the complicated problem of Florentine gold currency. Consult Florence Edler, *Glossary of Medieval Terms of Business—Italian Series, 1200-1600* (Cambridge, Mass., 1934), and the brief description in de Roover, *The Rise and Decline* . . . , pp. 31-34. Throughout this study the term florin has been used as a standard unit of account. Only a few of the accounts used here are kept in *fiorini di sugello*, which were eliminated by legislation in 1471, and these values have all been converted to *fiorini larghi*. In 1501 the *fiorino largo di grossi* was replaced by the *fiorino largo d'oro in oro*, which was 19 percent better; and on those tables which compare figures before and after 1501, this revaluation must be kept in mind. Only on Table 25 have figures been converted from the kind of florin used in the source.

LIST OF WORKS CITED

ARCHIVAL SOURCES

1. Archivio di Stato
   Aquisti e doni
   Archivio Capponi
   Archivio Gondi
   Arte del Cambio
   Carte dell'Ancisa
   Carte strozziane
   Catasto
   Manoscritti
   Mercanzia
   Miscellanea repubblicana
   Monte delle Graticole
   Tratte
2. Archivio Guicciardini,
   Florence
3. Biblioteca Nazionale,
   Florence
   Archivio Capponi
   Manoscritti Passerini
4. The Folger Shakespeare
   Library, Washington,
   D.C.
   The Folger Strozzi
   Transcript

PRINTED SOURCES

Acciaioli, Vincenzo. "Vita di Piero di Gino Capponi," *ASI*, IV, Pt. 2 (1853), 13-71.

Alberti, Leon Battista. *I primi tre libri della famiglia.* Ed. F. C. Pellegrini. Florence, 1946.

Cambi, Giovanni, *Istorie.* Vols. XX to XXIII of *Delizie degli eruditi toscani.* Ed. Ildefonso di San Luigi. Florence, 1786.

Certaldo (da), Paolo. *Libro di buoni costumi.* Ed. Alfredo Schiaffini. Florence, 1945.

"Consigli sulla mercatura di un anonimo trecentista." Ed. Gino Corti, *ASI*, CX (1952), 114-19.

Delizie degli eruditi toscani. Ed. Ildefonso di San Luigi. 25 vols. Florence, 1770-89.

Desjardins, Abel, ed. *Négociations diplomatiques de la France avec la Toscane.* 6 vols. Paris, 1859-86.

Guicciardini, Agnolo. *Tre lettere di Agnolo Guicciardini mandate da Cosimo I a Venezia nel 1519.* Florence, 1906.

Guicciardini, Bongianni. "Lettere." Ed. I Del Lungo, *Almanacco dell'amico del contadino,* 1887, 1889-90, 1891, 1892, 1893.

Guicciardini, Francesco. *Ricordanze inedite.* Ed. Paolo Guicciardini. Florence, 1930.

Guicciardini, Francesco. *Scritti autobiografici e rari.* Ed. Roberto Palmarocchi. Bari, 1936.

——. *Selected Works.* Ed. Cecil Grayson; trans. Margaret Grayson. London, 1965.

Guicciardini, Giovanbattista. *Lettere di Giovan Battista Guicciardini a Cosimo e Francesco de' Medici (1559-77).* Ed. Mario Battistini. Brussels-Rome, 1949.

Guicciardini, Isabella. *Lettere di Isabella Guicciardini al marito Luigi, 1535-1542.* Florence, 1883.

Guicciardini, Luigi. *Del Savonarola, ovvero dialogo tra Francesco Zati e Pieradovardo Giachinotti il giorno dopo la battaglia di Gavinana.* Ed. Bono Simonetta. Florence, 1959.

Journal de l'Étoile pour le règne de Henri III (1574-1589). Ed. L.-R. Lefèvre. Paris, 1943.

Landucci, Luca. *A Florentine Diary from 1450 to 1516: Continued by an Anonymous Writer till 1542.* Ed. Iodoco Del Badia; trans. Alice de Rosen Jervis. London, 1927.

Lapo da Castiglionchio. *Epistola.* Bologna, 1753.

Letters and Papers, Foreign and Domestic, 1509-1546. Ed. James Gairdner. 21 vols. London, 1864-1912.

Machiavelli, Niccolò. *Lettere.* Ed. Franco Gaeta. Milan, 1961.

Macinghi negli Strozzi, Alessandra. *Lettere di una gentildonna fiorentina del secolo XV ai figliuoli esuli.* Ed. Cesare Guasti. Florence, 1877.

Masi, Bartolomeo. *Ricordanze.* Ed. Gius. Odoardo Corazzini. Florence, 1906.

Morelli, Giovanni di Pagolo. *Ricordi.* Ed. Vittore Branca. Florence, 1956.

Nardi, Jacopo. *Istorie della città di Firenze.* Ed. Agenore Gelli. Florence, 1888.

Niccolini, G.-B. *Filippo Strozzi, tragedia.* Florence, 1847. Contains Lorenzo Strozzi, "Vita di Filippo Strozzi," and many relevant documents, ed. Pietro Bigazzi.

Niccolini di Camugliano, G. *The Chronicles of a Florentine Family, 1200-1470.* London, 1933.

Raccolta di cronichette antiche. Ed. Domenico Maria Manni. Florence, 1733.

Relazioni degli ambasciatori veneti al senato. Ed. Arnaldo Segarizzi. 3 vols. Bari, 1912-16.

Rerum italicarum scriptores. Ed. Lodovico Antonio Muratori. 25 vols. Mediolani, 1723-51.

List of Works Cited

Rossi, Tribaldo de'. *Ricordanze tratte da un libro originale*. Vol. XXIII of *Delizie degli eruditi toscani*. Ed. Ildefonso di San Luigi. Florence, 1785.

Rucellai, Giovanni. *Il zibaldone quaresimale*. Ed. Alessandro Perosa. London, 1960.

Sanuto, Marino. *I diarii*. 58 vols. Venice, 1879-1902.

Segni, Bernardo. *Storie fiorentine*. 3 vols. Florence, 1835.

———. "Vita di Niccolò Capponi," *Storie fiorentine* (3 vols.; Florence, 1835), III, 219-303.

Strozzi, Lorenzo. *Le vite degli uomini illustri della casa Strozzi*. Florence, 1892.

———. *Vita di Filippo Strozzi il Vecchio scritta da Lorenzo suo figlio*. Eds. Giuseppe Bini and Pietro Bigazzi. Florence, 1851.

Varchi, Benedetto. *Storia fiorentina*. 3 vols. Florence, 1888.

Velluti, Donato. *La cronica domestica di Messer Donato Velluti*. Ed. I. Del Lungo and G. Volpi. Florence, 1914.

Vespasiano da Bisticci, *Vite di uomini illustri del secolo XV*. Eds. Paolo d'Ancona and Erhard Aeschlimann. Milan, 1951.

SECONDARY WORKS

Ady, C. M. "Morals and Manners of the Quattrocento," *Proceedings of the British Academy* (London, 1942), pp. 179-96.

Albertini, Rudolf von. *Das florentinische Staatsbewusstsein im Übergang von der Republik zum Prinzipat*. Bern, 1955.

Ammirato, Scipione. *Delle famiglie nobili fiorentine*. Florence, 1615.

Antonelli Moriani, Margherita. *Giovanni Guicciardini ed un processo politico in Firenze (1431)*. Florence, 1954.

Anzilotti, Antonio. *La crisi costituzionale della Repubblica fiorentina*. Florence, 1912.

Archivio Mediceo avanti il principato. Inventario. 4 vols. Rome, 1951-63.

Ariès, Philippe. *Centuries of Childhood. A Social History of Family Life*. Trans. Robert Baldick. New York, 1962.

Bandini, Angelo Maria. "Vita di Filippo Strozzi," *Magazzeno toscano d'istruzione e di piacere*, II (1755-56), 17-33, 49-66.

Bardi, Alessandro. "Filippo Strozzi (da nuovi documenti)," *ASI*, Ser. V: XIV (1894), 3-78.

Battara, Pietro. "Botteghe e pigioni nella Firenze del '500: un censimento industriale e commerciale all'epoca del granducato mediceo," *ASI*, xcv (1937), II, 3-28.

Becker, Marvin B. *Florence in Transition*. Vol. I: *The Decline of the Commune*. Baltimore, 1967.

———. "Florentine Popular Government (1343-1348)," *Proceedings of the American Philosophical Society*, CVI (1962), 360-82.

———. "Problemi della finanza pubblica fiorentina della seconda metà del Trecento e dei primi del Quattrocento," *ASI*, CXXIII (1965), 433-66.

Bensa, Enrico. *Francesco di Marco Datini*. Milan, 1928.

Berengo, Marino. *Nobili e mercanti nella Lucca del Cinquecento*. Turin, 1965.

Besta, Enrico. *La famiglia nella storia del diritto italiano*. Padua, 1933.

———. *Le successioni nella storia del diritto italiano*. Milan, 1935.

Borghini, Vincenzio. *Discorso di Monsignore D. Vincenzio Borghini intorno al modo di far gli alberi delle famiglie nobili fiorentine*. Florence, 1821.

Braudel, F. and Romano, R. *Navires et marchandise à l'entrée du port de Livorne (1547-1611)*. Paris, 1951.

Brésard, Marc. *Les foires de Lyon aux XVᵉ et XVIᵉ siècles*. Paris, 1914.

Brucker, Gene A. *Florentine Politics and Society, 1343-1378*. Princeton, 1962.

———. "The Medici in the Fourteenth Century," *Speculum*, XXXII (1957), 1-26.

Burckhardt, Jacob. *The Civilization of the Renaissance in Italy*. London, 1951.

Camerani, Sergio. *Bibliografia medicea*. Florence, 1964.

Canestrini, Giuseppe. *La scienza e l'arte di stato*. Florence, 1862.

Capasso, Carlo. *Firenze, Filippo Strozzi, i fuorosciti e la corte pontificia*. Camerino, 1901.

Capponi, Gino. *Storia della repubblica di Firenze*. 3 vols. Florence, 1888.

Carmona, Maurice. "Aspects du capitalisme toscan aux XVIᵉ et XVIIᵉ siècles: les sociétés en commandite à Florence et à Lucques," *Revue d'histoire moderne et contemporaine*, XI (1964), 81-108.

————. "Sull'economia toscana del Cinquecento e del Seicento," *ASI*, cxx (1962), 32-46.

Charpin-Feugerolles, le comte de. *Les florentins à Lyon*. Lyons, 1893.

Cherubini, Giovanni. "Qualche considerazione sulle compagne dell'Italia centro-settentrionale tra l'XI e il XV secolo (in margine alle ricerche di Elio Conti)," *Rivista storica italiana*, LXXIX (1967), 111-57.

Cipolla, Carlo M. "Il declino economico dell'Italia," *Storia dell'economia italiana: saggi di storia economica*, ed. Carlo M. Cipolla (Turin, 1959) I, 605-23.

Clough, Cecil H. "The Archivio Bentivoglio in Ferrara," *Renaissance News*, XVIII (1965), 12-19.

Coleman, D. C. *Sir John Banks, Baronet and Businessman*. Oxford, 1963.

Conti, Elio. *La formazione della struttura agraria moderna nel contado fiorentino*. Vols. I and III. Rome, 1965.

Coornaert, Émile. *Les français et le commerce international à Anvers (fin du XVᵉ-XVIᵉ siècle)*. 2 vols. Paris, 1961.

Corbinelli, Monsieur de. *Histoire généalogique de la maison de Gondi*. 2 vols. Paris, 1705.

Cosenza, Mario Emilio. *Biographical and Bibliographical Dictionary of the Italian Humanists and of the World of Classical Scholarship in Italy, 1300-1800*. Boston, 1962.

Damsholt, Torben. "Some Observations on Four Series of Tuscan Corn Prices, 1520-1630," *Scandinavian Economic History Review* (1964), pp. 145-64.

Davidsohn, Robert. *Forschungen zur Geschichte von Florenz*. 4 vols. Berlin, 1896-1908.

————. *Geschichte von Florenz*. 4 vols. Berlin, 1896-1927.

Davis, James Cushman. *The Decline of the Venetian Nobility as a Ruling Class*. Baltimore, 1962.

Della Torre, Arnaldo. *Storia dell'accademia platonica di Firenze*. Florence, 1902.

Delumeau, Jean, *Vie économique et sociale de Rome dans la seconde moitié du XVIᵉ siècle*. 2 vols. Paris, 1957-59.

de Roover, Florence Edler. "Andrea Banchi, Florentine Silk Manufacturer and Merchant in the Fifteenth Century," *Studies in Medieval and Renaissance History*, III (1966), 223-85.

————. "Early Examples of Marine Insurance," *Journal of Economic History*, V (1945), 172-200.

de Roover, Florence Edler. "Francesco Sassetti and the Downfall of the Medici Banking House." *Bulletin of the Business Historical Society*, XVII (1943), 65-80.

———. "Restitution in Renaissance Florence," *Studi in onore di Armando Sapori* (Milan, 1957), II, 775-89.

de Roover, Raymond, *The Medici Bank: Its Organization, Management, Operations and Decline.* New York, 1948.

———. *The Rise and Decline of the Medici Bank.* Cambridge, Massachusetts, 1963.

———. "A Florentine Firm of Cloth Manufacturers—Management and Organization of a Sixteenth-Century Business," *Speculum*, XVI (1941), 3-30.

———. "Aux origines d'une technique intellectuelle: la formation et l'expansion de la comptabilité à partie double," *Annales d'histoire économique et sociale*, IX (1937), 171-93, 270-98.

———. "Gli antecedenti del Banco Mediceo e l'azienda bancaria di messer Vieri di Cambio de' Medici," *ASI*, CXXIII (1965), 3-13.

———. "La balance commerciale entre les Pays-Bas et l'Italie au quinzième siècle," *Revue Belge de philologie et d'histoire*, XXXVII (1959), 374-86.

———. "The Development of Accounting Prior to Luca Pacioli According to the Account-Books of Medieval Merchants," *Studies in the History of Accounting*, eds. A. C. Littleton and B. S. Yamey (London, 1956), pp. 114-74.

Doucet, Roger. "La banque en France au XVIe siècle," *Revue d'histoire économique et sociale*, XXIX (1951), 115-23.

———. *La banque Capponi à Lyon en 1556.* Lyons, 1939.

———. "Le grand Parti de Lyon au XVIe siècle," *Revue historique*, CLXXI (1933), 473-513; CLXXII (1933), 1-41.

Edler, Florence. *Glossary of Medieval Terms of Business—Italian Series, 1200-1600.* Cambridge, Mass., 1934.

Ehrenberg, Richard. *Capital and Finance in the Age of the Renaissance (A Study of the Fuggers and Their Connections).* Trans. H. M. Lucas. New York, n.d.

Fanfani, Amintore. "Effimera la ripresa economica di Firenze sul finire del secolo XVI?" *Economia e storia*, XII (1965), 344-51.

———. *Indagini sulla "rivoluzione dei prezzi."* Milan, 1940.

———. *Un mercante del Trecento.* Milan, 1935.

Febvre, Lucien. "Ce que peuvent nous apprendre les monographies familiales," *Mélange d'histoire sociale*, I (1942), 31-34.

Ferrieri, Pio. *Rime inedite di un cinquecentista*. Pavia, 1885.

———. *Studi di storia e di critica letteraria*. Milan, 1892.

Ferrai, Luigi Alberto. *Filippo Strozzi, prigioniero degli Spagnuoli*. Padua, 1880.

Fiumi, Enrico. "Fioritura e decadenza dell'economia fiorentina," *ASI*, cxv (1957), 443-510; cxvi (1958), 385-439; cxvii (1959), 427-502.

———. *L'impresa di Lorenzo de' Medici contro Volterra (1472)*. Florence, 1948.

Francastel, P. "Imagination et réalité dans l'architecture civile de '400," *Homage à Lucien Febvre—Éventail de l'histoire vivante*, ii (Paris, 1953), 195-206.

Gandilhon, René. *Politique économique de Louis XI*. Rennes, 1940.

Gilbert, Felix. *Machiavelli and Guicciardini: Politics and History in Sixteenth-Century Florence*. Princeton, 1965.

Gombrich, E. H. "The Early Medici as Patrons of Art," *Italian Renaissance Studies: A Tribute to the Late Cecilia M. Ady*, ed. E. F. Jacob (New York, 1960), pp. 279-311.

Goris, J. A. *Étude sur les colonies marchandes méridionales (Portugais, Espagnols, Italiens) à Anvers de 1488 à 1567*. Louvain, 1925.

Guicciardini, Paolo. *Un parentado fiorentino nei primi del Cinquecento e riflessi di vita umanistica della campagna valdelsana*. Florence, 1940.

———. *Il ritratto vasariano di Luigi Guicciardini*. Florence, 1942.

———, and Emilio, Dori. *Le antiche case ed il palazzo dei Guicciardini in Firenze*. Florence, 1952.

Gutkind, G. S. *Cosimo de' Medici*. New York, 1938.

Heers, Jacques. *Gênes au XVe siècle: activité économique et problèmes sociaux*. Paris, 1961.

———. *Le livre de comptes de Giovanni Piccamiglio, homme d'affaires génois, 1456-1459*. Paris, 1959.

———. *L'occident aux XIVe et XVe siècles: aspects économiques et sociaux*. Paris, 1963.

Hirsch, Rudolf. "Gondi-Medici Business Records in the Lea Library of the University of Pennsylvania," *Renaissance News*, xvi (1963), 11-14.

List of Works Cited

Jones, P. J. "Florentine Families and Florentine Diaries in the Fourteenth Century," *Papers of the British School at Rome*, XXIV (New Series, XI) (1956), 183-205.

Julien de Pommerol, Michel. *Albert de Gondi, Maréchal de Retz*. Geneva, 1953.

Karmin, Otto. *La legge del catasto fiorentino del 1427*. Florence, 1906.

Kominsky, Eugen S. "Peut-on considérer le XIVe et le XVe siècles comme l'époque de la décadence de l'économie européenne?" *Studi in onore di Armando Sapori*, I (Milan, 1957), 553-69.

Kristeller, P. O. *Iter italicum*. Vol. I. London, 1963.

————. *Studies in Renaissance Thought and Letters*. Florence, 1956.

————. *Supplementum Fincinianum*. Florence, 1937.

Lane, Frederic C. *Andrea Barbarigo, Merchant of Venice, 1418-1449*. Baltimore, 1944.

————. "Family Partnerships and Joint Ventures in the Venetian Republic," *The Journal of Economic History*, IV (1944), 178-96.

Lapeyre, Henri. *Une famille de marchands: les Ruiz*. Paris, 1955.

Limongelli, Luigi. *Filippo Strozzi, primo cittadino d'Italia*. Milan, 1963.

Litta, Conte Pompeo (ed.). *Le famiglie celebri italiane*. 15 vols. Milan, 1819-1902.

Lugli, Vittorio. *I trattatisti della famiglia nel Quattrocento*. Bologna-Modena, 1909.

Lupo Gentile, Michele. "Sulla paternità della vita di Niccolò Capponi," *Giornale storico della letteratura italiana*, XLIV (1904), 126-36.

Luzzatto, Gino. *An Economic History of Italy from the Fall of the Roman Empire to the Beginning of the Sixteenth Century*. Trans. P. Jones. New York, 1961.

————. "Les activités économiques du Patriciat vénitien (Xe-XIVe siècle)," *Studi di storia economica veneziana*. (Padua, 1954), pp. 125-65.

Mallett, M. E. "Anglo-Florentine Commercial Relations, 1465-1491," *Economic History Review*, XV (1962), 250-65.

————. "Pisa and Florence in the Fifteenth Century: An Economic Background to the Pisan War," unpublished D. Phil. thesis, Oxford University, 1959.

————. *The Florentine Galleys in the Fifteenth Century*. Oxford, 1967.

Mandrou, Robert. *Introduction à la France moderne (1500-1640): Essai de psychologie historique.* Paris, 1961.

Mansfield, M. *A Family of Decent Folk: 1200-1741.* Florence, 1922.

Mariani, Marisa. "Gino Capponi nella vita politica fiorentina dal 1393 al 1421," *ASI,* cxv (1957), 440-84.

Marks, L. F. "La crisi finanziaria a Firenze dal 1494 al 1502," *ASI,* cxii (1954), 40-72.

————. "The Development of the Institutions of Public Finance at Florence during the Last Sixty Years of the Republic c. 1470-1530," unpublished D. Phil. thesis, Oxford University, 1954.

————. "The Financial Oligarchy in Florence under Lorenzo," *Italian Renaissance Studies: A Tribute to the Late Cecilia M. Ady,* ed. E. F. Jacob (New York, 1960), pp. 123-47.

Martin, Alfred von. *Sociology of the Renaissance.* New York, 1963.

Martines, Lauro. "La famiglia Martelli e un documento sulla vigilia del ritorno dall'esilio di Cosimo de' Medici (1434)," *ASI,* cxvii (1959), 29-43.

————. "Nuovi documenti su Cino Rinuccini e una nota sulle finanze della famiglia Rinuccini," *ASI,* cxix (1961), 77-91.

————. *The Social World of the Florentine Humanists, 1390-1460.* Princeton, 1963.

Masetti-Bencini, Ida. "Neri Capponi: note biografiche tratte da documenti," *Rivista delle biblioteche e degli archivi,* xvi (1905), 91-100, 136-54, 158-74.

————. "Note ed appunti tratti da documenti sulla vita politica di Neri Capponi," *Rivista delle biblioteche e degli archivi,* xx (1909), 15-31, 33-56.

Masi, Gino. "La struttura sociale delle fazioni politiche fiorentine ai tempi di Dante," *Il giornale dantesco,* xxxi, New Series: i (1930), 3-28.

Mecatti, Giuseppe Maria. *Storia genealogica della nobiltà e cittadinanza di Firenze.* Naples, 1754.

Melis, Federigo. *Aspetti della vita economica medievale (studi nell'archivio Datini di Prato).* Vol. i. Siena, 1962.

————. "La formazione dei costi nell'industria laniera alla fine del Trecento," *Economia e storia,* i (1954), 31-60, 150-90.

Mini, Paolo. *Discorso della nobiltà di Firenze, e de Fiorentini.* Florence, 1593.

Mira, Giuseppe. *Vicende economiche di una famiglia italiana dal XIV al XVII secolo*. Milan, 1940.

Mylonas, Alexander George. "Francesco Guicciardini: A Study in the Transition of Florentine and Bolognese Politics, 1530-1534," unpublished Ph.D. thesis, Harvard University, 1960.

Negri, Giulio. *Istoria degli scrittori fiorentini*. Ferrara, 1722.

Niccolai, Franco. "I consorzi nobiliari ed il Comune nell'alta e media Italia," *Rivista di storia del diritto italiano*, XIII (1940), 116-47, 292-342, 397-477.

Nicora, Mario. "La nobiltà genovese dal 1528 al 1700," *Miscellanea storica ligure*, II (Milan, 1961), 219-310.

"Notizie degli archivi toscani," *ASI*, CXIV (1956), 414-40; CXVIII (1960), 359-73.

Ottokar, Nicola. *Il comune di Firenze alla fine del Dugento*. Florence, 1926.

Paatz, Walter and Elizabeth. *Die Kirchen von Florenz*. 6 vols. Frankfurt, 1952-55.

Pagnini della Ventura, G. F. *Della decima e di varie altre gravezze imposte dal comune di Firenze; della moneta e della mercatura de' fiorentini fino al secolo XVI*. 4 vols. Lisbon and Lucca, 1765.

Pampaloni, Guido. *Palazzo Strozzi*. Rome, 1963.

Panella, Antonio. *Storia di Firenze*. Florence, 1949.

Parenti, Giuseppe. *Prime ricerche sulla rivoluzione dei prezzi in Firenze*. Florence, 1939.

Pertile, Antonio. *Storia del diritto italiano*. 6 vols. Turin, 1896-1903.

Peruzzi, S. L. *Storia del commercio e dei banchieri di Firenze in tutto il mondo conosciuto dal 1200 al 1345*. Florence, 1868.

Picot, Émile. *Les italiens en France au XVIe siècle*. Bordeaux, 1902.

Pieri, Piero. *Intorno alla storia dell'arte della seta in Firenze*. Bologna, 1927.

Poggi, Enrico. *Cenni storici delle leggi sull'agricoltura dai tempi romani fino ai nostri*. 2 vols. Florence, 1845-48.

Pontieri, Ernesto. "La giovinezza di Ferrante I d'Aragona," in *Studi in onore di Riccardo Filangieri* (Naples, 1959), I, 531-601.

Power, Eileen. *Medieval People*. London, 1946.

Ramsey, Peter. *John Isham, Mercer and Merchant Adventurer:*

List of Works Cited

Two Account Books of a London Merchant in the Reign of Elizabeth I. Durham, 1962.

———. "Some Tudor Merchants' Accounts," *Studies in the History of Accounting.* eds. A. C. Littleton and B. S. Yamey (London, 1956), pp. 185-201.

Ranke, Leopold von. *Sämmtliche Werke.* 54 vols. Leipzig, 1875-1900.

Renouard, Yves. *Les relations des papes d'Avignon et des compagnies commerciales et bancaires de 1316 à 1378.* Paris, 1941.

Reumont, Alfred von. *Beiträge zur italienischen Geschichte.* 6 vols. Berlin, 1853-57.

———. *Lorenzo de' Medici the Magnificent.* Trans. Robert Harrison. 2 vols. London, 1876.

Ridolfi, Roberto. *Gli archivi delle famiglie fiorentine.* Florence, 1934.

———. *Vita di Francesco Guicciardini.* Florence, 1960.

———. "Francesco Guicciardini e Cosimo I," *ASI*, CXXII (1964), 567-606.

Rodolico Niccolò. "Il ritorno alla terra nella storia degli italiani," *Atti della R. Accademia dei Georgofili di Firenze*, Ser. V: XXX (1933), 323-40.

Romano, R. "À Florence au XVIIe siècle, industries textiles et conjoncture," *Annales: économies—sociétés—civilisations.* VII (1952), 508-12.

Roon-Bassermann, Elizabeth von. "Die Rossi von Oltarno: ein Beitrag zur mittelalterlichen Sozial- und Wirtschaftsgeschichte von Florenz," *Vierteljahrschrift für Sozial- und Wirtschaftsgeschichte*, LI (1964), 235-48.

Roth, Cecil. *The Last Florentine Republic.* London, 1925.

Rubinstein, Nicolai. *The Government of Florence under the Medici, 1434-1494.* London, 1966.

———. "The 'storie fiorentine' and the 'memorie di famiglia' by Francesco Guicciardini," *Rinascimento*, IV (1953), 171-225.

Rubinstein, Nicolai, and Ricci, Pier Giorgio, eds. *Checklist of Letters of Lorenzo de' Medici.* Florence, 1964.

Ruiz Martín, F. *Lettres marchandes échangées entre Florence et Medina del Campo.* Paris, 1965.

Rutenburg, Victor. "La compagnia Uzzano (su documenti dell'archivio di Leningrado)," *Studi in onore di Armando Sapori*, I (Milan, 1957), 689-706.

Salvemini, Gaetano. *La dignità cavalleresca nel comune di Firenze.* Published with *Magnati e popolani in Firenze dal 1280 al 1295.* Turin, 1960.

Santini, P. "Società delle torri in Firenze," *ASI*, Ser. IV: XX (1887), 25-58, 178-204.

Sapori, Armando. *Le marchand italien au moyen âge.* Paris, 1952.

————. *Studi di storia economica, secoli XIII-XIV-XV.* 2 vols. Florence, 1955.

————. "Luci ed ombre sui mercanti fiorentini del Rinascimento," *Nuova antologia*, XCIII (1958) 19-40.

Sereno, Renzo. "The *Ricordi* of Gino di Neri Capponi," *American Political Science Review*, LII (1958), 1118-22.

Sieveking, Heinrich. "Aus genueser Rechnungs- und Steuerbüchern," *Sitzungsberichte der Kais. Akademie der Wissenschaften in Wien. Philosophisch-historische Klasse*, 162 (Vienna, 1908-9).

Silva, José-Gentile da. "Aux XVIIᵉ siècle: la stratégie du capital florentin," *Annales: économies—sociétés—civilisations*, XIX (1964), 480-91.

Silva, José-Gentile da, and Corti, Gino. "Note sur la production de la soie à Florence au XVᵉ siècle," *Annales: économies—sociétés—civilisations*, XXX (1965), 309-11.

Spini, Giorgio. "Politicità di Michelangelo," *Rivista storica italiana*, LXXVI (1964), 557-600.

Spreti, Vittorio, ed. *Enciclopedia storico-nobiliare italiana.* 6 vols. Milan, 1928-32.

Stahl, Berthold. *Adel und Volk im Florentiner Dugento.* Cologne, 1965.

Stone, Lawrence. *The Crisis of the Aristocracy, 1558-1641.* Oxford, 1965.

Tabarrini, Marco, "Le consorterie nella storia fiorentina del medio evo," *La vita italiana nel Trecento* (Milan, 1904), pp. 98-127.

Tamassia, Nino. *La famiglia italiana nei secoli decimoquinto e decimosesto.* Milan, 1910.

Tiribilli-Giuliani, Demostene. *Sommario storico delle famiglie celibri toscane.* 3 vols. Florence, 1855-63.

Trollope, T. Adolphus. *Filippo Strozzi: A History of the Last Days of the Old Italian Liberty.* London, 1860.

List of Works Cited

Ugurgieri della Berardenga, Curzio. *Gli Acciaioli di Firenze*. 2 vols. Florence, 1961.

Upton, Anthony F. *Sir Arthur Ingram, c. 1565-1642: A Study of the Origins of the English Landed Family*. Oxford, 1961.

Ventura, Angelo. *Nobiltà e popolo nella società veneta del '400 e '500*. Bari, 1964.

Villari, Pasquale. *Life and Times of Girolamo Savonarola*. Trans. Linda Villari. New York, 1898.

Vita privata a Firenze nei secoli XIV e XV. Florence, 1966.

Wackernagel, Martin. *Der Lebensraum des Künstlers in der florentinischen Renaissance*. Leipzig, 1938.

Watson, W. B. "The Structure of the Florentine Galley Trade with Flanders and England in the Fifteenth Century," *Revue Belge de philologie et d'histoire*, XXXIX (1961), 1073-91; XL (1962), 317-47.

Weber, Max. *Zur Geschichte der Handelsgesellschaften im Mittelalter*. Stuttgart, 1889.

Wee, Herman van der. *The Growth of the Antwerp Market and the European Economy (Fourteenth-Sixteenth Centuries)*. 3 vols. The Hague, 1963.

Woodward, William Harrison. *Vittorino da Feltre and Other Humanist Educators*. New York, 1963.

Woolf, Stuart J. *Studi sulla nobiltà piemontese nell'epoca dell'assolutismo*. Turin, 1963.

INDEX

Index